"Miss Spain in Exile"

The Cañada Blanch / Sussex Academic Studies on Contemporary Spain

General Editor: Professor Paul Preston, London School of Economics

A list of all published titles in the series is available on the Press website. More recently published works are presented below.

Concha Alborg, *My Mother, That Stranger: Letters from the Spanish Civil War*.

Peter Anderson, *Friend or Foe?: Occupation, Collaboration and Selective Violence in the Spanish Civil War*.

Germà Bel, *Disdain, Distrust, and Dissolution: The Surge of Support for Independence in Catalonia*.

Carl-Henrik Bjerström, *Josep Renau and the Politics of Culture in Republican Spain, 1931–1939: Re-imagining the Nation*.

Darryl Burrowes, *Historians at War: Cold War Influences on Anglo-American Representations of the Spanish Civil War*.

Andrew Canessa (ed.), *Barrier and Bridge: Spanish and Gibraltarian Perspectives on Their Border*.

Kathryn Crameri, *'Goodbye, Spain?': The Question of Independence for Catalonia*.

Pol Dalmau, *Press, Politics and National Identities in Catalonia: The Transformation of La Vanguardia, 1881–1931*.

Mark Derby, *Petals and Bullets: Dorothy Morris – A New Zealand Nurse in the Spanish Civil War*.

Francisco Espinosa-Maestre, *Shoot the Messenger?: Spanish Democracy and the Crimes of Francoism – From the Pact of Silence to the Trial of Baltasar Garzón*.

María Jesús González, *Raymond Carr: The Curiosity of the Fox*.

Helen Graham, *The War and its Shadow: Spain's Civil War in Europe's Long Twentieth Century*.

Arnau Gonzàlez i Vilalta (ed.), *The Illusion of Statehood: Perceptions of Catalan Independence up to the End of the Spanish Civil War*.

Xabier A. Irujo, *GERNIKA: Genealogy of a Lie*.

Mandie Iveson, *Language Attitudes, National Identity and Migration in Catalonia: 'What the Women Have to Say'*

Gabriel Jackson, *Juan Negrín: Physiologist, Socialist, and Spanish Republican War Leader*.

Nathan Jones, *The Adoption of a Pro-US Foreign Policy by Spain and the United Kingdom: José María Aznar and Tony Blair's Personal Motivations and their Global Impact.*

Xavier Moreno Juliá, *The Blue Division: Spanish Blood in Russia, 1941–1945.*

David Lethbridge, *Norman Bethune in Spain: Commitment, Crisis, and Conspiracy.*

Antonio Miguez Macho, *The Genocidal Genealogy of Francoism: Violence, Memory and Impunity.*

Carles Manera, *The Great Recession: A Subversive View.*

Nicholas Manganas, *Las dos Españas: Terror and Crisis in Contemporary Spain.*

Jorge Marco, *Guerrilleros and Neighbours in Arms: Identities and Cultures of Antifascist Resistance in Spain.*

Emily Mason, *Democracy, Deeds and Dilemmas: Support for the Spanish Republic within British Civil Society, 1936–1939.*

Soledad Fox Maura, *Jorge Semprún: The Spaniard who Survived the Nazis and Conquered Paris.*

Martin Minchom, *Spain's Martyred Cities: From the Battle of Madrid to Picasso's* Guernica.

Olivia Muñoz-Rojas, *Ashes and Granite: Destruction and Reconstruction in the Spanish Civil War and Its Aftermath.*

Linda Palfreeman, *Spain Bleeds: The Development of Battlefield Blood Transfusion during the Civil War.*

Fernando Puell de la Villa and David García Hernán (eds.), *War and Population Displacement: Lessons of History.*

Rúben Serém, *Conspiracy, Coup d'état and Civil War in Seville, 1936–1939: History and Myth in Francoist Spain.*

Gareth Stockey, *Gibraltar: "A Dagger in the Spine of Spain?"*

Maggie Torres, *Anarchism and Political Change in Spain: Schism, Polarisation and Reconstruction of the* Confederación Nacional del Trabajo, *1939–1979.*

Dacia Viejo-Rose, *Reconstructing Spain: Cultural Heritage and Memory after Civil War.*

Antoni Vives, *SMART City Barcelona: The Catalan Quest to Improve Future Urban Living.*

This book is dedicated with all of a son's love to the memory of my mother Conchita, known as Isa Reyes during her artistic career.

It is also dedicated to the memories of her mother (my Tita) and her sister (my Aunt Nuria).

Os quiero mucho y os hecho muy de menos.

The book from which the poem "Dicen . . . " is excerpted is entitled: *Canto Llano*, published 1959 by Tezontle Mexico Press, Mexico City. Author: Nuria Parés.

"Miss Spain in Exile"
Isa Reyes' Escape from the Spanish Civil War
Flamenco and Stardom in 1930s Europe

DORIAN L. (DUSTY) NICOL

Copyright © Dorian L. (Dusty) Nicol, 2021.

The right of Dorian L. (Dusty) Nicol to be identified as Author of this work has been asserted in accordance with the Copyright, Designs and Patents Act 1988.

2 4 6 8 10 9 7 5 3 1

First published in 2021 in Great Britain by
SUSSEX ACADEMIC PRESS
PO Box 139
Eastbourne BN24 9BP

Distributed in North America by
SUSSEX ACADEMIC PRESS
Independent Publishers Group
814 N. Franklin Street
Chicago, IL 60610

All rights reserved. Except for the quotation of short passages for the purposes of criticism and review, no part of this publication may be reproduced, stored in a retrieval system, or transmitted, in any form or by any means, electronic, mechanical, photocopying, recording or otherwise, without the prior permission of the publisher.

Published in collaboration with the Cañada Blanch Centre for Contemporary Spanish Studies, London School of Economics.

British Library Cataloguing in Publication Data
A CIP catalogue record for this book is available from the British Library.

Library of Congress Cataloging-in-Publication Data
To be applied for.

Paperback ISBN 978-1-78976-086-6

Typeset and designed by Sussex Academic Press, Brighton & Eastbourne.

Contents

Cañada Blanch Centre for Contemporary Spanish Studies   viii
Series Editor's Preface by Paul Preston   x
Author's Preface   xiii
Acknowledgments   xv

Introduction   1

1	A Village in the High Sierra	8
2	The Burning Fields	23
3	The Airbase at Sariñena	33
4	Crossing the Pyrenees and Becoming Isa	48
5	Three Painters	61
6	The Duchess' Palace	74
7	On the French Riviera	85
8	In Poland	108
9	Miss Spain	122
10	Sharing a Hotel with the Russians	129
11	The Miss Europe Contest	141
12	A Christmas Holiday	152
13	Father is Alive!	164
14	Two Weeks in Venice	173
15	Berlin	185
16	A Trip to Greece	199
17	The New World	212

Epilogue   222

Index   224

The Cañada Blanch Centre for Contemporary Spanish Studies

In the 1960s, the most important initiative in the cultural and academic relations between Spain and the United Kingdom was launched by a Valencian fruit importer in London. The creation by Vicente Cañada Blanch of the Anglo-Spanish Cultural Foundation has subsequently benefited large numbers of Spanish and British scholars at various levels. Thanks to the generosity of Vicente Cañada Blanch, thousands of Spanish schoolchildren have been educated at the secondary school in West London that bears his name. At the same time, many British and Spanish university students have benefited from the exchange scholarships which fostered cultural and scientific exchanges between the two countries. Some of the most important historical, artistic and literary work on Spanish topics to be produced in Great Britain was initially made possible by Cañada Blanch scholarships.

Vicente Cañada Blanch was, by inclination, a conservative. When his Foundation was created, the Franco regime was still in the plenitude of its power. Nevertheless, the keynote of the Foundation's activities was always a complete open-mindedness on political issues. This was reflected in the diversity of research projects supported by the Foundation, many of which, in Francoist Spain, would have been regarded as subversive. When the Dictator died, Don Vicente was in his seventy-fifth year. In the two decades following the death of the Dictator, although apparently indestructible, Don Vicente was obliged to husband his energies. Increasingly, the work of the Foundation was carried forward by Miguel Dols whose tireless and imaginative work in London was matched in Spain by that of José María Coll Comín. They were united in the Foundation's spirit of open-minded commitment to fostering research of high quality in pursuit of better Anglo-Spanish cultural relations. Throughout the 1990s, thanks to them, the role of the Foundation grew considerably.

In 1994, in collaboration with the London School of Economics, the Foundation established the Príncipe de Asturias Chair of Contemporary Spanish History and the Cañada Blanch Centre for Contemporary Spanish Studies. It is the particular task of the Cañada Blanch Centre for Contemporary Spanish Studies to promote the understanding of twentieth-century Spain through research and teaching of contemporary Spanish history, politics, economy, sociology and culture. The Centre possesses a valuable library and archival centre for specialists in contemporary Spain. This work is carried on through the publications of the doctoral and post-doctoral researchers at the Centre itself and through the many seminars and lectures held at the London School of Economics. While the seminars are the province of the researchers, the lecture cycles have been the forum in which Spanish politicians have been able to address audiences in the United Kingdom.

Since 1998, the Cañada Blanch Centre has published a substantial number of books in collaboration with several different publishers on the subject of contemporary Spanish history and politics. An extremely fruitful partnership with Sussex Academic Press began in 2004. Full details and descriptions of the published works can be found on the Press website.

Among the books about the Spanish Civil War published in the series, there have been many biographical studies. The subjects have ranged widely from major political figures – Juan Negrín on the left, Gonzalo Queipo de Llano on the right, to leading lights of the art world – Luis Quintanilla and Josep Renau, to influential academics – Raymond Carr and J. B. Trend, and to volunteers on the Republican side – Patience Darton, Dorothy Morris, Tom Wintringham, and Norman Bethune. The present volume, Dorian (Dusty) Nicol's edition of the memoirs of his mother Isa Reyes, is not an academic study but rather a compellingly readable and utterly unique contribution to the wider history of the travails of Republican Spain.

Series Editor's Preface by Paul Preston

The Cañada Blanch Series on Contemporary Spain is principally concerned with the country's political, social and economic conflicts over the last one hundred and fifty years. Accordingly, the memoirs of a beauty queen and dancer who performed in a Paris nightclub attended by the Duke and Duchess of Windsor and other denizens of Parisian high-society might be thought to sit uncomfortably with the rest of the series. All the more so, it could seem, when the names that fly out of its star-spangled pages are those of major figures of French stage and cinema including Sacha Guitry, Jean Gabin, Charles Boyer, Fernandel, Jean-Paul Belmondo and Maurice Chevalier.

A similar conclusion might be indicated by the descriptions of her jaunts to the Longchamps horse races, to Monte Carlo, Cannes, Saint Tropez and the Cap d'Antibes. Even greater puzzlement might be sparked off by the references to fashion and fashion designers, to jackets and coats from Lanvin, to suits and dresses from Patou, to evening gowns from Schiaparelli, to a gold wristwatch from Cartier, to diamond earrings from Van Clef, to silk scarves and luggage from Hermès and to perfume from Guerlain. And yet this fascinating volume is no anomaly within the series. The memoirs of Concepción Balcells de los Reyes, 'Conchita', constitute an important, albeit unusual, contribution to the history of the Spanish Republican exile.

It is difficult to imagine more kaleidoscopic experiences than those of 'Conchita'. Aged fifteen, she accompanied her family on holiday from Madrid just before the outbreak of the Civil War. The tensions of the capital they were leaving behind are atmospherically described. The family was staying in the village of Pedro Bernardo in the province of Ávila, which was still in the Republican zone. When war broke out, her father, who was a liberal Republican lawyer, tried to save local rightists from marauding

Series Editor's Preface by Paul Preston

mobs. At the same time, he was training the farmers and peasants of the area in the use of firearms, military drills and trying to prepare them for the fight to defend the Republic. As the war rapidly intensified, Ricardo Balcells sent his wife and daughters to Paris to stay with relatives. He himself returned to Madrid to serve the Republic.

Despite his loyalty, when he was away from Madrid on duty as an officer in the Republican army, his home was ransacked by anarchists. This senseless looting was a response to the fact that, as a prosperous lawyer, he was simply assumed to be a fascist. The consequence was that valuable paintings, antique furniture, cabinets filled with silver and exquisite pieces of old china and a library of rare books were either destroyed or stolen. In the meanwhile, the rest of the family, now in Paris, had to earn a living. Conchita would be their savior. Her first job was as a juvenile fashion model but soon she was picking up work as an artist's (clothed) model. An introduction to Sacha Guitry led to a bit part in a movie as a gypsy. Her cinema career was curtailed by a bout of measles, but it was at this time that she adopted the stage name Isa Reyes. Her major financial success was to come as a dancer. Very musical, as proficient with castanets as her sister Nuria was with guitar, she was an accomplished flamenco dancer. With her cousin Alma, a record-player and some records, she learned the tango and foxtrot. After appearing at a high-society charity ball, the 'Alma et Isa' duo began to receive invitations to dance, first in Paris, then on the French Riviera and finally all over Europe.

Conchita's account of her adventures in that period is both funny and exciting. Isa and Alma danced together in Venice in the presence of Mussolini and Count Galeazzo Ciano. When she threw a flower into the audience that landed on Ciano's table, it set off an effort to seduce her by the inveterate womaniser. He was thwarted only when Alma warned him off by telling him that Isa was secretly the mistress of a high-ranking Nationalist official in Spain and that if were revealed that Count Ciano became involved with her, there would be serious diplomatic repercussions.

In Paris, Isa danced at a benefit to raise money to buy medical supplies and provisions for the Spanish Republic. An unlikely consequence was that she took part in, and won, the "Miss Spain in Exile" competition organized by *Le Monde*. Her success entitled her to compete in the finals of the Miss Europe pageant that was held in Denmark. Refusing to carry the Francoist flag and being prevented from carrying the Republican flag, she opted for a white banner simply worded 'España'. Her audiences understood the gesture and cheered enthusiastically.

Isa's account of her travels across a Europe on the verge of war are vivid and disturbing. This is particularly true of the description of the return journey through Nazi Germany from a tour of Poland that she, her mother and Alma had to undertake without valid passports. The horrors of being in the Third Reich were relived in April 1939, shortly after the end of the Spanish Civil War. Now in a flamenco trio with the dancer Antonio Arcaraz, she was invited to perform in Berlin at Hitler's 50th birthday celebration. She felt great distress at contractually being obliged to participate in an event intended to commemorate the German contribution to Franco's recent civil war victory. Despite a lavish stay in the luxurious Hotel Adlon, the hugely successful performance left nightmare memories. For the rest of her life she would speak of 'looking out from the stage and seeing the gallery of Twentieth Century Evil spread in front of me'.

Back in France, the family underwent agonies while waiting for Ricardo Balcells finally to get out of Spain when Valencia was about to fall. Like so much of the book, Conchita's evocation of that experience sheds light on a little known aspect of life for Republican exiles.

By turns informative, moving and funny, this fascinating book is as perceptive about what Chamberlain's Munich betrayal meant for Czechs and Spaniards as it is about the wild vodka-fueled antics of White Russian exiles in Paris. It fully merits its inclusion in the Cañada Blanch Series on Contemporary Spain.

Author's Preface

This book is based on real events.

Most of the narrative in Isa's voice is adapted from the draft memoirs that she wrote near the end of her life. Isa wrote the bulk of her memoirs within a few years after her husband died, when sitting at a typewriter and writing her story helped to pass the time and ease the sadness of her loss.

Gaps or inconsistencies in the story were resolved using my memories of conversations with her or with her sister Nuria, during which they shared with me their recollections of what had occurred. In some cases, I used my imagination combined with my knowledge of what had really transpired to fill in the gaps and to lend some continuity to the story. In these cases, I can vouch that what I added is plausible based on what I know of the real events that occurred.

I have been faithful to her written words and to their recollections as much as possible and I have changed none of the facts of the story. Where appropriate, I have added some comments for context, particularly historical context. These historical comments are accurate to the best of my knowledge, but I make no pretense of objectivity when it comes to writing about Hitler or the Fascists or the betrayal first of Spain and later of Czechoslovakia by the western democracies during the 1930s. The western democracies stood idly by and allowed Hitler and Mussolini with their fascist legions to support Franco and his Nationalist forces while doing nothing to support the legitimate government of Spain. I consider this a betrayal as great as the infamous betrayal of Czechoslovakia at Munich only a few years later, when England and France broke their promise to defend Czechoslovakia and left that country to her fate at the hands of the Nazis.

There can never be any justification for the policy that became known as "Appeasement" and one can only hope that we can learn from history. As an epigraph for his book 'The Rise and Fall of the Third Reich', William L. Shirer paraphrases the philosopher George

Author's Preface

Santayana: "Those who do not remember the past are condemned to relive it." It seems to me that those lessons of the 1930s are no less apt for today's world.

But this book does not pretend to be a history book or a researched work of scholarship. Nor does it presume to add a new interpretation to the well-known events in Europe during the late 1930s.

This is the story of a family that lived through those years. In particular, it is the story of that family's older daughter, Conchita, who later took on the stage name Isa. Isa's story is that of a young girl who had to grow up quickly when war turned her world and her life upside down. Somehow, despite everything she went through, she never lost her optimism or her sense of humor. As the darkness was descending upon Europe, she was not content simply to survive. She dared to dream, and she dared to try to realize her dreams. This is a story of how even during a tragic time, one can make one's dreams and aspirations come true. This is also a story of how love can triumph even during the darkest of times and through a tumultuous period when world events make one's own fate impossible to control.

Acknowledgments

My deepest gratitude is extended to Sir Paul Preston CBE, noted author and historian *y un hombre muy caballero*, without whose help and encouragement the publication of this book would have remained an unfulfilled dream. Paul's careful review caught several historical errors, the inevitable result of a work written by an amateur historian. Equally, my gratitude to Anthony Grahame, Editorial Director, and his colleagues at Sussex Academic Press, for publishing this book and honoring me with its inclusion in the Cañada Blanch series.

To my friend Lynne Cox, thank you as always for the friendship and support and for reminding me from time to time that the process of writing and publishing a book is not unlike completing a marathon swim. You and I have always understood each other.

My brother George and my sister Dina were lovingly supportive and encouraging of my efforts to write this book. George helped me select the photographs that appear in this book and he made them available from his collection of our mother's photos.

Zed Chance cleaned up and edited the photographs to make them suitable for inclusion in the book.

Sylvia Parés, *mi querida prima*, encouraged me to tell this story about my mother and her mother, my Aunt Nuria, and graciously gave permission for me to include the excerpt from her mother's poem "Dicen" as an epigraph. Marta Bechhoefer, Don Margolis, and Victoria Dougherty read portions of different drafts at various times and improved the manuscript with their suggestions. My Finnish sister Jeanne C. Drake, whom my mother loved dearly, helped with the final proofing. *Kiitos ja sisu!*

Finally, and most importantly, to Karen, who gives meaning to all I do and who makes the sun rise every morning: *Gracias por todo*, Kiki. Your loving encouragement and support made finishing this project possible and your suggestions improved the way the story was told.

Epigraph

"Even the olives are bleeding."

Remark attributed to the Irish poet Charles Donnelly, who volunteered to fight for the Spanish Republic, shortly before he was killed by gunfire at the Jarama Front during the Battle for Madrid, February 1937.

*"Anda por todas partes. Lo he leído
Y lo sigo leyendo todavía.
Anda por todos lados,
Anda en todos los ojos que lo miran
brillar en la blancura de las páginas
con su cándida luz inofensiva.
Que soy, que somos (nos lo dicen)
'la España peregrina' . . . "*

Nuria Parés, from her poem "Dicen . . . ", in her collection of poems "Canto Llano".

Introduction

In July of 1936, a fifteen-year old Spanish girl from Madrid went on her annual summer vacation to the mountains with her father, her best girlfriend from school, and her younger sister. Her mother was not as enamored of the country life as was her father, so she stayed behind in their comfortable home in Madrid. This had become an annual tradition, to spend a month in the mountains of the Sierra de Gredos, in the Province of Ávila, northwest of Madrid. The girl's father would hunt with his friends and the girls would swim and hike and read and enjoy the fresh, cool air of the mountains.

The young girl's name was Conchita Balcells de los Reyes. Her friend's name was Carmen and her younger sister's name was Nuria. Conchita had just turned fifteen the month before. She was a pretty girl with long black hair and huge brown eyes, through which she looked at the world with innocent wonder and curiosity. She still dressed like a schoolgirl most days, wearing knee-length skirts and knee socks and with her hair in braids, as demanded by the nuns of the Catholic school that she attended, and which had only a few weeks earlier entered the summer recess. She almost always had a smile on her face and could find humor or something to laugh at in almost any situation. She adored her little dog Tosca, whom she had named after the Puccini opera, and she and little Tosca were a well-known sight at Madrid's Retiro Park, only a few blocks from her home near the Puerta de Alcalá in the center of Madrid.

Their family home occupied the top two floors of a residential building on Calle Velasquez. The home was full of art that Isa's cultured parents had collected over the years, mostly oil paintings and small sculptures, as well as family pictures and mementos. The large living room was lined with bookshelves as was her father's office. A large piano dominated a corner of the living room, near the tall window that looked out on Calle Velasquez.

"Miss Spain in Exile"

Conchita enjoyed reading and studying, particularly history and literature, but she was not overly bookish. She was extroverted and always happy, with an incurable optimism about life and her future. Even at a young age, she had developed the sense of humor that she would have for her whole life. As much as a sense of humor, it was a sense of the ridiculous, an ability to look at situations and see the comical or ridiculous aspects and find a way to laugh at them.

Conchita's slim figure belied her love of sweets. Her favorite meal of the day was the afternoon "merienda" or snack, usually comprising a bowl of café con leche or the thick hot chocolate for which Madrid is famous, accompanied by churros or almond cookies. During autumn or winter, she also loved the roasted chestnuts that she could buy by the bagful from any of the carts along the Paseo de la Castellana where she would go for walks with her family and with Tosca, the little dog bundled and somewhat uncomfortable in the little sweater she had knitted for her. For the rest of her life, anywhere she was, the smell of roasting chestnuts would evoke a powerful memory of her youth in Madrid.

Her family was well-to-do, what would be considered upper middle class. She had spent her childhood comfortably and carefree in Madrid, attending school and, as was normal for girls of her age and social standing in Madrid, taking additional classes after school to polish her French and to take music lessons, in her case piano. From an early age, she loved music and dancing and begged her parents to let her study the traditional folk dances of Spain, including the fiery gypsy-inspired Flamenco dances of Andalucía in the south of Spain. Her dance teachers recognized her passion and her natural talent as a dancer and encouraged her to develop her skills, adding some classic ballet training and tap dancing to her repertoire. Secretly but often, she dreamed of one day performing on a stage in front of an audience. She would lie awake at night dreaming of the applause and ovations she would receive someday on the stages of European capitals.

As much as Conchita loved to dance, she loved equally playing the castanets. She became fascinated by the rhythms of point and counterpoint with which the castanets weave their way into and out of the melodies of Spanish dance music, particularly Flamenco, and she would practice incessantly. When the click-clacking of the castanets would begin to wear on the nerves of her family, she would practice silently, tapping her foot gently on the floor or

Introduction

quietly tapping her hands on her knees until she could switch effortlessly back and forth between the complex and ever-changing rhythms of even the most complex melodies. For the rest of her life, she could pick up a pair of castanets at a moment's notice and tap out an accompaniment to any piece of music. In fact, she couldn't listen to music without her hands, with castanets or without, tapping and playing rhythmical games with point and counterpoint to the beat.

Her father's name was Ricardo Balcells Pinto. He was an attorney, originally from the Canary Islands by way of Barcelona. He had a successful law practice in Madrid which brought him enough income to provide a comfortable life for his family. He was a cultured Spanish gentleman of the old school, always immaculately dressed in his hand-made suits, generally with a pipe in his hand, smoking nothing but the finest Virginia tobacco. He considered himself a gourmet in both food and wine and insisted on obtaining the finest delicacies at every opportunity. He had a keen wit and was fond of entertaining his friends for hours at a time with his stories and with his ability to recite from memory extensive passages from the classics of Spanish literature and poetry. His real passion, though, was music. He used to say that he didn't really listen to beautiful music with his ears, he heard it through his heart and stomach. He would be moved to tears by music he loved, particularly the delicate music of Debussy or the piano pieces of Chopin. He could sit at his piano and play by ear most pieces of music after hearing them just once.

Quite rarely for a man of his social class in Spain at that time, his political leanings were somewhat to the left of center. He sympathized with the plight of the workers and of the poor and landless peasants who comprised much of the population of Spain in those days. He was often teased by his more right-leaning friends that he was a firm believer in socialism for the masses, as long as he could continue dressing in his suits from Savile Row and enjoying his Danish hams and French cognac. Although that characterization was in some ways accurate, it neglected to take into account the kindness and empathy that were at the heart of his soul and that did not allow him to ignore the plight of the disenfranchised.

Conchita's mother was named Concepción de los Reyes y Gonzalez Cardenas. She had been born in Girona, in Catalonia near Barcelona, and had grown up speaking fluent Catalán as well as Castilian Spanish. She had been educated by the nuns of the Sacred Heart and as a result also spoke a beautiful and literary French and was conversant with all the classic works of Spanish and French literature. Her family was upper middle class with certain pretensions to nobility. The right to append the name "de los Reyes" to the family name had been granted by a king of Spain centuries earlier. The story of the events that had led to this privilege had become part of the family lore. Although the story was perhaps apocryphal, it was passed on generation to generation and the name "de los Reyes" continued to be part of the family name. The details of the legend were told somewhat differently by each generation, but the gist of the story was that some few hundred years earlier, one of the family's distant ancestors had been a soldier in the service of the Spanish King and happened to be riding next to the king as they forded a shallow river. The King's horse tripped on a rock and the king fell off of his horse into the shallow water. He was wearing a heavy suit of armor, which began to fill with water, and supposedly the king would have drowned had not this ancestor, whose name was Salvador, pulled him up and saved him from a rather inglorious death. The King knighted him on the spot, with the name Salvador de los Reyes ("Savior of the Kings") and the family name had retained those words since.

Concepción lived the life of a well-to-do Spanish lady in Madrid, watching over the household with the aid of a handful of servants who had been with the family for so long that they had become part of the family. She was not terribly interested in politics, but she supported Ricardo's views. She was, like him, at heart a kind person who could not ignore suffering in others, though she stopped short of supporting the more ardent socialists and anarchists, whom she simply considered vulgar and uncultured. It says a lot about her that the worst insult she was capable of bestowing on anyone was to refer to that person as "vulgar". Occasionally when seeing a group of people behaving in a manner that she considered vulgar or in any way not appropriate for a lady or gentleman in that setting or occasion, she would repeat the saying she had learned from her mother: "It is a good thing those people are wearing trousers and jackets. Otherwise, their tails would be visible."

The younger sister Nuria was two years younger than Conchita. She was also pretty, with red hair that she liked to wear in a bob and with eyes that were curious and bright and expressive of her every emotion. She was bit more cerebral than Conchita, even at an early age, and tended to go through life with a pensive and questioning expression on her face rather than with the innocently joyous countenance of her older sister. As a child, she already displayed the love of words and language that would later in life make her a published and acclaimed poet in Spanish, as well as a respected translator of poetry between Spanish, English, and French. Her real passion, though, especially during her youth, was guitar. She began studying classical guitar at an early age and would play the Spanish guitar music to which Conchita would practice her dances. She later studied under the great classical guitarist Carlos Montoya and only stopped playing guitar in her old age when she developed arthritis and her fingers became too stiff to continue playing. Nuria and Conchita were very close, with little of the normal rivalry that commonly causes rifts between siblings so close in age. Where Conchita was always smiling and ready to indulge her father in his taste for practical jokes, Nuria was quieter and more serious. If she wasn't practicing guitar, she was happiest when left alone to read quietly.

Conchita's friend Carmen came from a similar family background, in Carmen's case from an old Madrid family. She and Conchita had been in school together since they had been six years old and were inseparable friends. They shared the same sense of humor and laughed easily at the same things. It had become a tradition that Carmen would accompany the family every year on their summer vacation. Carmen was a bit more socially precocious than Conchita. She had begun to discover boys and was developing an interest in them, whereas to Conchita boys were still boring and somewhat annoying. Carmen had also discovered grown-up wonders like smoking cigarettes, which she convinced Conchita to try one day. The resulting fit of coughing kept Conchita from trying smoking again for a long time. Carmen's family's politics were considerably to the right of the Balcells family's politics, but by tacit agreement, politics were not allowed to interfere with the girls' friendship and both families felt that the friendship was good for both girls. They remained friends for the rest of their lives and when they would reunite, sometimes with a spell of years and once of decades since last having seen each other, they would simply continue the conversation they had abandoned in mid-sentence and continue.

"Miss Spain in Exile"

It was a tumultuous time in the world as the girls left for their summer vacation. Hitler had been in power in Germany for three years and his Nazis and their increasingly aggressive posturing were casting a pall over Europe. Only four months earlier, Hitler's Wehrmacht had re-occupied the Rhineland in violation of the Treaty of Versailles and the Nazis were openly rearming, again in violation of the Treaty of Versailles. Mussolini had been in power in Italy since 1922 and his fascist legions had a year earlier invaded Abyssinia (present day Ethiopia) while the impotent League of Nations stood idly by and watched and did nothing.

The democracies of Europe had not really recovered from the trauma of World War One. They were still wary of war and were firmly committed to pacifist policies. Although the word "appeasement" was not yet in vogue, the spirit of appeasement was very much in the air. Only three years earlier, the students of the Oxford Union Society in Britain had overwhelmingly approved the motion "This house will under no circumstances fight for its king and country." One of the few English politicians who recognized the Nazi threat and was prepared to speak against it was Winston Churchill, but he was in political exile and his was a voice in the wilderness. The French Third Republic was in its final throes and the French people were in no mood to take on the risk of another war.

The United States was wrestling with its own problems, stemming from the Great Depression, and was in the middle of one of its particularly isolationist periods. Americans in general were in no mood to become embroiled in the affairs of another continent, not when the Atlantic Ocean stood as a barrier between them and the age-old conflicts of the Old World.

So, in general, the rest of the world sat back and watched as Europe marched inexorably toward war. Spain was one of the first focal points of the inevitable conflict between fascism and democracy. The Spanish Civil War, fought between 1936 and 1939, was in many ways the crucible of World War Two and the battles that raged on Spanish soil were the opening act of the world war that was soon to follow.

The Spanish Civil War broke out while that 15-year old girl was on her vacation. As a result, her childhood would come to an end

Introduction

during that summer. She would leave Spain for Paris to escape the war, where, taking the stage name Isa Reyes, she was "discovered" as a model and dancer, selected as "Miss Spain in Exile", and she would dance in the cities and capitals of Europe as the world marched toward World War Two. Dancing in Athens, she would meet a Greek man with whom she would fall in love, and together they would escape Europe just as the continent was being engulfed by war.

They fled Europe and came to the New World, first to Cuba, then to Mexico, then finally to the United States. They married in Mexico and eventually settled in Northern California, near San Francisco, where they would raise their family, a daughter and two sons.

That young Spanish girl was my mother and the Greek whom she married was my father.

This is her story. It is a story of resilience during a time of tragedy, of love and compassion during a time of cruelty, and of hope during a time of darkness.

A friend of mine asked my mother once how she could always stay so happy and always be in such a good mood? She answered, "You have to remember that by the time I was 18 years old, I had survived a civil war and a world war, had lost everything, and started my life over on a new continent. Since then, there is very little the fates can throw at me that will faze me very much."

CHAPTER 1

A Village in the High Sierra

July 1936
Author's Note (the author's historical notes and comments will appear in italics through the rest of this book, to be distinguished from Isa's narrative):

Madrid was unusually quiet on the Sunday morning that the girls left Madrid for the Sierra de Gredos. Perhaps the buildup to the tragic events that were about to occur was to blame for the stillness and the silence. There was a palpable air of uncertainty in Madrid, a strange and eerie uneasiness that seemed to envelope the city like a shroud. On the afternoon of July 12, right-wing gunmen shot and killed a leftist officer of the Republican Assault Guards, Lieutenant José del Castillo. Castillo was number two on a blacklist of pro-Republican officers drawn up by the Unión Militar Española, the ultra-right conspiratorial organization preparing the military uprisisng that would take place some days later. His fellow officers soon carried out a swift and merciless revenge against the purported right-wing organizers of the assassination. In retaliation, Calvo Sotelo, the prominent right-wing politician, was abducted from his home and cruelly murdered. Both burial processions, as they marched through the streets of Madrid, provoked dozens of demonstrations, from rightist and leftist parties alike. There were scuffles in the street as protesters of conflicting ideologies encountered each other.

As the political situation in Spain continued to deteriorate, people began to believe that it would take a miracle to prevent this chain of events from ending in disaster. The people were right in fearing an imminent disaster. The Spanish Civil War, with all of its horrifying consequences, was but a few weeks ahead.

The Spanish Republic had been proclaimed on April 14, 1931, when the Spanish king, Rey Alfonso XIII, was deposed. From the beginning, the existence of the Republic was fraught, as it was always threatened by imminent conflicts between various factions of both the left and right wings. Many of Spain's problems stemmed from the great inequalities in wealth and land ownership that existed. There were parts of Spain (particularly Andalucía in the south and Extremadura in the southwest), where virtually all the land and wealth were in the hands of a few families and the peasants lived lives hardly better than those of animals, with no hope of a better life for themselves or their descendants. Despite the fact that the Republic was a secular government, the Catholic Church exerted a strong influence on society and in most villages, it was the local landowner(s) and the village priest who were the best fed.

In the industrial and mining towns, various unions or "sindicatos" were in constant conflict for control of the workers' loyalties. Strikes were frequent and were often suppressed violently. The most violent of these suppressions had been the one in the mining province of Asturias, in the north of Spain, in 1934. Striking miners led a rebellion and occupied the capital of the province, Oviedo, for two weeks. The army was sent in, under the leadership of General Francisco Franco. Franco brutally suppressed the rebellion, destroying much of the city in the process and earning him the nickname "The Butcher of Asturias". Other workers' rebellions throughout Spain met similar fates.

There were attempts at land reform, but major structural reform had failed to be enacted. As a result of this failure, and of the failure of the workers' strikes to improve the lot of the laborers, the parties of the left began to turn toward more radical platforms. The rightist parties were turning more and more to the right in reaction to this, and as a result, the moderate center began to disappear as the country became almost totally polarized between left and right.

The elections of February 1936 saw the installation of a government that called itself the Popular Front, an unlikely coalition of socialists, communists, and what was left of the Madrid- and Barcelona-based moderate left-wing parties. In the coming months, there was increasing violence between left-wing and right-wing parties in the streets of Madrid and other Spanish cities. As a result of this unrest, and inspired by Mussolini's and Hitler's fascist parties, there developed a nationalist party that called itself the "Falange Española" or the "Nationalists". This became a magnet for the reactionary right-wing groups that wanted to return Spain to its past and undo what reforms had been possible under the Republic. It also became a magnet for those attracted by the fascist ideologies of Hitler and Mussolini. Among those most attracted to the Falange was General Franco, who by then had been sent back to the Canary Islands in the hopes that in this relative isolation, he would be harmless.

As Spain entered the month of July that summer, the tensions affecting Spain began to boil over.

Isa's narrative begins now, as, in the midst of the tumult and unrest affecting all of Spain, she travels to the little village in the Sierra where she is to spend the summer holiday.

Soon after crossing the mountain pass, the tiny houses of the village came into view, huddled against the hillside and dwarfed by the high tower of the village's ancient church, perched high above the rooftops of the neighboring houses. The village had an odd name. It was called Pedro Bernardo. It had changed little since the times when the legendary El Cid was seen roaming across these lands.

I had asked my father several times, during previous vacations there, who Pedro Bernardo was. He had asked around the village, but no one knew with certainty. The most common legend, which was recounted with very little if any supporting detail and in a slightly different way by each villager who told the story, was that he had been a valiant knight who had ridden with El Cid. We were never able to confirm this, but I enjoyed believing the legend. I still do.

The houses in Pedro Bernardo were very old. The ruinous, lopsided dwellings had been built long ago from the sepia-colored stone of a nearby quarry. The houses seemed to cling to each other for protection from the harsh winds of the Sierra. In a corner of the village plaza, nestled in among the tall elms and poplars, and within the crumbling wall that had been built around it, was the Inn.

The biggest room in the Inn was the dining room, whose floors were made of red tile. There were no carpets and very little furniture, other than a huge dining table and its chairs, but large vases full of fresh flowers were everywhere. Huge oak beams traversed the ceiling from side to side, dark now with centuries of smoke and waxing. Old, frayed portraits lined the walls and a

A Village in the High Sierra

gigantic fireplace, large enough to roast an ox, its logs cold and covered with dust, sat in the far corner of the room. Its logs were ready and waiting to be lit again, as soon as the cold winds from the Sierra started blowing in autumn. The bedrooms were on the second floor. From their windows, we could see the village clustered at the foot of the mountain. On the crystal-clear mornings, we could see the ancient and noble town of Talavera de la Reina looming in the distance.

Fig trees in full bloom provided a canopy of green foliage over the front entrance to the Inn. There was a cobblestoned courtyard at the back of the Inn, which looked out onto the mountains in one direction and the sun-bleached houses of the village in the other. Behind the courtyard was an orchard, reached by crossing an arched gateway with massive iron doors and a medieval coat of arms carved high on its façade.

We were there for our summer vacation and had just arrived from our home in Madrid. My father was with us, my younger sister Nuria, and my best friend Carmen. Like me, Carmen was 15 years old. Nuria was two years younger than us, but already precocious.

We had departed on our journey from Madrid early that morning, soon after daybreak. Mother did not share my father's enthusiasm for the outdoors and so she had not accompanied us. She would stay in our home in Madrid, near the Puerta de Alcalá, and await our return. Although we were only going away for two weeks, she could not hide from her pretty face a worried look of concern as she hugged and kissed us goodbye. My father's car was waiting for us by the front door and the driver was busy placing the luggage in the back of the automobile and tying it onto the roof rack.

Mother hugged me extra tightly as she said goodbye to me that morning.

"Promise to be careful," she said.

"About what, Mamá?"

I was too young to fully understand the political unrest affecting the capital. She did not want to frighten me and quickly changed topic.

"You will have a nice time in the mountains with your father, as you always do, and I will be waiting for you to come back and tell me about all your adventures."

She did not intend for me to hear her whispered words to my father, "Please be careful and watch the girls and please promise to come home immediately if there is any trouble." Father replied that of course he would and off we went on our vacation.

We left Madrid and drove northwest toward the mountains. How beautiful appeared ahead in the distance the sight of the Sierra de Gredos! Soon we were in the province of Ávila and rushing toward the Sierra, the fresh smell of thyme, rosemary, and a dozen aromatic herbs perfuming the clean mountain air around us. The mountains were still capped with snow, contrasting starkly with the bright blue sky of summer. We could see flocks of partridges and pheasants taking cover from the bright sunshine by hiding under the shrubs of the sulfur-yellow mimosa that covered the fields.

Our automobile zig-zagged its way up along the tortuous road and soon we were at Pedro Bernardo. We passed the church and crossed the plaza and arrived at the entrance of the Inn. As he had every summer that I could remember of my youth, my father's best friend, Rafael Romero, was there to greet us at the front entrance, flanked by his two huge hunting dogs. He was tall and lean and handsome with an aristocratic bearing. I had had a schoolgirl crush on Don Rafael all of my young life, and I blushed as he gallantly took my hand, bowed, and raised my hand to his lips to kiss it in welcome. Carmen and Nuria giggled as they saw me blushing.

"I am so happy to see you, Don Rafael," I said in what I imagined was my most grown up and sophisticated voice.

"And I equally happy to see you, little girl," he replied, somewhat deflating me and causing Carmen and Nuria to giggle just a little bit more.

We went upstairs to our room to get ready for lunch. After quickly washing our faces and changing our clothes, Carmen, Nuria, and I ran down the steps of the stone stairway from the second floor to join my father and the others who were already seated at the dining table, drinking wine and chatting animatedly among themselves. Responding somewhat shyly to the greetings of "Buenos dias" loudly proffered to us from every corner of the room, we went to take our places at the table. Among the dozen or so guests, we were the only children vacationing at the Inn that summer.

Lunch was the usual hearty fare of Ávila. We started with "fabada", a stew of white beans with ham, then a plate of the veal chops for which that region of Spain was so well-known. I remembered that my father, who so loved good food, used to say, "For suckling pig, Segovia. For lamb, León. But for veal, there is nothing like the veal of Ávila!" With the veal was a plate of green beans cooked with garlic and for dessert my favorite, a custard flan. The conversation at table revolved around the political situation in Madrid and whether there was any hope of things calming down or would the unrest continue. I tried to follow the conversation as best I could, but I did not understand all of the things the adults were discussing. I could recognize some names and words, including "Franco" and "Fascists" and I heard the phrase "Do you think this will mean civil war?" several times. I could tell that my father was worried about all of the issues that they were discussing, and later, over their coffees, he and Don Rafael held a whispered conversation.

After the big lunch, we all went to our rooms upstairs for a siesta. As I fell asleep for my nap, I tried to make some sense of the discussion the adults had been having.

The bright, sunny days that followed could not have been more perfect. The three of us girls would wake up early, have our breakfast, and be at our favorite spring by mid-morning. After a swim in the clear, fresh waters of the pond below the spring, we would walk over to the nearby meadow and sit under the protective shade of its elm trees, talking and reading. Sometimes Nuria would bring her guitar and I my castanets and we would play music. If we played Flamenco music, Carmen would do her best exaggerated imitation of a gypsy wailing the dramatic lyrics and we would howl with laughter.

Letting the day slowly roll by, when we got hungry, we would eat the lunch that had been packed for us. Lunch was always hearty portions of the local "jamón serrano" and creamy goat cheese and thick slices of the delicious local bread, baked daily at the Inn, "Ávila style", in an oven filled with aromatic pine needles. Returning back to the Inn in the afternoons, we would take detours through the countryside so we could take figs and apples from the neighboring orchards. By sunset, the three of us girls would always be stationed by the Inn's main gate, there to await, in the courtyard, the return of my father and his hunting companions. They soon would come strolling toward us, carrying shotguns on their shoulders, followed by their dogs. They always looked tired but happy, and my father's face would blossom into a huge smile when he would see us waiting for him.

"Miss Spain in Exile"

"What did you get today, Papá?" I would ask him.

"Dinner!" he would always reply with a laugh.

On Sundays, when the church bells began to toll at dawn, I would lie still in bed and let my eyes follow the fragile light of early morning as it began to flood the room the moment the sun's rays struck the glazed pane of the window. Outside my window, flocks of larks and nightingales were already flying high, heading for the open fields. Carmen, Nuria, and I, after attending Mass in the village church, would hurry back to the Inn for breakfast with Father and Don Rafael. Breakfast was the same every day. A big bowl of steaming café con leche would be accompanied by toast, made from bread that was still warm from the oven when it was sliced. On this toast, we would spread tomato that had been crushed with salt and olive oil and accompany this with a little bit of cheese and jamón serrano and the Manchego cheese that was my father's favorite and that the Inn always kept in supply for him. With this, we would have little bowls of fruit that had been picked from one of the local orchards, usually figs, which I loved, and which were then just beginning to ripen.

After the morning meal was finished, Father and Don Rafael would sit down outdoors in the shade and play chess for a couple of hours. Later, we would all depart for a ride on horseback to the dark castle that lay in the shady woods some distance away from Pedro Bernardo on the road to Talavera de la Reina. How much fun it was for us to ride with them, the horses bounding along, following a narrow trail across the valley, gradually climbing up toward the distant hill! As soon as we emerged from the woods, we would see the craggy towers of the castle silhouetted against the sky.

After a lazy afternoon exploring the surroundings, we'd imagine we could hear El Cid riding toward us, perhaps accompanied by his loyal knight Pedro Bernardo. Eager to search for hidden treasures among the moss-covered stones, we would sit on the grass on the banks of a stream, its banks bordered with oaks and carob trees which provided a cool and welcome shade for us. Our packed meal had been prepared earlier by the Innkeeper's wife, Doña Maria, and it was wonderful. There was an entire round loaf of bread, ham and cheese, olives, roasted peppers, and my favorite, a big slab of Spanish "tortilla", a potato and onion omelette that had been cooked that morning. Rafael would fill his and Father's glasses with wine and pour a few drops in Carmen's, Nuria's, and my glasses

A Village in the High Sierra

and we would all clink glasses and say "Salud!". Then the five of us would eat with a hearty appetite everything that Doña Maria had placed in the basket. As the first star of the evening appeared in the sky, we would begin to make our way back to Pedro Bernardo, our horses carrying us gently along the path. Above us, the sky was crystal clear, the firmament sparkled with glittering stars, and the crisp breezes of the night filled our lungs with the heavy and bittersweet scent of the eucalyptus trees.

The small, well-tended garden that lay at the back of the Inn, next to the orchard, was my favorite place for reading and for studying my lessons. I would go there at the end of the afternoons, once the heat of the day had begun to fade. Sometimes, I would remain there for a long time reading and studying and daydreaming. Before going back into the Inn, I would help the old woman who did most of the work at the Inn gather the flowers which she later would place on the dining room tables and in our rooms.

One particular afternoon, I immediately sensed, on reentering the Inn, that something out of the ordinary had taken place while I had been outside. The radio was on and all the guests, including my father and Don Rafael, were seated around it and thoroughly engrossed in listening to the news bulletins being broadcast by Radio Madrid. The mayor of Pedro Bernardo, Don Felipe, was there. So was Santiago, the young schoolteacher sent recently from the capital, the two local priests, and a score of others. The radio announcer spoke in a nervous and high-pitched voice as he related the startling series of events which had occurred during the last twenty-four hours. A general of the Army, Francisco Franco, had begun a military uprising with the aim of overthrowing the government of the Republic of Spain and replacing it with a fascist, military dictatorship. The long-feared rightist revolt was finally taking place. Soon, the army from the Spanish military garrison in Morocco would be airlifted into Málaga, in the south of Spain to spearhead the attack. Thus, on that fateful summer day began one of the cruelest struggles in the history of mankind, the Spanish Civil War. This was a war that would pit village against village, family against family, and even brother against brother.

The date was July 17, 1936.

The rebel forces of General Franco, the Nationalists as they called themselves, had begun their military uprising that morning and were preparing to invade Spain, coming from Morocco. Landing in the south of the country, they erupted northward as had the Moors centuries earlier. The Spanish Civil War had begun, pitting the insurgent Nationalists against the "Loyalists", those who remained loyal to the Republic. The Nationalists quickly swept across the southern plains toward Castilla and Madrid. Many officers of the armed forces of the Republic sided with Franco, so that within days there were army units throughout Spain loyal to the invading Nationalists. Soon the Republic, in order to survive, would have no choice but to improvise its own army of Loyalists. Considering the insurmountable obstacles that it faced, the Republic did a remarkable job.

The Nationalists were winning major early victories and soon controlled almost all of the southern province of Málaga, with the exception of the city of Málaga itself. That city would later pay a terrible price as Franco's forces terror-bombed it in retribution for its resistance. The Loyalists were struggling as hard as they could to defend the government against the rebels and the battle lines were being drawn. Both sides were now setting up to face each other across the plains of Castilla.

Within days, most of the roads leading to and from Madrid had been cut off or closed, the thoroughfares to Talavera and Toledo being used and fought over by both Loyalist and Nationalist forces. Loyalists and Nationalists were each trying to gain control of the nearby cities and fighting was erupting everywhere. So, at least for the time being, there was no choice for us but to remain in the remote, isolated village. The telephone line from the mayor's office had been our only link with the outside world and it was no longer working. As the days went by, the daily news broadcasts on Radio Madrid became more and more important to us and these broadcasts were the focus of our days. We soon learned that the Nationalists were being victorious in most of the southern provinces of Andalucía.

One morning, for some reason I had decided to forgo our usual morning swim. Carmen and Nuria set off as usual and I decided to stay nearer the Inn so that I could have a quiet morning of reading. The sun felt unusually hot for so early in the morning that day as I walked across the courtyard and stepped into the garden with my book. The air was so clear and the atmosphere so transparent that the distant hills and the rocky peaks of the Sierra appeared to be within a short walk. Bees were humming frantically among the rose bushes and small lizards, their little heads tilted toward the sweltering sun, lay motionless on the veranda. I found a comfortable spot in the shade and sat down to read.

I was distracted from my reading by the sight of two mules that approached the iron gate and began nibbling at the rows of daisies and marigolds that grew next to it. I started to walk toward the mules to see if I could lead them toward shade and bring them some water. I gasped in terror when, as I started to get near them, I saw the corpses of two men lying sideways on the backs of the animals, their limp arms and legs dangling over their sides. Where the mules had stopped, the dusty path underneath them was swiftly being tinted scarlet by the blood dripping from the corpses. Tied to the back of each body was a sign with the words "Traidor a España" ("Traitor to Spain") crudely written on it.

I had never seen a dead body before, and I screamed. Hearing me scream, Don Benito, the Innkeeper, came running outside, closely followed by two other men. Once they reached the gate, they approached the animals and, without speaking, they began to secure the lifeless bodies more tightly to the mules' backs with pieces of rope. I watched them as they led the animals away toward the center of the village and I saw them disappear a few minutes later behind the little house near the church where the local Guardia Civil was stationed. It was later that day, in the evening, that we learned that those two men, after being shot, had been draped over the mules' backs with those signs attached to them and then the mules had been left to wander aimlessly throughout the fields, the corpses on their backs a warning to other perceived "traitors".

"Why did they do this?" I asked my father.

He replied, "Those men refused to swear loyalty to Franco and the Nationalists. They were killed and their bodies left like that to scare others so that they will be afraid to fight back."

That was my first sight of death and my first dim understanding that those events everyone listened to on the radio were not just words.

Meanwhile for us in Pedro Bernardo, the days, and even more so the nights, were never to be the same as before. Our carefree lives had become considerably restricted. We could still visit the spring and we were allowed to ride horseback along the paths of the nearby meadow, but we had to be back at the Inn as the first rays of the sun began to fade away into the western horizon. Father did not want us staying out after dark for any reason.

The village mayor and a handful of other men were shot at dawn one morning. When the unexpected news of their deaths reached us at the Inn, a terrible and unforeseen omen seemed to suddenly cast a grim and ugly shadow upon everyone present. It was clear that Don Rafael's life was also in danger now. His life was seriously threatened as men from the neighboring towns began to appear more and more often, demanding to be taken to meet with "the dirty aristocrat". Finally, my father, in spite of Don Rafael's extreme reluctance to do so, convinced him that he should hide in one of the Inn's underground cellars. My father told him to remain in hiding there until such a time as it would be feasible to arrange his escape to safety. Carmen, Nuria, and I were sworn to secrecy, each of us solemnly promising that from then on, we would take turns taking his food down to the cellar for him and that we would not breathe a word to anyone about his whereabouts. Of the three of us, of course, I was the one that took on this responsibility the most wholeheartedly, because I still had my schoolgirl crush on him. I had had a crush on him since I first met him when I was a child, when he had come to visit my parents at our home in Madrid. He was never too affectionate toward any of us children. Quite the contrary, there was always a certain air of arrogance about him which even I, at times, found annoying. But now, I felt sorry for him, as he began to look increasingly haggard and pale from his confinement in that dark and humid cellar.

Carmen and Nuria soon began to find excuses to avoid visiting him in the cellar. Before long, I was left with the sole responsibility for caring for him and looking after him. During my daily walks through the countryside, I would gather fruits and berries and later in the evening, I would bring these to him, together with sweets and pieces of cake which I would take from the dining table. When I would descend into the cellar, a faint smile would settle on his lips as he greeted me, and I would go and sit next to him, keeping him company until he had finished his meal. It was during one of these visits that he gave me his ring, now too big for him to wear. It had his family crest engraved on it and he helped me place it onto the little gold chain that I always wore around my neck.

After a tearful and agonizing debate, Don Benito and my father finally agreed that Don Rafael's two beautiful dogs had to be killed. They were becoming increasingly restless, barking incessantly by the entrance to the cellar where they knew their master was hiding. Carmen and I went along with my father when he went to inform his friend about this decision. While Don Rafael listened in silence to my father's words, not a single muscle seemed to move on his lean, handsome face. His expression remained unchanged. Only his hands betrayed his emotions as they began to shake uncontrollably. Tears welled in my eyes as I watched him. Seeing me watching him, he turned away and buried his face in his hands. I stood there wanting to say something, but not knowing what to say.

Father took Carmen and me by our hands and led us up the stairs and out of the cellar. He guided us outside to a little bench in the courtyard behind the Inn and told us to wait there and not go anywhere until he came back for us. I burst into uncontrollable crying as I saw him walk into the Inn and get Don Benito. Through a window I could see the two of them going out the front door and around toward the side of the Inn. I was still crying when I heard the two gunshots.

As we reached our spring one morning, we were surprised to find the place crowded with people. A group of university students from nearby Salamanca was having a picnic there. It seemed incredible to us that as the country was falling into a civil war, they would find the time to travel for a picnic in the country, but there they were. As we got nearer the pond, we could hear their voices and their laughter. Some were swimming and others were playing guitar and singing at the top of their lungs. We could see their car parked in the shade under a tree by the side of the road. Upset at the thought that what we considered our private domain had been invaded by strangers, we turned back toward the Inn. The old professor in charge of the students followed us and asked us to join the group and eat with them. Soon we were sharing their food and merrily joining them in their singing. We stayed with them until sunset and then started hastily making our way back to the Inn, anxious to return before dark as we were supposed to. Two of the older boys gallantly volunteered to escort us back to the village. As we walked together, so that they could have their hands free to help us pick the blackberries that grew by the side of the road, they carefully wrapped up their swimming shorts and white towels, like turbans around their heads. This was a trivial act which almost cost them their lives.

At the entrance to Pedro Bernardo, a few women were still busy washing clothes in the public fountain. At the sight of the boys, they began to scream hysterically, their shouts and screams piercing the stillness of the evening as they pointed their fingers in sheer terror at the boys.

"Moros!" they screamed. "Vienen los Moros!" ("Moors! The Moors are coming!")

With their heads covered by what appeared to be white turbans, the women had mistaken the students as being Moors, the North African Muslims who had occupied Spain for so many centuries until their expulsion during the "Reconquista" (the Reconquest). Carmen, Nuria, and I could do little else but simply stare at the women in bewilderment. The women by now had knelt on the ground and seemed to be fervently praying to the heavens. The boys did not know what to do either and simply stood there looking dumbfounded.

Soon we were surrounded by a group of men who seemed to have appeared out of nowhere, some carrying rifles while others, reaching into their pockets, were flashing knives at the startled and now terrified students. After a tense few seconds, we finally became aware of what was happening, and we began to laugh nervously. Finally, the boys removed the towels from their heads and one of them started singing out loud an old Castilian song that we all knew by heart. Little by little, the whole group, including we girls, joined him in his singing and as the voices rose and became louder, the tension lessened and the fear, as if by magic, disappeared.

It was not too long afterward when, amid a clamor of jubilant voices and much shaking of hands and hugs, the boys were led away in the direction of the old taverna. The three of us resumed our walk back to the Inn alone, still shaking somewhat from the experience. From the taverna, the sound of men's' voices singing and laughing could be heard from kilometers away.

When we told our father about what we thought to be a comical incident, he was not in the least amused by it.

"But Papá," I said, "It was funny in the end. When the boys took the towels off their heads, and started singing in Spanish, everyone realized that they weren't Moors. And how could Moors be in Spain in 1936 anyway? Those villagers were just being silly!"

A Village in the High Sierra

My father was quiet for several moments as he searched for the words to explain things to us. He looked at all three of us very seriously as he puffed on his pipe.

"Yes, you are correct, in the end it was funny," he said to us. "But it could have ended not so funny. Everyone is worried about what might happen. Don Rafael is in hiding because we cannot predict how people will behave toward him, simply because of who he is. The village mayor has been shot for not having the correct loyalties, whatever those are supposed to be. And these villagers are not so silly. General Franco commanded brigades of Moorish soldiers in Morocco. If he brings them to Spain, he will turn them loose on villages like this."

"But why? Why would he bring the Moors back to Spain?"

"You saw how terrified these villagers were at the mere thought that the Moors were coming. That is why. Franco will want to frighten everyone who opposes him. That is the way the Fascists gain power and keep it. Through fear."

From that day on, we were forbidden to return to the spring.

Those two men whose bodies I had seen tied to the mules were the first victims of the civil war in the village of Pedro Bernardo. They were merely a token number among the many throughout Spain who would die during the Spanish Civil War, not to mention the countless lives disrupted and families uprooted during that civil war. The violence throughout Spain continued to escalate, fueling reprisals, which in turn fueled yet more violence. Hideous atrocities were committed by both sides. Some elements of the Republicans, in a rampage of hate and frustration, turned against the Catholic Church, whom they felt had betrayed them by siding openly with Franco, killing nuns and priests and all others presumed to be Franco's sympathizers. Landowners and members of the aristocratic class, or those perceived to be of the aristocratic class, were also targeted. The Nationalists in turn, as they advanced, rounded up all those whom they believed had supported the Republic, or who had not demonstrated allegiance to the Nationalists with sufficient fervor, stood them against the wall, and shot them on the spot without mercy. It was not uncommon for the Nationalists to torture and publicly humiliate their victims before executing them.

As the villagers of Pedro Bernardo had feared, and as my father had predicted, the Moors did indeed return to Spain during that fateful summer. Franco brought contingents of them from Morocco to fight alongside his Nationalist troops, knowing how the presence of these Moorish mercenaries would terrorize the villagers of Spain. A large segment of the population was immediately terrified and for good reason, as tales began to spread all over the land of these foreign soldiers ransacking towns, raping women, and killing villagers indiscriminately. The Moorish troops were generally attached to units of the Spanish Foreign Legion, those fanatical supporters of Franco who were known for their ruthlessness and cruelty and who were proud of their sobriquet "El Novio de la Muerte" ("The Bridegroom of Death") and their battle cry "Viva la Muerte" ("Long Live Death"). Franco's use of the Moors in this way was one more cynical ploy designed to instill terror in the populace. Their presence touched upon the deep-seated fear that rural Spaniards still had of those former occupiers of the Spanish Peninsula.

Chapter 2

The Burning Fields

August 1936
General Franco's troops had reached the Castilian Plateau (the "Meseta"). The province of Ávila, to which Pedro Bernardo belonged, was still Loyalist, under control of the Government of the Republic, but most of the neighboring province of Toledo had already fallen into the hands of Franco's Nationalists.

Hitler and Mussolini had by now agreed overtly to help the Nationalists and it was now known that it was German and Italian airplanes that had airlifted Franco's army to the Spanish mainland from Morocco the previous month. More and more of the regular army was defecting to Franco and as a result, the government in Madrid disbanded the regular army. That became a more or less irrelevant decision, though, as most of the regular officers had already defected and taken their troops with them. Franco brought the rest of the Spanish Foreign Legion forces to the mainland, under the command of his fanatical supporter General José Millán Astray. They included in their ranks the Moorish mercenaries who, together with the Legionnaires, instilled terror everywhere they went due their reputation for bloodlust and cruelty.

As the Republic began to rely more and more on its militias, having been abandoned by most of the regular army, the first of the international volunteers began to arrive in Spain. They would be organized into the five International Brigades, numbered XI to XV, with British and American volunteers incorporated into the Fifteenth International Brigade, which included the Americans of Lincoln Battalion. In response to Hitler's and Mussolini's support of the Nationalists, Stalin expressed support for the Republic and its Loyalist forces. But where the fascist support was massive and significant from the beginning, support from the Soviet Union only trickled in at the beginning and consisted more of propaganda than arms. Even later, while the fascists were concerned entirely with putting Franco in power, the Soviets were more concerned with preserving the ideological purity of the Spanish Leftists. George Orwell wrote about this in detail in his memoirs of his time fighting as a volunteer in Spain, 'Homage to Catalonia'. Hitler and Mussolini not only viewed Franco ideologically as one of their own, they had a long-term strategic reason for supporting him. A Spain sympathetic to them might be willing to seize Gibraltar from the British and thus give a fascist ally control of the entrance to the Mediterranean.

Carmen, Nuria, and I shared a large bedroom that looked down on the orchard. At night, we would lie in bed for hours, awestruck by the view through the narrow frame of our window. The far-away distance, up to the horizon, was strangely and eerily aglow with the reflections from dozens of fires burning across the dry wheat fields.

My father's biggest concern was to find transportation to get us all back to Madrid. My mother, as well as Carmen's parents, had not had any news from us for weeks and he was well aware of the anguish and the terrible anxiety they must be going through. He spent countless hours trying to locate someone, somewhere, willing to provide an automobile in which we could attempt to make a safe journey back to the capital.

Although the nightmare of war was getting dangerously close to us, the three of us girls did not fully appreciate this. Carmen, my sister Nuria, and I did not fully comprehend what was happening around us. Although frightening, in some ways it was also exciting for us. Several times each day, we could distinctly hear the sounds of the artillery and the canons as they were being fired, sometimes as close as just a few kilometers away from us. We would lie flat on the ground to listen to and feel the waves of tremors rumbling through the earth, echo after echo of the tremendous battles that were taking place between Toledo and Talavera de la Reina.

My father's nightly disappearances were becoming more and more frequent. Although we asked him several times about this, he never volunteered any information about where he was going off to every evening or why. It was my sister Nuria who overheard the women in the kitchen talking and commenting about my father and she relayed their conversation back to Carmen and me to satisfy our ever-increasing curiosity. From then on, we could hardly wait for nightfall to arrive. As soon as it was dark, we would go to our upstairs bedroom, put out the light, and wait there, in darkness, until we began to hear the whispering of voices in the courtyard and the bustling and snorting of the horses as they were being saddled. Among the shadows, we could identify those of my father, of Don Santiago, and of a third man, all three wrapped in the heavy capes worn by the local farmers and their heads covered by wide-brimmed hats. We watched them as they slung blankets and leather bags over the animals' backs. In a matter of minutes, they were on horseback and disappearing quickly into the darkness.

Although my father was a staunch Loyalist, a supporter of the Spanish Republic, he was a deeply compassionate man who could not abide the cruelties that were being inflicted by both sides of the rapidly expanding civil war. Also, he had been raised as a gentleman, and despite his somewhat leftist political leanings and his support for the Republic, he had friends on both sides. He took it upon himself to save as many lives as he could from the senseless slaughter that was becoming more and more prevalent.

Riding for hours through the night, my father and his companions would visit the surrounding villages and lend a helping hand to the local priests and certain landowners whose lives were now in jeopardy. They helped them to escape and reach "the other side", Franco's territory, where they would be safe. By cutting through mountain passes, across isolated paths, and traveling only at night, my father was able to bring many such rescue missions to a successful and happy ending.

I was enthralled yet confused by my father's exploits. I had read the novel 'The Scarlet Pimpernel' in school that year and I thought of my father as a modern-day Sir Percy, riding gallantly in the night to rescue would-be victims before it was too late. At the same time, I knew that he was loyal to the Republic and that the men he was saving were not. He did not like to speak of these missions, even when I asked him repeatedly to tell me more, but one morning after breakfast he explained his motives to me.

"But Papá," I asked, "Aren't these men enemies of the Republic?"

"Yes, Conchita," he explained patiently. "But that does not mean they deserve to be killed. There will be enough cruelty and death before this is done. Remember, our friend Don Rafael is also opposed to the Republic. But he is still our friend."

I was beginning to understand, at my tender age, that perhaps the world was not as black and white as I had thought.

After our daily siesta, holding a thick slice of crusty bread and a bar of chocolate in our hands, we would walk over to the esplanade situated at the western edge of the village. Looking out over the massive blocks of granite that encircled the esplanade, we could see the impressive cliff and the ravine that dropped off from its edge. To the right, the cascading waters of the river rushed along the huge crevices that formed the bottom of the gorge and led to a waterfall that, fed by the perennial snow and ice that covered the Sierra de Gredos, ran year-round.

The esplanade served as the meeting place for the villagers. In the late afternoon, it was always crowded with men and women, country people, gathered in small groups or strolling under the chestnut trees that lined the square. They would meet and gather there for hours, the voices of adults and children mingling with the sounds of the waterfall, discussing all the matters that are of great import to country life and trying to make sense of the chaos of civil war that was erupting around them.

I loved the time we spent there, the three of us girls perched atop a stone fence, joining the old men and women who, like us, were already taking their places around the square to watch my father and the other two men, who had been sent from Madrid, as they did their work. They were training the farmers and peasants of the area in the use of firearms, teaching them military drills, trying in the shortest possible time to transform them into Loyalist soldiers of the Republic. From the surrounding towns and villages, men would arrive on foot, a few on horseback, waiting patiently in the brightness of the summer afternoon for their turn to be called.

I can still see their faces. Their skin had been turned a deep mahogany color by the sun and by the fierce winds of the Sierra, their lean bodies were erect, and they all had a strange look of anticipation in their eyes. Proud people, they would learn fast, trained as quickly as possible a few at a time. They were told to march in unison, step in step, to turn right or left over and over again. They followed orders silently, lifting thick clouds of dust with their rope-soled "alpargatas" (espadrilles). As we watched these men train and prepare for war, we could hear the distant rumbling thunder of the cannons being fired in the battles of

Toledo and Talavera de la Reina. If these men were feeling any fear that soon they would be facing those cannons themselves, their faces did not show it.

In time, these men that my father helped to train would become the fearless militia of the Spanish Republic. Like their brothers across the land, they would fight valiantly to try to defend the Republic at all costs and against insurmountable odds. This would be a militia consisting mainly of raw recruits, poorly equipped and only quickly and insufficiently trained. When told that they were to fight fascism, many among them did not know what this word meant. They just knew that men they trusted, men like my father, were telling them it was an evil force that had to be fought and beaten. And they believed them. How could they possibly have emerged victorious against the more numerous and by far much better equipped forces of Franco's Nationalists? They did not have adequate supplies, as these were denied the Republic by almost all the western democracies, including the United States. Only later, to the dismay of many, too little and too late and too dominated by Stalinist ideology, did the Soviet Union send military and propaganda specialists and airplanes to aid the forces of the Republic. Some aircraft were also bought from France, but all of this paled in comparison to the massive military aid that Hitler's Germany and Mussolini's Italy were providing to Franco.

Meanwhile, in Pedro Bernardo, the specter of war seemed to be growing inexorably closer every day. Although we girls were not fully aware of it, the "Four Horsemen of the Apocalypse" were riding toward us at a fast pace and soon the whole country would be engulfed by civil war. By now, the little church next to the square was seldom empty. Women were gathered there at almost all times and the flicker of candles constantly illuminated the altar as well as the image of Santa Teresa, the patron saint of the province.

Rather unexpectedly, my father announced to us one morning, right after breakfast, that we must gather all of our things and be ready at a moment's notice as we would be leaving for Madrid soon. In the next town, several kilometers away in the next valley, some "milicianos" had commandeered a couple of automobiles in which they were making daily trips back and forth to the capital. One of these men knew my father well and had agreed to take us along on his next journey. Although happy at the opportunity that was being offered to us, we were also concerned and reluctant to leave the village. We knew the trip would not be exempt from danger. The Nationalists had taken control of all the provinces along the flanks of the nearby mountains. Their troops controlled the neighboring towns and hamlets and almost all the main thoroughfares were also in their hands. To travel to Madrid in relative safety, we would have to traverse the countryside along unused roads, first crossing the high mountain pass on foot until we could reach the valley that lay beyond. Once there, we could continue the journey by road in the automobile.

On the day of our departure, I waited for Carmen to join me to go down to the cellar for a last visit with Don Rafael. As usual, we found him reading by candlelight, the unventilated cellar foul with the smell of tobacco and the rancid fumes emanating from the old wine barrels stacked high along the walls.

"I came to say goodbye, Don Rafael," I said.

Lacking his usual aloofness, he smiled and pointed at the ring he had given me, with his family crest engraved on it, which I still wore around my neck.

"You won't forget me, will you Señorita Conchita?" It was the first time he had called me "Señorita" and not "little girl". I blushed and he smiled at noticing. "You have been a good friend to me. Thank you. I shall always remember you."

Something in his bearing told me it would be unseemly to cry in his presence and I fought back the tears as he kissed my hand and said "Vaya con Dios" a final time. He said goodbye to Carmen, and we left.

Back in the courtyard, we waited for the four men and two women who would be travelling with us over the pass and to the next valley, where the automobile would be waiting for us. When we finally saw them descending the slope behind the Inn, it was already late afternoon. The final preparations for our trip were being made, and I turned to my father to ask him if I could go back once more to the cellar to say another goodbye to Don Rafael and to give him some of my books. My father did not answer right away, but taking me by the arm and looking distraught, in a hushed tone of voice out of earshot of the others he told me that Don Rafael had decided to make his escape. He had done so during the last hour, unnoticed by anyone.

"Will he be alright, Papá?" I asked.

My father was quiet for several seconds and then whispered,

"I only hope and pray, for his sake, that he will be able to reach 'the other side' safely."

After an emotional and tearful farewell to Don Benito and his family, our little group began the long and hazardous walk. Night had arrived and we were totally engulfed by darkness by the time we reached the little shepherd's refuge hut at the summit of the pass where we were to spend the night. After a few hours of much needed rest, we would continue our journey at sunrise.

The moon had not risen yet and a dark firmament was suspended above us, its dome sparkling brightly with a shining tapestry of millions of stars. All around us, the landscape was bare, except for some scrubby vegetation. The peaks of the mountains dominated the valley, their granite boulders silvery in the shadows and obscurity of the night. The air was freezing cold. Wrapped up in a blanket, it felt good to sit by the fire that the men had made outside the hut. From a basket, one of the women extracted some cheese, green peppers, and olives, which she handed to us, together with slices of bread, while the "bota" filled with wine was passed around. When our meager but tasty meal was finished, the men remained outside the hut, but the two women, followed by we three girls, went into the hut. It was getting colder and we tried to get some needed sleep by bundling close to each other for warmth. At the far end of the hut, a half dozen sheep were grouped together next to a pile of hay, and all through the sleepless night, I could see the amber pupils of their eyes shining in the darkness.

Finally, huddled together like the sheep, we managed to fall asleep.

It was right at about dawn that, hearing noise and commotion from outside, I was woken up. I got up and went outdoors to see what was going on. The sun's warming rays had not yet reached the summit of the pass, which was still in the shadow of the night, and I could see my breath in the cold mountain air. I was wrapped in my blanket and shivering with cold as I tried to accustom my eyes to the dim light of the early morning. There were still stars visible in the dark sky to the west as the sky to the east began to lighten. The first thing I saw in the dim light was the figure of my father hurriedly walking toward the two strangers that were approaching the refuge, carrying between them what looked like the limp body of a dead man. Soon, they were surrounded by all the others, who helped them to lay the body on the ground.

Somehow, instinctively, I knew that this was Don Rafael's body, even before I could get close enough to recognize his features. When my father saw me, standing only a few feet away, he tried to pull me gently back. But I could not move, remaining there as if glued to the ground, all the while staring in front of me in disbelief and too stunned to cry.

Watching silently, I saw the women approach and cover the body with a blanket, then kneel down to pray beside it. Two of the men were already busy trying to dig a hole in the ground in which to bury him, on the little knoll that rose from the pass. The ground was frozen, and this proved to be an arduous task. They found some tools inside the hut and they proceeded with their grim work. It took almost half the morning for the men to dig the grave, the shovels in their hands almost useless in their attempts to break through the frozen earth, but my father could not leave his friend's body unburied. Afterward, when Don Rafael had been buried, Nuria helped my father to place a few rocks on top of his grave, while Carmen and I looked amid the underbrush for some wildflowers to lay by the gravesite.

After we had put the rocks on top of the hastily dug grave to mark it and spread the flowers at its head, my father stood silently at the grave as though he was about to speak. But no words came. He just stood silently, tears streaming gently down his face as he cried silently. Nuria and Carmen and I stood behind him, holding hands and watching, not knowing what we could say or what we should do.

Finally, Father straightened his back, tilted his head down toward the grave, and in a clear voice he said, "Vaya con Dios, mi amigo. Vaya con Dios."

He motioned for us to come to him and he hugged all of us as we stood there in silence for a few more minutes saying our silent goodbyes to Don Rafael. As were standing there together, the sun finally rose high enough to bathe the mountain pass in its rays and for a moment, Don Rafael's grave was bathed in golden sunlight.

When my father finally gave the signal that it was time for our march to resume, I turned my head to look at him, and I was amazed at the sudden change that had taken place on his face. He was a handsome man who always had a gentle expression in his large, brown eyes. But when I saw him now, as he descended from the knoll where his friend now lay buried, he looked to me like a different man. The sunlight was now striking his face and I could see his features clearly. A sudden pallor and an expression of grief were there, as would be expected, but what struck me the most now was the rictus, full of bitterness, that had settled on his lips and the strange new look in his eyes, which now appeared to be burning with a feverish intensity. Nuria ran to be next to him, and I could see him take her hand, holding it tightly in his, as they began their descent together. I followed closely behind them, but I stopped after taking only a few steps to look back for the last time at the little knoll with its solitary grave. Tears streamed down my face as I walked and hurried to catch up with the group.

As we dropped into the valley and reached the village where we were to be met, the first thing we saw was the top of a black sedan parked by the side of the road, its black top gleaming under the bright sun. The first and most arduous part of the journey home to Madrid was behind us, but we still had a potentially very dangerous drive in front of us.

Under the bright sunshine of noontime, we rode toward Madrid with the farewell wishes of the villagers still ringing in our ears. We drove southeast, gradually descending from the high altitudes of the Sierra to the valley below and the Meseta of Castilla. We left behind us dense thickets of burned woods and scores of fire-charred hills. In the distance, the sky was blackened by smoke. The fields on both sides of the road were still smoldering. As we got closer to Madrid, we could see entire villages in flames, gigantic columns of smoke shielding the sun from our view. The hoarse and roaring sound of the cannons thundered intermittently, that terrible and terrifying noise shattering and destroying the otherwise quiet of the afternoon.

For the rest of my life, the autumn smell of burning leaves evoked a memory of these burning fields and of the sight of villages in flames as I heard the thunder of the cannons. Others may associate the smell of burning leaves with autumn and the approach of the holiday season. For me, it would always be the aroma of war and tragedy.

As we entered Madrid, night had fallen upon the city. People were everywhere, overcrowding the sidewalk cafés along the avenues, while throngs of men and women seemed to be moving around aimlessly. In the sky, there was not a single cloud to dim the extraordinary brilliance of the full moon. An air of unsettledness and anticipation permeated the city and seemed to affect everyone.

"Miss Spain in Exile"

After dropping Carmen at her parents' house and bidding her, and them, a tearful goodbye, we headed home toward the Puerta de Alcalá. Soon we were home, on Calle Velasquez, and in our mother's arms. She held us tightly to her while crying silently at our safe return. Marta, the cook, was also crying from relief at seeing us, as was her husband Manuel, who was also employed by the household. Our little dog Tosca was totally beside herself from excitement at seeing us and kept jumping at our feet and barking incessantly.

I was exhausted and my emotions were drained. I was anxious to go to my room and as I closed the door behind me, I rushed and fell onto my bed. I buried my face in the pillows and wept uncontrollably for a long time. Every time I closed my eyes, I could not rid myself of the sight of Don Rafael's corpse or of the burning villages we had seen during the drive home. I was afraid that I would have nightmares if I fell asleep and I struggled to stay awake as I thought about all the events that had occurred and struggled to make sense of them.

All of a sudden, from the street below my window, I could hear noise and the clamor of shouting voices. Opening the balcony doors, I stepped outside. Opposite our house, men were busy raising a huge banner and streaming it across the street from the third floor of the buildings on either side of Calle Velasquez. With my vision still obscured by the tears streaming from my eyes, I read what was clearly written across the banner in bold, black letters:

NO PASARAN
("They Shall Not Pass")

Chapter 3

The Airbase at Sariñena

Autumn 1936
Despite the failure of the governments of the western democracies to provide aid to the Spanish Republic, foreign volunteers began to arrive in Spain to fight on the Loyalist side. These were formed into the International Brigades, among them the Fifteenth International Brigade, which included among its ranks the American volunteers of the Lincoln Battalion. But these brave and idealistic volunteers (George Orwell, Andre Malraux, and Arthur Koestler were among them) were no match for the thousands of well-armed Italians fighting alongside the Nationalists, nor for Goering's Condor Legion, with German pilots flying and testing the latest German warplanes.

The main body of the Republican army, though, was composed of Spaniards who fought with the tenacity and bravery for which the Spanish people have always been known. If the United States, France, and Britain had shipped arms and matériel to the Spanish Republic when Franco first invaded, as they had every right to do, for the Republic was the legitimately elected government of Spain, the Republic would have survived. But at the time, Hitler cast a tremendous and terrifying shadow over the world and the western democracies were not willing to risk a major war over Spain. Only a few years later, a similar aversion to risking war over the fate of Czechoslovakia led to the debacle of Munich. But war came anyway. As Winston Churchill said after Czechoslovakia was betrayed at the Munich Conference in 1938, "You were given the choice between war and dishonor. You chose dishonor, and you will have war." And so, the world war came anyway, but at a time when Hitler and his allies were ready for it. Many historians agree that if the war had come in 1936, when Hitler was far from fully prepared for it, the Allies would have had a far easier time defeating him and millions of soldiers and civilians would not have perished.

"Miss Spain in Exile"

It is also now well recognized that the Spanish Civil War was not merely a struggle between two factions within the country. It was an international conflict in which Germany, Italy, and the Soviet Union all took part, to a greater or lesser degree, using Spain as a battlefield and testing ground for their arms and bombs and tactics. The barbarous techniques of modern warfare, including terror bombing of civilian populations, were rehearsed and perfected during the Spanish Civil War. Madrid itself was bombed mercilessly, targeting civilians, in a campaign designed to instill terror. In addition to the terror bombing of civilians, Goering used Spain as a training ground for the air support of ground forces that characterized German Blitzkrieg warfare during World War Two.

Modern techniques of wartime propaganda were also developed during the Spanish Civil War, by both sides. These involved the issuance of disinformation, the spreading of rumors with the objective of instilling fear and unrest in the civilian population, and the tainting of the opposing force as being unpatriotic and unfit to live in Spain.

The Second World War was shamelessly rehearsed on Spanish soil, with Spanish blood and with Spanish tears, while the world at large closed its eyes and did nothing to intervene on the side of the legitimate government against the rising fascist tide.

By autumn of 1936, the civil war had spread, and fighting was raging throughout Spain. In places, there were clear battle lines with Loyalist forces on one side and the Nationalists on the other. In other places, though, it was village against village and even city block against city block. Later on, when the battle for Madrid raged, the international volunteers were instructed to take the subway to the fighting but were cautioned to remember to get off at the right stop, or they could exit the subway behind enemy lines!

The military junta led by Franco had officially proclaimed him as Head of State of Spain and Commander in Chief of the Spanish Armed Forces. By November, both the governments of Nazi Germany and Fascist Italy had recognized Franco as the head of Spain's government and were pouring military aid and matériel into Spain to support Franco and his Nationalists. The first military aid had begun to arrive from the Soviet Union in support of the Spanish Republic, but it was no match for what would be provided by Hitler and Mussolini. France was allowing the purchase of some warplanes, but these were old and surplus planes. In general, the western democracies continued to sit back idly and watch as the tragedy in Spain unfolded. They termed their policy "Non-Intervention", but it was a policy that allowed Hitler and Mussolini to intervene as they wished on the Nationalist side while prohibiting intervention on the side of the Republic. It was the population of Spain that paid the price for this policy.

France did ship Spain some surplus airplanes, purchased in haste by the Republic. Curiously, these airplane sales from the French were arranged by France's Air Minister in contravention of the official non-intervention policy of the French government. Then, the Soviet Union began to send Spain some aircraft of their own. On the other side, the Nationalists would soon have on their side the aircraft of Goering's Condor Legion, a thinly disguised arm of Hitler's Luftwaffe, with modern warplanes being flown by well-trained German pilots.

With the civil war now in full gear, living in Madrid was becoming increasingly hazardous. The city was practically isolated from the rest of the country. The German planes, shamelessly and openly aiding Franco's Nationalists, were dropping bombs all over Republican Spain, Madrid of course being their main target. By now, it had become routine for us to rush to the relative safety of the basement at the first sound of the air raid sirens, my sister holding Tosca in her arms and I following with the servants, making sure, following instructions from my mother, that all the doors were tightly shut behind us. We would then spend the entire evening in our makeshift bomb shelter, in semi-darkness, listening first to the whistling sound made by the bombs as they were being dropped and a few seconds later shivering in terror on hearing the deafening noises and feeling the reverberations made by the explosions. The basement floor and walls would shake so much that it felt as though the whole building might collapse on top of us. Mother, the servants, the building's concierge and her family would all eventually emerge, with Nuria and I not far behind, as soon as the distant sirens let us know that the airplanes had gone away. For now.

For the rest of my life, I had a horror of dark spaces and could not stand loud noises or explosions. These brought back too many terrifying memories of waiting through the air raids, cowering in a basement, hearing the loud thumps and booms of the explosions, feeling the ground shake under me, and fearing that the entire house might collapse on top of me. I could not endure holiday fireworks celebrations without shaking and trembling, and I developed a claustrophobia that I had never experienced before then. After those air raids, I could never enter small closets or dark rooms without remembering the terror I had felt as a child during those bombardments.

Father had volunteered to serve as an officer in the Loyalist forces of the Popular Militia and was now on a temporary assignment in Valencia. The living quarters in our spacious home on Calle Velasquez were now confined to the main floor. All the rooms on the second story were closed, the furniture covered with meters of white cloth and the heavy draperies carefully drawn on all the windows. For mother, separated now from her husband and living in the inferno that Madrid had become, dealing alone with all kinds of problems, life must have been almost unbearable. Emotionally, she was growing increasingly distressed, with her closest friends either killed or imprisoned, and most of her relatives living now in exile in Portugal or France. Most of all, though, she lived with the constant fear that her aristocratic background was a source of continual danger for all of us. In spite of all her worries, she tried her best to be cheerful, always trying to reassure us that no matter how bad things were for us at the moment, the nightmare would soon be over, and life would resume as it had been before. We so wanted to believe her!

When the letter from my Aunt Encarna arrived from Paris, my father was home from Valencia on a short leave. In her letter, my aunt again suggested, as she had several times during the previous weeks, the idea for us to leave Spain and stay with her in Paris until the present turmoil subsided and things returned to normal. The decision for my mother, my sister, and me to go to Paris to live with her was finally agreed upon by my parents. Getting us out of the city was becoming an obsession to my father, who refused to return to his post in Valencia until all our papers were in order and our exit visas were secured. While waiting to leave the country, we could go to Barcelona and stay with my father's side of the family, or accept my Uncle Alfonso's (my mother's brother) invitation to join him and his family at the Air Force base in Sariñena, outside the city of Zaragoza, where he was stationed as an officer of the Air Force of the Spanish Republic. Of my mother's two brothers, Uncle

The Airbase at Sariñena

Alfonso was the older. The other brother, Uncle Julio, was also a high-ranking military officer who, like Alfonso, had served in the Spanish Foreign Legion during the Moroccan Wars. Like almost all the officers of the Spanish Foreign Legion, Uncle Julio had sided with Franco and was now commanding Nationalist forces in Sevilla. Alfonso, however, had remained loyal to the Republic. Uncle Alfonso was a bigger than life character and Nuria and I both loved him.

The decision that my parents had to make as to whether we should wait in Barcelona or in Sariñena until we could leave for Paris was not an easy one. For the moment, Barcelona appeared to be relatively peaceful and was not being bombed by the Nationalists, but who could know how long that would last? If the bombing started, Barcelona was a defenseless civilian city. Like Madrid, it did not have adequate defenses against attacks from the air. Sariñena was a military base and so could any day become a target for the Nationalist bombers, but we would be under the care of Uncle Alfonso there, and at least as an Air Force base it would not be such a defenseless target. Or so my parents thought.

When Mother and Father announced that they had decided upon the second alternative, that we would be going to stay with Uncle Alfonso at his Air Force base until we left for Paris, Nuria and I could not have been happier. They made that decision as much as anything because Mother had not seen her brother in a long time, and she did not want to leave Spain without being able to have some time together with him.

After several days of hectic preparations, the day arrived for our departure from Madrid. On the other side of the ornate iron gate that separated the garden at ground level of our building from the street, several milicianos were, as usual, stationed near the front door. There were four of them, shotguns draped over their shoulders, with wide, red badges encircling their upper arms. They had been posted there not only for our personal safety, but also to guard our house and protect everything in it. As autumn approached and the air of Madrid became crisp, they would build a little fire at the farthest corner of the garden and stand their vigil next to it all day and all night long. The maids were no longer with us, having gone back to their respective villages. Mademoiselle Yvonne, our French tutor, had also returned to her native France, after an emotional farewell. Only Marta, our faithful cook, and Manuel, her husband, were still with us. Marta, while helping Mother with the packing, continued to talk to Nuria and me, giving us advice on how we should always be careful to keep our knee socks straight and our hair properly combed and away from our eyes. As she watched us get into the car to leave, she began to sob while drying her tears with a corner of her apron. "Vayan con Dios", she kept repeating as the family car, driven by Manuel, began to pull away from the curb. Nuria and I, with our heads halfway out the window of the car, waved back to her until the automobile turned sharply at the next corner and she and our house disappeared from our view.

It was only months later I would learn that less than twenty-four hours after our departure, an unruly crowd composed of communists and anarchists had pushed its way in through the gate from the street. Seeking vengeance against anyone or any family they perceived as aristocratic, they had entered our building and ransacked every apartment. They were deaf to the appeals of the milicianos who tried to stop them, explaining that not only was our family Loyalist, but the head of the family was fighting for the Republic. The mob did not care. They took with them everything they could carry that was of value, and burned or destroyed the rest, leaving hideous knife scars on the paintings and pictures, smashing the statues, and destroying Father's beloved piano. We never learned what had happened to Father's priceless collection of old books, some of which had been in the family for generations.

Manuel was driving us for the last time that afternoon. In silence, we crossed the beautiful Paseo de la Castellana, where Nuria and I had spent so many happy hours as younger children. Soon we had passed the gates of the El Retiro park, the foliage of its centuries-old trees already painted with the vibrant gold and red colors of autumn and arrived at the Atocha Train Station.

Father, taking Mother gently by the arm, led her into the railway station, with Nuria and me following close behind, fearful of losing sight of them amid the tremendous crowd that filled the lobby. He had recently been given the rank of Captain in the Popular Brigade, and he was due back in Valencia that evening. The military train in which he would travel was on the opposite side of the tracks. None us knew that then, but he would be back in Madrid before long to take an active part in the defense of the capital. Like his fellow Republican militiamen, he carried a rifle, wore rope-soled "alpargatas" (espadrilles), and the sleeves of his shirt, open at the neck, were rolled all the way up to the elbow. This was quite a contrast to the way in which he used to dress, wearing only suits tailor-made for him by the best tailors of Savile Row in London! Mother, on the other hand, was her usual self, elegantly dressed from head to toe, her only concession to the leftist spirit of the day in Madrid being that she no longer wore a hat or gloves.

As Mother and Father embraced to say goodbye to each other, they seemed to be oblivious to everything around them, sensing only themselves. In the noisy and chaotic confusion that surrounded us, Nuria was having trouble keeping little Tosca quiet. She handed her over to Manuel only at the last minute, when the departure of our train was announced. We both threw our arms around the old man's neck in tears, while he kept on blowing his nose and swallowing hard, trying to control his weeping. Taking our little dog in his arms, he promised us for the hundredth time that he would take good care of her during our absence. We kissed Father one more time before boarding the train and going to our compartment. The gaiety, fun, and excitement that had always preceded our trips in the past was absent on this occasion. Mother regained her composure as the train began to pull away from the station. With Nuria and me by her side, we continued to look out the window until we lost sight of Father and Manuel and the station became a blurred, tiny spot in the distance. Slowly at first but gradually picking up speed, we traversed the outskirts of the city heading east. Madrid's lights were shining brightly, its thousands of luminous reflections blending at the horizon with those of the stars.

Mother had sat down and she remained motionless for a long time with her eyes closed. I knew she was not asleep. A short while later, the conductor entered our compartment and gave us strict orders not to lift the black canvas shade that covered the window. All kinds of precautions had to be taken to lessen the chances of being attacked by enemy planes.

It was eerie to be traveling in almost total darkness, with only a dim, bluish light shining faintly from the ceiling above our heads. As we lay down, trying to sleep on the compartment's couch, neither Mother, nor Nuria, nor I suspected then, as the train continued its journey kilometer after kilometer, that we were not only leaving Madrid behind for many years to come. We were also leaving behind a way of life, a sunny and carefree existence that was being lost forever. My happy childhood came abruptly to an end on that day, the moment we boarded the train bound for Zaragoza on our way to Sariñena.

Sariñena was an old and prosperous town, situated not far from the Ebro River. It belonged to the province of Aragón, which together with the provinces of Valencia and Catalonia were still controlled by the Loyalists.

My Uncle Alfonso was waiting for us at the railroad station. He was wearing the uniform of the Republican Air Force, with the stars and gold braid on the sleeves denoting his rank as Commanding Officer and he looked as handsome as ever. He was of medium height, but slim despite the approach of middle age. He always stood ramrod straight but with an easy smile on his lean face. Jet black hair poked out from under his cap and his brown eyes were always mirthful, as though smiling at a joke that only he knew.

Teniente Coronel Alfonso de los Reyes y Gonzalez Cardenas was an extraordinary man who had led an adventurous life, a romantic and highly dangerous one as well, ever since the time when, as a young man, he had graduated from the prestigious Military Academy of Toledo. He had fought in North Africa as a young officer of the Spanish Army throughout the campaigns of the war in Morocco. He then enlisted and served for a while in the Spanish Foreign Legion, fighting and earning medals for valor in the continuing Moroccan Wars. After leaving the Foreign Legion, he became involved and had an active role in a plot to stage a coup d'état and overthrow the Spanish monarchy. The plot was exposed, and he spent some in a military prison outside Madrid. King Alfonso XIII issued a pardon for him, because of his numerous medals. He had lived notoriously in many parts of the world, among them Washington, D.C., where he met and later married, after getting her pregnant and not without a great deal of scandal and publicity, the daughter of the Irish ambassador to the United States. She had been killed tragically in a car accident not long after their marriage. His current wife, Elvira, was a Spanish beauty, blonde and green-eyed and with whom he seemed to be very much in love. My Uncle Alfonso was a unique man with a unique personality, well-liked and greatly admired by his subordinates.

After hugging and kissing Mother and saying, "Sister, how happy I am to see you here!", he saw me and pretended not to recognize me.

The Airbase at Sariñena

"Who is that grown up young lady who looks so much like my little niece Conchita?" he said to me in a loud voice, wrinkling his brow in feigned confusion. "And who can this other young lady be, who looks so much like my niece Nuria?" Pretending to only then have recognized who we were, he said, "How lovely you both look and how much you have grown since the last time I saw you!"

He kissed first my hand then Nuria's, like the Spanish caballero that he was, then clicked his heels and gave us a formal military salute. Mother couldn't stop smiling and did not attempt to hide her joy at seeing her brother. Just seeing him made us feel that we were once again safe.

We climbed into the big automobile that was waiting for us outside the gates of the railroad station. It was a clear, fair morning, and as the car passed through the last bend in the road, Sariñena suddenly appeared, an old and noble-looking town hunched against a wall of brownish rocks, basking under the sun. The nearby fields were bordered with low stones forming stockades, and inside their enclosures, herds of bulls and a few scattered Merino sheep were quietly grazing.

The Air Force base was situated a few kilometers outside of the town. As we drove alongside the sage-covered countryside, I looked around me with increasing curiosity, not knowing how long we would be remaining in this place, only knowing that it would be for an indeterminate period of time.

My uncle and his lovely wife lived in a comfortable house inside the base. The house also served as his headquarters. Separate barracks provided lodging for his officers and for the cadets and the rest of the personnel that lived and worked on the base. The flyers that were stationed there under his command were a mixed and interesting group of men. The younger ones were fresh from the Air Academy. The others, older and more experienced, had completed their training either in France or in Britain. As a whole, they were a colorful group of carefree men who took their dangerous daily air missions in stride and who seemed to enjoy the difficult work that had been assigned to them in spite of the dangers involved.

Close to the hangars, the airplanes were lined up next to each other in perfect, neat rows. These aircraft were old and ill-kept, since there was a continuous lack of spare parts for their proper maintenance. Many of them were World War One surplus. As soon as they were airborne, everyone became aware of the fact that from that moment on, the lives of the pilots depended more on plain good luck, and the grace of God, than on anything else. Nevertheless, those aviators flew in these planes to conduct their assigned missions, day after day, regardless of the danger or the ever-shrinking margin of safety.

My uncle could hardly restrain himself from cursing the airplanes often, especially when at the end of the day he was informed of the number of casualties suffered during the day's missions. Clenching his hand into a tight fist and chewing nervously on his lower lip, we would hear him shout out loud obscenities, cursing those airplanes that, he said, were only good to be used for scrap. His disappointment must have been tremendous when, after inspecting the "new" planes sent over to him from Madrid, he realized that they were scarcely better than the ones he already had at hand.

But there was more than one reason why Teniente Coronel Alfonso de los Reyes y Gonzalez Cardenas was so well-liked, and indeed worshipped, by his men. Whenever a new airplane arrived, and it was not sure whether the plane was safe to fly, he would always volunteer to be the first pilot to take the plane up and make sure it was airworthy. Similarly, whenever there was an especially dangerous mission to be flown, for example an air assault on an enemy position, with little chance of returning safely to the base, he would invariably always be the first one to step inside a cockpit, his perennial grin as always present on his well-tanned face. In either case, a test flight of a new plane or a dangerous mission over Nationalist territory, as soon as the plane he was flying was off the ground, my Aunt Elvira together with my mother would go inside the tiny chapel on the base. There they would remain, praying to the "Virgen del Pilar" for his safe return, until he had once again defied the odds and landed safely back at the base.

Meals at the base were served in a spacious, rectangular hall that had been converted into a dining room. Our family sat apart from the airmen, at a round table next to one of the few windows located at the rear of the room. To be on time for the meals was an absolute requirement and Nuria and I would rush indoors as soon as we heard the bell announcing it was time for a meal. The comradeship that reigned in that place, especially during meals, was contagious. The stories recounting the events and adventures that had occurred during the course of the day were told and commented upon from

The Airbase at Sariñena

table to table and the happy, or more often sad, experiences of the day's missions were shared by all.

It was during the course of one such meal that the base was attacked from the air for the first time. Although we were aware of the possibility that this could happen, and drills were conducted frequently to prepare us for the possibility, when it finally did occur and bombs began exploding all around us, we were taken by surprise. There had been no time even for the sirens to sound out the air raid alert and warn us of the imminent danger. It was all so sudden, and everything happened so quickly, that it felt like a nightmare. The defenses at the Sariñena Air Force base proved to be totally inadequate for the task of defending against an attack by modern warplanes.

When the attack was over, several on the base had been killed. The hangars and almost all the airplanes had been destroyed. It was terrifying to look around and see so much havoc and so much damage created in such a short time. Wounded airmen lay sprawled on the ground under benches and tables, and the ones who were seriously wounded were moaning in agony. The main building, in spite of having been hit severely, had not collapsed. But a large portion of its roof had been blown off by the impact of bombs and through the huge gap in the ceiling, a portion of the bright, blue sky could be seen from indoors. Debris was everywhere and dense smoke and dust filled the air.

Doctors and nurses began arriving, sent over from a nearby clinic. Mother, Aunt Elvira, and most of the officers' wives were keeping themselves busy by quickly setting up makeshift hospital beds and bandaging and attending to the wounded. One of the doctors instructed me to stay in the kitchen and help the women who were there keeping the big kettles constantly filled with boiling water.

Since that first air strike, we lived in constant fear, dreading the subsequent bombings that we knew would follow. Mother was becoming increasingly anxious that we leave for Paris. It was with a huge sigh of relief that only a few days later we finally received word from the French Consulate in Barcelona that our visas to enter France had been granted. Uncle Alfonso helped us to make plans to depart for Barcelona the very next day, in a military automobile with a military driver that he was able to arrange on short notice.

After dinner that last evening at the Sariñena Air Base, we all sat down next to the fireplace as usual but gone was the merriment and the gaiety that used to prevail at such times, when guitar music and singing would last through the evening. Now, instead we simply stared in silence at the flames, unable to erase from our minds the tragedy of the past few days. The empty places around us were mute evidence and a constant reminder of those among our friends who were gone forever. My Uncle Alfonso took particularly hard the loss of any of his men, but it was easier for him to accept their loss in air combat than on the ground from bombing. He felt as though he had let them down by failing to protect them.

I remember our last night at the base. I can still hear the soft, nocturnal noises that pierced the stillness of the evening, the chirping of crickets and cicadas hidden in the wheat fields. Suddenly, out of nowhere, like monstrous and evil black birds, the shadows of enemy planes on a bombing mission appeared in the sky. The muffled, rattling sound of their engines filled the pit of my stomach with anguish and apprehension as they flew over us, on the way to their target. Some minutes later, from far away, we could hear the distant rumbling thunder of the bombs that they had dropped. Then they flew over us again, looking just as monstrous and evil even though now we knew that they had already dropped their deadly bombs and were just returning to their base behind the Nationalist lines.

The next morning, when the time came to say goodbye, Mother led Nuria and me by the hand to where Uncle Alfonso and his wife and the officers who had now become our friends were waiting outside the to say "adios". The big automobile outside was being loaded with our luggage and my sister and I ran over toward the spot where Uncle Alfonso had gone to open the door for us. As we said "adios" to him, he gave us each a big hug and, reaching into one of the pockets of his worn leather flying jacket, he drew out two small medals which he placed in the palms of our hands.

"These medals are for being so brave and courageous", he said, his habitual grin lighting up his whole face. Then he and his officers gave us a formal salute. He kissed Mother goodbye and we got in the car and drove off the base and toward Barcelona.

A storm had been brewing since early morning. It wasn't raining yet, but dark clouds were massing, and the wind was beginning to pick up. As the wind moved the clouds quickly across the sky,

The Airbase at Sariñena

bright flashes of sunshine burst sporadically through the ever-shifting gaps in the clouds.

We had scarcely been driving for half an hour when we were forced to halt in the middle of a narrow road. A funeral procession was blocking the way, heading for the cemetery, the hearses closely followed by the local authorities and by the families of the victims. The same airplanes that only days ago had dropped bombs on the base had also dropped their lethal cargo of explosives on the defenseless town of Sariñena, leaving behind a score of dead and injured. Some of the injured, we were told, had died within days of the bombing. By the time our journey resumed, big drops of rain were starting to fall, quickly soaking the dry, reddish earth.

The contours of the hills were hardly discernible through the rain, hidden by the menacing clouds that hung heavily above them. Ahead of us, the Ebro River unfolded itself, its yellow waters flowing smoothly under the arches of the ancient bridges that spanned it. As we entered the fertile plain in which the city of Zaragoza lies, the sun was once more shining brightly, painting with golden colors the dome and the towers of the old church of Zaragoza, the whole city enclosed by the winding river. It was a beautiful and peaceful sight that was hard to reconcile with the savage bombings to which we had been subjected only days before or to the funeral procession we had seen just that morning.

We continued on our journey to Barcelona uninterrupted and arrived before nightfall.

We stayed in Barcelona for ten days. I was happy to be back in that beautiful city, where I had been born fifteen years earlier.

From the balconies of my father's family's ancestral home, I could see the magnificent buildings and the tree-lined avenues that extended from the foot of the mountains down to the Mediterranean. Our family's home was located in the heart of the city, only minutes away from the "Paseo de Gracia", one of the major avenues of Barcelona. We spent our time in the company of countless uncles, aunts, and cousins of all ages. Life in this home was considerably more formal and structured than we were used to. Meals took forever, everyone seated at his or her assigned place at the long dining room table. The long and formal meals were presided over by Aunt Antonieta, the matriarch of the Balcells (my father's) family. Surrounded by a continuous flow of new acquaintances, Nuria and I could hardly wait for the chance to run outside.

Chaperoned by one or two servants, we would go down to the street and sit down on one of the many marble benches that lined the avenue. From our vantage point, we watched in fascination all the strange and unfamiliar happenings that were taking place before our eyes.

Barcelona was preparing for the civil war to arrive. Barricades were being erected and sand-filled bags were being placed along the buildings and around all the monuments. The streets were terribly noisy with the constant humming and bustling of people. A battalion of "milicianos" was being drilled nearby by a group of their comrades. The shrill voices of loudspeakers were a deafening clamor of political slogans and martial music. It was in Barcelona then that I heard for the first time the stirring music of the "Internationale", the international anthem of the communists, and heard its Russian verses sung in Spanish.

Finally, the long-awaited day came that we were to leave for Paris. Uncle Alfonso had sent two military men from Sariñena to accompany us to the railway station and to ensure that we boarded our train safely. We drove to the station with them, the journey delayed every few blocks by mobs of people that came from every direction. We found ourselves surrounded by and in the middle of a demonstration, thousands of people grouped together in a show of solidarity with the government of the Republic. Men and women were passing by us, walking arm in arm, some of them carrying weapons of various kinds. Crowds waving the yellow, red, and purple flag of the Republic marched past, singing the fighting songs of the Republic, which by then every Loyalist knew by heart. With all sorts of banners being held high above the crowd, all the numerous and different factions of the Spanish political parties of the left and workers' unions, the "sindicatos", were taking part in that seemingly endless procession.

We finally arrived at the railway station. The station was overcrowded with groups of soldiers and "milicianos" traveling in all directions. Refugees of all kinds were grouped together, like us on their way to France. And there were many little Spanish children, boys and girls, being sent away by their parents for their own safety. Some were going to France or to distant Mexico, from where many of them would eventually return. Some were being sent to the Soviet Union. Most of these never came back and many of them were never heard from again.

The Airbase at Sariñena

As our train left Barcelona and we headed toward Paris, I couldn't help but wonder what lay ahead for me. I had no way of knowing what direction my life would take and that it would be twenty-five years before I would set foot on Spanish soil again.

For the rest of her life, Isa would be moved to tears at hearing the old fighting songs of the Republic. When I learned to play guitar, I learned many of the songs by listening to recordings. She especially loved the songs sung by the Americans of the Lincoln Battalion, which I learned by listening to the recordings that Pete Seger made. She would get a faraway look in her eyes when I would sing these for her, and then she would want to talk about "those courageous and idealistic young Americans who came to fight for Spain in her hour of need."

CHAPTER 4

Crossing the Pyrenees and Becoming Isa

Autumn 1936–Winter 1937
As the civil war continued to be fought savagely between Loyalist and Nationalist forces, the whole province of Aragón, from Huesca to the mouth of the Ebro River, had become a huge battlefield. Some of the most savage battles of the Spanish Civil War were fought in this province as that winter of 1936 set in. There were very few clear frontlines in this war. Village fought village and sometimes the battle lines were drawn between different factions within single villages.

As autumn turned into winter, the Nationalists continued to consolidate territory as they prepared for the concerted attack they would launch on Madrid in February. It was during the months before this attack that the Nationalist general Emilio Mola told a journalist that he and his three fellow rebel generals (Franco, Varela, and Queipo de Llano) had in addition to their four columns of soldiers that would attack Madrid, a "fifth column" of sympathizers in the capital that would rise to help defeat the Republic and ensure victory for the Nationalists. This was the origin of the phrase "Fifth Column" to refer to traitors or sympathizers, and became the title of Hemingway's only play, written while he was in Madrid during the Nationalist bombardment of the city.

In February 1937, Franco started his major ground forces assault on Madrid. Through the bitter fighting, Nationalist forces made it to the suburbs of Madrid and there was fighting so close to the center of the capital that Loyalist militiamen could take the Madrid subway to and from the front. The International Brigades played a major role in resisting this Nationalist offensive. In March, at the Battle of Guadalajara, some 60 kilometers northeast of Madrid, Italian

Crossing the Pyrenees and Becoming Isa

"volunteers" fighting with the Nationalists were soundly defeated, again with significant participation by the international volunteers, in particular here the Italians of the XII Brigade and the Poles of the XIII Brigade. As a result of this defeat, Franco for the moment abandoned his plans to capture Madrid and focused his war plans on consolidating his control of the rest of Spain.

There was a song of the Spanish Civil War entitled "Los Cuatro Generales" ("The Four Generals"), referring to Franco, Mola, Varela, and Queipo de Llano. My mother used to love for me to sing her this song when I would come to visit her later in her life and she would play her castanets while I played the guitar and sang. She particularly loved the verses that went:

> Madrid que bien resistes,
> Madrid que bien resistes,
> Madrid que bien resistes,
> Mamita mia, los bombardeos.
> De las bombas se ríen,
> De las bombas se ríen,
> De las bombas se ríen,
> Mamita mia, los Madrileños.

As sung in English by the Americans of the Lincoln Battalion, the words are:

> Raining bombs on our cities,
> Raining bombs on our cities,
> Raining bombs on our cities,
> Mamita mia, they tried to defeat us.
> But the brave Madrileños,
> But the brave Madrileños,
> But the brave Madrileños,
> Mamita mia, they laugh in defiance.

These words would always make my mother emotional as she remembered the bombardments she had endured as a young girl and the siege to which the beloved city of her birth had been subjected. The song "Los Cuatro Generales" was based on the melody of the traditional Spanish song "Los Cuatro Muleros", but with updated lyrics adapted to the Civil War. At least some of these lyrics were written (in German) by Ernst Busch, a German singer and actor who left Nazi Germany with the Gestapo on his heels.

"Miss Spain in Exile"

He joined the International Brigades to fight on the Loyalist side during the Spanish Civil War. There was a small band of such anti-Nazi Germans who formed a contingent within the International Brigades. Though small in number, this unit fought against the fascists with bravery and distinction on the battlefields of Spain.

Our train left Barcelona and we slowly gathered speed northeastward and entered the province of Girona, where my mother had been born. Our path paralleled the Mediterranean coast, passing through small towns and picturesque fishing villages, as yet untouched by the war. We gazed in wonder at the beautiful coastline of the Costa Brava, which later would become such a destination for tourists from all over the world, with its sandy beaches and little coves sparkling like crystals under the radiant sun. Soon, we were approaching the Pyrenees, their foothills swooping down toward the sea below. As we climbed into the foothills and turned inland, the blue immensity of the Mediterranean was lost from our view. We entered the Pyrenees through narrow passages and our train climbed steadily. The forbidding mountains were brown and purple, crowned with wild, white clouds, the snow-covered ridges towering over the valleys and ravines that sloped down from the heights. It was a dazzling landscape of breathtaking beauty, the memory of which I would keep in my heart forever.

The train slowed as it reached the French border. Luckily for us, despite the careful search and close inspection of our luggage, first by Spanish customs agents and then by the "gendarmes" on the French side of the border, the stash of jewels Mother had hidden in her luggage was not discovered. The customs officials on either side of the border would happily have confiscated these jewels had they found them. This was the first of several frightening encounters with border officials that we would go through during the next few years. As nerve-wracking as this border crossing was, it was nothing compared to the fear we would feel in the future when it was not French gendarmes inspecting our papers and examining our luggage, but the cold-eyed men of the Gestapo.

When the gendarmes had left our compartment and our train resumed its journey toward Paris, Mother let out an audible sigh of relief. She was counting on those jewels to help us survive through

Crossing the Pyrenees and Becoming Isa

the exile and inevitable hardships that lay ahead. My parents' wealth had gone up in smoke as the first shots of the civil war were fired. The Madrid house with its beautiful and valuable paintings, antique furniture, and cabinets filled with silver and exquisite pieces of old china, would never be recovered. Wardrobes full of clothing and expensive linens were left behind, as were fur coats neatly stored away inside monogrammed covers. My father's library, stocked with hundreds of volumes including his father's priceless collection of rare books, some of which had been in the family for generations, was lost forever. Father's lucrative law practice simply ceased to exist. He had sacrificed everything when he made the decision to join the forces of the Republic to fight the Fascists.

Nonetheless, as we left Spain behind and gradually drew near Paris, my mother's face looked happier and more serene than I had seen it in a long time. I took her hand and said, "Don't worry, Mamá. Everything will be fine."

She looked into my eyes and smiled and said, "Of course it will be, Conchita. As long as we are together, we will all be fine."

The locomotive started to slow down as we approached the station in Paris. When it finally came to a halt, Nuria and I jumped to our feet and began helping Mother collect our luggage. As we stepped off the train onto the platform, we were met by Aunt Encarna and my two cousins. They all looked as beautiful and elegant as I remembered them from when they had last visited us in Madrid. My cousins Alma and Nanita were a few years older than me and they certainly looked considerably more sophisticated than me, with my hair still in braids and wearing my knee socks.

The six of us with our load of suitcases managed to get into a taxi. As we rode, we talked excitedly in Spanish, trying not to pay too much attention to the rude grumblings of our driver, who seemed annoyed by our ceaseless chattering in a language he did not understand. After the long train journey, I was tired, but nevertheless I managed to keep my eyes open as our taxi made its way through the streets, crossing broad avenues and passing awesome, magnificent buildings. It was my first time in Paris and the city appeared so wonderful and beautiful to me, the most marvelous city I had ever seen or could have imagined!

Aunt Encarna's fashionable apartment was located near the Avenue Mozart, in the heart of the elegant and toney 16th

Arrondissement. It was a fairly large apartment with three spacious bedrooms, a big parlor, and a dining room separated from the living room by tall, glass-paneled doors. Aunt Encarna was renting the apartment from its owner, a wealthy Jewish widow who had spent the last several years touring Europe before settling in Venice. They had known each other from years earlier, when their husbands had been friends. She allowed Aunt Encarna to pay a greatly reduced rent for the fashionable apartment, knowing that she could be trusted to take care of it for her.

Mother and Nuria shared a room next to Aunt Encarna and Nanita, while Alma and I took the room situated in the corner. Our room was not as large as the other two, but, as Alma was quick to point out to me, it had a balcony from which we could get a nice view of the not too distant Bois de Boulogne.

From the day we arrived, Paris would be our home until the approach of yet another war – the greater conflagration of World War Two – would force us to abandon it and seek asylum and safety somewhere else. I fell in love with Paris from the beginning and felt a special bond with the city, as do all those who arrive as foreigners but before long become Parisians. In this fair and beautiful city, and in a totally new environment for us, we began to settle into our new lives. We tried as best we could among the six of us to cope with the realities and problems that our new life brought us, not least of these our financial situation.

Nuria was soon admitted to the Lycée Molière, where she continued with her education. She was a bright and pretty girl, fourteen years old now, with thick, chestnut colored hair, and bangs that invariably half-covered a pair of mischievous eyes. She still practiced her guitar at every opportunity and dreamed of being a concert guitarist one day. The renowned Spanish guitarist Carlos Montoya, who revolutionized Flamenco guitar and was responsible for making this a mainstream form of music for its own sake, not solely an accompaniment for the dancing and singing of Flamenco, was often in Paris in those days. Through the connection of a family friend, Nuria was able to take lessons with Montoya when he would be in the city. Eventually, Nuria would play concerts and recitals in Paris and in other European cities.

My cousin Nanita was tall, blonde, and very beautiful. She was working as a model for Jean Patou, the famous designer. To earn some badly needed money, I too began to do some modeling for

Patou, for his "junior collection". I was a bit nervous about this at first, as I felt like an immature schoolgirl in the presence of the other models, all of whom had what appeared to me to be an almost magical Parisian sophistication. With a little practice, though, I developed the poise and confidence that allowed me to feel comfortable as I posed for photographs or walked down the runway showing off the collection. Alma was working part time at a fashionable boutique, Chez Coty, selling perfume, and Mother and Aunt Encarna kept themselves busy all day and brought in some money knitting and crocheting various items which could be sold to various boutiques.

We faced our first serious crisis when Mother told us that she had sold the last piece of jewelry. From then on, our economic situation became extremely difficult. The "femme de ménage" (housekeeper) who used to come regularly to clean our apartment was let go, and the six of us took turns doing the housework. Between all of us, we were able to bring in enough money to pay the rent and live a comfortable, if in no way luxurious or extravagant, life. Aunt Encarna and my cousins would have had to give up their large and fashionable apartment in such a nice neighborhood had not the rest of us been able to pitch in and help with expenses.

I often went with my mother and my aunt to shop in the nearby market where we bought our groceries. When the weather allowed it, we would stop at the corner café on our way home and sit outside and share a little treat. Sometimes it was a little cake to share with our tea, or sometimes it was a "citron pressé" (a freshly made lemonade). These little snacks together did not cost very much, and it was always fun to sit outside and watch the world go by.

My French had quickly improved, and I had enriched my vocabulary surprisingly fast. I had also picked up a considerable amount of Parisian slang, or "argot", much to the dismay and annoyance of my mother and my aunt, both of whom spoke the impeccable and proper "Sacre Coeur" French that they had been taught by nuns as children.

With Alma's help, I was learning other new things besides my newly enriched vocabulary. She taught me how to apply lipstick and how to cover my eyelashes with mascara. To me the most exciting thing she taught me was how to smoke, especially the proper and chic way to hold a cigarette in my left hand with an air of nonchalance. Hiding in the secrecy of our balcony and trying as best we could to suppress the fits of coughing that invariably accompanied these sessions, we would remain there for a long time, practicing trying to look grown up and sophisticated.

With the aid of a few phonograph records, we also practiced dancing. We learned the tango and the foxtrot and soon became quite expert, at least in our young eyes, at all these popular dances, including the new ones from South America whose rhythms were becoming so popular. We spent a lot of time together, Alma and I, and became very close. She had a quick temper and a somewhat unpredictable disposition, but she liked me and took me under her wing. It was always great fun to be in her company.

Neither my aunt nor my cousins had seen their father, my Uncle José, for years. My aunt had separated from their father when the girls were very young, and they had not seen him since then. José M. Carretero was a monarchist and a well-known journalist and writer in Spain. He now had become an important literary celebrity in Franco's Nationalist circles. Although well to do financially, he had through all those years refused to provide any help to my aunt or to his children. Lately, though, after my Aunt's imploring him to help, he had started sending a small check every month, which was immediately put aside to pay the rent.

We heard very little from my father. His letters would only reach us weeks after they had been posted. With all the telephone lines to Madrid and almost all the rest of Spain cut off, it was virtually impossible to communicate with him. Mother was so happy the day she received a call from a friend of my father's, who was in Paris on an official trip, and he was able to tell her that he was alright. He had returned to Valencia after participating in the defense of Madrid in February and was still attached to his same militia unit.

My Aunt Encarna's friends were, for the most part, Franco sympathizers. When they came to our apartment to visit, they would invariably turn the conversation to the events happening in Spain, boasting how well the war was going for Franco and his Nationalists, and how slim by now was any hope for the Republic to survive, much less prevail. Usually in these situations, I would leave the room in tears. Other than on those occasions, we lived among ourselves in harmony, rarely discussing politics, and with our innermost thoughts seldom brought out into the open.

When we learned that Mother's other sister, Aunt Marina, was

Crossing the Pyrenees and Becoming Isa

moving from Nice to join us in Paris, we were overjoyed. My Aunt Marina was a charming woman, still attractive though perhaps in a somewhat odd way, her taste in clothing bordering on the ridiculous. She habitually dressed in silks and handmade laces, with long strands of pearls dangling down almost to her waist. She loved to wear old-fashioned "Empress Eugénie" hats, which leant her a certain almost ethereal air. She looked like a character in the romantic novels that were popular at the turn of the 20th century. As fond as we were of our Aunt Marina, we absolutely adored her husband, Uncle Aldo, a dashing, elegant Italian from Milano. They moved into a stylish, if somewhat overstuffed, house in the Passy neighborhood, the most exclusive corner of Paris' 16th Arrondissement. We would gather there for supper every other Sunday. Aunt Marina was an accomplished gourmet cook. Uncle Aldo was a self-described "dilettante of the school of haute-cuisine". This combination made even a simple meal served at their house something extraordinary. Seated at our customary positions around the dining table, our eyes would follow Uncle Aldo's every move, as he proceeded to serve us the succulent food, while their old, grumpy Italian maid would come in bringing the wine, properly set to chill in a silver bucket filled with ice.

Uncle Aldo was a fanatic about classical music as well as opera. I enjoyed going with him at every opportunity, when he would invite me to join him at a concert or at a performance at the Comédie Française. By now, I was taller than my mother and she would let me borrow her gowns for these occasions. I would often sneak into Alma's closet, where I would pick out the shoes with the highest heels. My hair was dark and very long and after seeing a couple of Dorothy Lamour movies, in which she appeared wearing a white flower pinned into her hair, I decided to copy her style. From then on, I would seldom go out without a gardenia pinned to the side of my head. The flower supply was provided by the neighborhood florist. The owner's son, a pale and unhealthy-looking teenager, would rush outside the shop, flower in hand, to meet me whenever I chanced to pass by the shop. Of course, now I realize that the poor boy had a crush on me. I was too naïve and innocent to be aware of it at the time.

Uncle Aldo always managed to obtain the best seats available at the theatre or concert hall. He knew many people in Paris, and during the intermissions, I would stroll with him into the foyer,

55

where he would proceed to point out to me who was who among the attending audience. It was during one of these events, at the Opera House, that my uncle introduced me to Monsieur Sacha Guitry, "Le Maître", as he was called. He was a famous actor and playwrite and in the Paris of the 1930s, he had become a successful theatrical producer as well. Now he had ventured into the relatively new field of cinema, and was producing and directing a movie which, in time, was destined to become a classic of French cinema. The film was *Les Perles de la Couronne*, a highly publicized epic, with a huge cast and a budget already into the millions of francs.

It was only a few days after meeting Monsieur Guitry that I received a telephone call from his secretary asking me to make an appointment with him at the Joinville Studios. The news plunged our little household into a chaotic state of anticipation and high hopes, with everyone discussing my future as a movie star. Alma of course immediately assigned herself the role of being my personal coach, making me read out loud for hours entire passages from Molière's plays. She would scold me, and not in a genteel manner, if my recitations lacked sufficient conviction or if my lines were not delivered flawlessly. After one recitation from "Le Misanthrope" she actually tried to rap my knuckles with a ruler, as though she were one of my nun teachers at school and I had misbehaved. I drew the line at that!

When the day for my interview arrived, my two cousins accompanied me to the movie studios. As we walked into the sound stage, we saw Monsieur Guitry surrounded by a dozen people, in the middle of an array of several huge movie cameras, and under the glare of several klieg lights, their beams converging from all angles onto the center of the set. It was fascinating to see him and to watch him direct the scene and to hear his powerful and commanding voice issuing instructions. After that scene had been shot, he got up to greet us and offered to guide us on a tour of the different sets where his epic was being filmed. One of his assistants took me aside and began to explain in some detail the reason for my interview. In the movie, there was a bit part that called for a girl to play the role of a gypsy, and Monsieur Guitry was interested in me for this role. If I would accept this role, I would have to return to the studio in a couple of days to be coached by one of the staff directors, as shooting for that particular scene was scheduled to start in a couple

Crossing the Pyrenees and Becoming Isa

of weeks. Of course, I agreed immediately!. My cousins stayed with me for moral support and we spent the rest of the day there, my head spinning. I met with all kinds of people and finally at the end of the day, we left the studios and boarded the metro to go home. Under my arm was a manila envelope containing my movie contract.

I had to get up early to take the metro and be at the studios every day by 7 a.m. For days, I rehearsed with my staff director the same scene, over and over again. He was a perfectionist! After a few days, not only did I know my lines perfectly by heart, but also those of the rest of the cast as well.

But for me, the best part of each day was not the time spent on the set and in front of the cameras, but the hour each day at lunchtime when I could join the other actors heading to the commissary. The restaurant adapted for this purpose was always crowded with well-known figures of French cinema. Sometimes, I was lucky enough to find an empty seat next to one of my idols: Jean Gabin or Michelle Morgan. I would be amused, like the rest of the diners, by the antics of the great comedian Fernandel and join in the laughter brought about by the other famous comedian of the day, Raimu. Raimu spoke with the "Midi accent" of the south of France and would keep the whole room entertained and laughing with his hilarious monologues. I often lingered there longer than necessary, fascinated by the nearby presence of a young, handsome, and very romantic-looking Charles Boyer.

Finally, my rehearsals were completed, and the day came for my shoot. I was quite nervous when, after being dressed in my costume as a gypsy, my face all covered with dark makeup, I entered the sound stage where Monsieur Guitry was waiting for the scene to begin shooting. A Renaissance Italian town had been constructed on the set. I was instructed to walk over and sit down next to a make-believe fountain next to a make-believe water well. After endless adjustments until the lighting just right, the handsome young actor who played one of the king's soldiers appeared on the set leading a beautiful white horse by its reins. I knew exactly what I was supposed to do next: approach the soldier and offer him a drink of water from the rustic jug that lay at the edge of the well. The soldier then began our dialogue and, as I had rehearsed a hundred times, I walked slowly toward the horse to lead him gently over to the fountain so that he too could quench his thirst.

"Miss Spain in Exile"

Everything up to that moment had gone smoothly, but then the stubborn horse, no matter how hard I pulled on his bridle, refused to budge from where he was standing.

We repeated the same scene at least a dozen times more, but to no avail. The horse's hooves seemed glued to the floor and his legs immobile, as he ignored the tempting cubes of sugar that I kept placing under his nostrils. Monsieur Guitry was becoming visibly exasperated with the lack of cooperation on the part of the horse. He let fly a few "zut alors", a couple of "merdes", and one or two more colorful French expressions. Finally, the crew reached the conclusion that the horse would just have to have his own way. The scene was hastily rewritten so that now, the young gypsy girl would walk over to the horse to let him drink from the water jug. This I did, and the horse drank the water most contentedly. The rewritten scene was filmed in one shoot. I could swear that all the while, the horse kept looking at me with a bemused twinkle in his eyes.

The film *Les Perles de la Couronne* had not yet finished filming when I received word that another studio wished to interview me. This time it was with Marc Allegret, the prestigious movie director, whose latest movie, "Le Lac aux Dames", had been an instant success. Now he was preparing to film a sequel and after seeing some of the "rushes" from Guitry's movie, he wanted me to play one of the leading parts.

But my dreams of becoming a movie star were cut short by an unfortunate circumstance. On the eve of my preliminary screen test in front of the cameras with the actor Jean Pierre Aumont, I came down with a severe case of the measles and was immediately placed in medical quarantine by my doctor. While I was ill, another young actress was given the part.

It was during this short experience with the world of the cinema that I acquired the stage name Isa Reyes. A friend of the family suggested it, the reason being that the popular folk songs of the Canary Islands are called "Isas". I liked the sound of the name. My father and my paternal grandfather had both been born In Santa Cruz de Tenerife, the prettiest of the Canary Islands, so the name was appropriate for me. I adopted it immediately and from then on, my nom de guerre was Isa Reyes.

Crossing the Pyrenees and Becoming Isa

By the time Isa had completed her short career in French films, it was almost spring of 1937. More than half of a year had gone by since that last summer vacation in Pedro Bernardo, those carefree days of her youth by now a distant memory for my mother. Europe continued its inexorable march toward war, though few in the western democracies seemed aware of or wanted to recognize the growing dangers posed by the Fascist powers. Hitler continued rearming his military, still in flagrant violation of the Treaty of Versailles, and finished consolidating his hold on power in Germany. By now, Goering had sent the infamous Condor Legion to Spain to fight on the side of Franco's Nationalists. His pilots continued rehearsing and perfecting in Spain the bombing and ground support techniques that would be used later during the Blitzkrieg campaigns and in the terror bombings of civilians in Poland and other countries. The most infamous of the bombing raids in Spain was the one on the defenseless Basque city of Guernica in April 1937. Multiple waves of bombing and strafing runs by the German warplanes devastated this town. The horror was later immortalized by Picasso in his painting "Guernica". In addition to the airplanes and pilots to fly them, both Hitler and Mussolini continued sending arms to the Nationalists and Mussolini also sent combat infantry and armor troops.

Germany itself continued its descent into Nazi totalitarianism. By 1937, German courts were not allowed to interfere with Gestapo activities in any way. German security forces were rounding up dissidents or anyone they deemed a threat and incarcerating them in concentration camps, including the infamous Dachau. The laws excluding Jews from all forms of public life and commerce had come into effect. Late in 1937, Hitler held the meeting with his military commanders in which he explicitly presented his expansionist plans to gain "Lebensraum" (room for living) for Germany by conquering and subjugating the lands to the east.

In late 1936, Hitler's Germany and Mussolini's Italy had signed the "Anti-Comintern Pact". Although not a formal alliance, this expression of mutual support was the beginning of what would become the Axis of Germany, Italy, and Japan during World War Two. Hitler expressed support for Mussolini's campaigns in Abyssinia (modern day Ethiopia) and the rest of the world turned a blind eye to the atrocities being committed there. In exchange, Mussolini agreed to give Hitler a free hand in Austria, the next target on the Fuehrer's list. In France, the Third Republic continued in the throes of its final years. The political leadership had moved back and forth between left and right for years. Various reforms were carried out, particularly with respect to labor laws, but neither the left nor the right were satisfied with the outcomes. France continued to refuse to support the Spanish Republic, principally out of fear of reaction from the right. A heavy sense of weariness from World War One continued to permeate the national psyche, as a result of which France in general aligned with Britain in pacifist policies and in the policy of non-confrontation with Hitler that in time would be called "Appeasement".

CHAPTER 5

Three Painters

Spring 1937
Paris in the 1930s was a center of artistic and literary creativity. It was home to many artists, and had become home to several Spanish painters, among them the trio of Pablo Picasso, Joan Miró, and Salvador Dali, the last holding court at the Hotel Scribe near the Opera. It was a vibrant milieu of creativity and artistic experimentation.

Between May 25 and November 25, 1937, Paris hosted the "Exposition Internationale des Arts et Techniques dans la Vie Moderne" (International Exposition of Art and Technology in Modern Life). Forty-five countries participated in this Exposition. The French government never gave military aid to the Spanish Republic, and in fact seemed during the course of the Spanish Civil War and its immediate aftermath to have trouble making up its mind what its policy toward Spain should be. Nonetheless, it was a political statement to invite the Spanish Pavilion at the Exposition to be arranged and organized by the Loyalist government of the Republic. It attracted a great deal of attention because of the civil war. The exhibit at the Spanish Pavilion included the first exhibition of Picasso's painting Guernica, capturing the horror of war and the atrocities committed by the Condor Legion bombers on that defenseless Basque town. The exhibit also featured Joan Miró's painting Catalán Peasants in Revolt and Alexander Calder's sculpture Mercury Fountain.

Two other notable participants in the exhibition were Nazi Germany and the Soviet Union. Implacable ideological foes that these two countries were at this time, before the signing of the infamous Ribbentrop–Molotov Pact in 1939, it was odd that the Exhibition's organizers chose to put these countries' respective pavilions across from each other. Or perhaps this was the French sense of humor at work. In any event, this juxtaposition turned much of the Exhibition into a visible competition between these two ideological rivals.

The Soviet Pavilion was huge and full of art of the Soviet Realist school, exhibiting smiling workers and peasants toiling jointly in earnest to build the Workers' Paradise promised to them by Marx and Lenin. The building was topped by a large statue of a male worker and a female peasant, their hands clasped together in solidarity, holding in their hands respectively a hammer and a sickle, which they seemed to be thrusting forward as they marched confidently into the future.

The Nazi architect Albert Speer designed the German Pavilion. He admitted later in his memoirs, written in prison after the war, that he had snuck a look at the plans for the Soviet Pavilion and that this affected his final design of the Nazi German counterpart. He designed it to appear to be a bulwark against the tide of communism. Crowned by the twin symbols of Nazi Germany, the swastika and the eagle, the German pavilion was presented as a monument to "German pride and achievement." Its objective was to demonstrate to the world that Germany was resurgent, and to do so in Paris, site of the signing of the treaty that less than three decades earlier had marked the end of the first world war and had, in the minds of the Allied victors of that war, condemned Germany to a future of weakness, poverty, and impotence. A sculpture stood outside the Nazi Pavilion, which was illuminated by powerful floodlights all night long, depicting two enormous nude males, hands clasped tightly together, standing together as if in defiance and solidarity against the world.

It took three weeks for me to recover from the measles attack that had ended my short career in the movies and knocked flat my dreams of becoming a movie star. I intended to go back to my aspiring career as a fashion model, hoping that I could graduate from the junior collection soon, when through my Aunt Encarna, I received an invitation to model for a painter. Although that first experience as a painter's model did not end well, it led to other offers from two additional artists. As a result of this, I spent that spring modeling for three different painters in Paris: first Federico Bertrán Masses, then Adrianus, and finally, Jean Gabriel Domergue.

Three Painters

Each of these men was a talented painter, although they had quite different artistic styles. Each was also an intense and colorful personality, though they could not have been more different from each other in temperament or behavior.

Federico Bertrán Masses

When I first met Federico Bertrán Masses, the Cuban-born Spanish painter, he must have been about sixty years old. His talent as an artist, although by no means diminished, had been, as of late, somewhat criticized for being too commercialized. In his youth, he had been rather avant-garde, experimenting with the use of color to highlight the contrast between the subjects he was painting and their surroundings, which were typically dark and nocturnal. He tended to place his human subjects against texturally rich fabrics and often painted in a darkened room lit by artificial light to allow him to create the light and shadow contrasts he was seeking to represent on the canvas. In Spain in 1915, he had painted a portrait of a Spanish countess (La Maja Marquesa), naked but for a white mantilla, seated between two fully clothed companions. This painting was a bit too scandalous for Spain at that time. It was refused by the committee of the Exposición Nacional de Bellas Artes (the equivalent of a Spanish jury for the arts) and this caused him to move to Paris, where he had been living since.

Now, he had moved on to painting almost exclusively portraits on commission for individual clients. He still had a unique and recognizable style and still liked to paint his subjects in contrast to dark surroundings and against rich fabrics, but the critics had started accusing him of pandering to his rich patrons for commercial success rather than remaining true to his art. In recent years, the subjects for most of his paintings had been men and women of so-called "high society", well-known personalities of the political world as well as those connected with the artistic and literary worlds. All of these subjects paid extravagant fees to have their images painted by him on canvas. As they were paying for them, they had the right to demand what they wanted their portraits to look like. Within broad limits, Bertrán Masses tried to accommodate them.

"Miss Spain in Exile"

Monsieur and Madame Bertrán Masses knew my Aunt Encarna from the time when they had all lived near each other in their native Spain. They had come to be good friends with my Uncle Aldo as well once they had met him in Paris. I met them both while attending one of his exhibits with my aunt at a private art gallery. Shortly after meeting him, during one of their frequent visits to our apartment, he asked me if I would like to work for him as a model. I refused at first, but later on I agreed, once properly and emphatically reassured that my modeling would not be in the nude. The fact that I would be earning some badly needed francs contributed greatly to my decision to accept his offer.

The Bertran Masses lived in magnificent opulence in the Passy district, not far from Uncle Aldo and Aunt Marina. Their home was an old palace that at one time had been the residence of one of Louis XIV's ministers. The décor was an odd and eclectic mixture of Spanish and Moorish style, all done in minute detail and, honestly in my opinion, in the worst taste imaginable! He used one of the salons of the palace as his atelier, or studio, the spacious room so cluttered with massive furniture and rare "objets d'art" that it was almost impossible to take two steps across the room without bumping into something. At the far end of the atelier stood an immense piano, its top half covered by a richly embroidered Spanish shawl. In the opposite corner, an ancient Japanese incense burner was constantly emitting strong, aromatic fumes which filled the entire room with what for me was the sickening smell of myrrh and other scents. The windows, hidden behind thick draperies of golden damask, were always kept tightly closed.

My young ego certainly suffered a blow when, on my very first visit to his atelier, I learned that the purpose of my being there was not to have my likeness painted. My job was to take the place of Madame Worth, the family scion of the famous French perfume industry, whose portrait he was in the process of finishing. The work just needed the final few touches here and there for its completion. I was needed only so that he could work on the lights and shadows of the different fabrics, the folds and creases of her gown, and to make sure he could properly capture the glitter and reflections from her jewelry. Madame Worth herself, now that her likeness had been achieved, did not wish to bother herself with sitting for the rest of the small details still needed for the completion of her portrait.

Three Painters

In the back room, next to the atelier, I took off my street clothes and slipped into her sumptuous ballgown and satin slippers, placing her magnificent jewels on my fingers and on both arms, finally pinning a magnificent tiara of emeralds and diamonds atop my head. That tiara felt like it weighed a ton when I started to walk back to the atelier. Her gown was heavy and several sizes too large for me and I felt anything but graceful as I walked back into the studio and reclined on a small sofa as instructed.

This work of modeling was at first not as exciting as I had expected. My main job was to sit as still as possible so that the painter could capture the precise details that he was striving to reproduce on the canvas.

I would have dozed off and fallen asleep more than once during those long, tedious sessions of sitting in for Madame Worth, had it not been for Bertran Masses' lively conversation. While painting, brushes and palette in his hands, he would regale me with amazing stories about the time when, as a younger man, he had lived in southern California. It was during the Roaring Twenties and there he had met many famous people connected with the movies, becoming a close friend of Charlie Chaplin, Douglas Fairbanks, senior, and Rudolph Valentino, among many others. He showed me a series of photographs taken of him with his Hollywood friends in Los Angeles and Santa Monica during those years. When Valentino became gravely ill, he would visit him and was by his bedside when he died. He described to me in minute detail everything that happened that day and how he had managed to make a death mask of his friend before he was taken away to be buried. That very same death mask was in his atelier, just a meter or so away from me, placed on top of an ornate Chinese cabinet and looking so incredibly real and lifelike that I could never bring myself to look at it too closely for fear that the eyes behind the closed eyelids would suddenly open wide and stare right back at me.

On one rainy, gloomy morning, I headed toward his house as usual. As I entered the front hall, Madame Masses was stepping out, dressed in black, as if in mourning. This seemed to be her favorite attire on some days. Although she never demonstrated a great deal of warmth to me, she was usually at least civil, if distant and reserved. This particular morning, though, she was icy cold in the way she greeted me as I walked in, and this disturbed me.

"Bonjour, madame," I said to her.

"Oui, bonjour," she replied, brushing past me on her way out, without even looking up at me.

In the atelier, the iron burner was as usual emitting tiny, twisted columns of bluish smoke, the heavily perfumed scent permeating the entire room. I took my assigned place next to the easel, reclining rather uncomfortably on the stiff Empire-style sofa, and letting my eyes wander around the room, taking in the varied collection of strange-looking objects that surrounded me. Bertran Masses did not seem to be in his usual talkative mood, and I was trying my best not to fall asleep. In a sort of a sleepy daze, I watched him stand up and put away his brushes and palette. He walked slowly toward the sofa where I was reclining in my pose and then suddenly dropped to his knees in front of me. I had no idea what was happening, and I sat there in utter confusion. To my utter confusion and amazement, he took both my hands in his and in a scarcely audible voice, stammering a little, he kept repeating that I was "his love, his passion", as he put it. I was completely unprepared for this declaration of love on his part. It took me a few seconds to fully understand the situation, and when I did, now fully awake, I became frightened and I began to struggle rather frantically to escape his tight grip on my hands. This was not an easy task, as I was wearing Madame Worth's heavy gown, which was about twice my size and hampered my movements.

Somehow, I managed to flee from the atelier into my dressing room. Locking the door behind me, I changed into my old skirt and sweater. A few minutes later, when I cautiously opened the door, Bertran Masses was still on his knees, sobbing while still in that ridiculous-looking posture, and mumbling something to the effect that he had already confessed the truth of his love for me to his wife and that if I did not return his love, he would kill himself. That explained his wife's attitude to me when I had arrived that morning! He remained on his knees, looking at me and continuing to mumble incoherently about how much he loved me and needed me to love him in return. As I looked at him, not sure what I should do or how I should behave, I was no longer nervous or afraid. I just felt sorry for the old man. As silly as he looked and sounded, still on his knees and now crying as he continued to mumble, my overwhelming emotion was one of pity for him.

As I had absolutely no interest in complying with his ardent wishes or romantic desires, I ran out of the house as fast as I could.

Three Painters

Once in the street, I ran for several blocks, scarcely aware of the steady rain that was now falling but feeling the chill of the cold water as it soaked through my clothes. I was dripping wet, frozen, and very tired by the time I reached our apartment. I was also feeling completely exhausted and drained emotionally. I had never expected anything like this to happen and I was totally unprepared to deal with it. Nothing in my young and rather sheltered life up to that point had prepared me for this sort of thing!

Although I never told anyone about this, of course my modeling for Bertrán Masses came to an end after this incident and our friendship, such as it had been, cooled considerably. I simply told my family that the portrait of Madame Worth was now finished, and my modeling was no longer required for this painting. The family never doubted or questioned my story. Inevitably, we continued to meet him from time to time at social gatherings of one kind or another, attended by my Aunt Encarna or Uncle Aldo and me. On these occasions, nothing in the perfectly polite and courteous but reserved manner in which he greeted me betrayed any indication of what had occurred that morning in his atelier or gave me any hint as to what emotions he may have still felt toward me. I did notice that his wife had stopped accompanying him to these social affairs. I learned to interact with him politely and no one ever suspected that anything untoward had occurred between us.

Other than the way in which it ended, and despite this, I had enjoyed my short stint of artistic modeling. The world of painting and art fascinated me, as did the act of painting itself. It was amazing to me that with brushes and dabs of paint from a palette, an artist could create such vivid reproductions of people or objects, infusing so much emotion and interpretation into their work, and I wanted to learn more about this world. However, the strange way that my modeling for Bertran Masses ended had left a bad taste in my mouth and I did not go out of my way to find a new painter for whom to model.

Isa kept this love of art and of painting for her entire life. She was especially fond (of course) of the classic Spanish painters, Goya and El Greco, and also of the Impressionists, particularly Claude Monet and Mary Cassatt. She would use artistic references frequently in daily conversation, for example, referring to a stormy sky by saying "it could have been painted by El Greco." She collected art to the extent she could, amassing later in her life a reasonable collection of work by competent artists. She would never miss an opportunity to visit an art museum and could usually discuss much of the art on display with as much knowledge and authority as the docents. She dabbled in painting herself, using both oils and watercolors. One of her oil paintings in particular was striking, of an old Indian in Mexico, with haunting eyes that seem to be staring right at the spectator no matter from what angle. My brother still has that painting.

Adrianus

His name really wasn't Adrianus. That pseudonym is used here because, for reasons known only to him, he never wanted the names of his models to be made public. He swore Isa to secrecy and when he painted her, as when he painted others, he changed their features just enough that they could not be positively identified as subjects of his paintings. I have tried a few times to identify this mystery painter for whom Isa modeled, but I have never been successful in doing so. In deference to what I knew were her wishes to honor the promise made to him many years earlier, admittedly I did not try terribly hard. His name and identity remain a mystery, as he wished and as Isa agreed.

When Maître Adrianus and his wife accepted our invitation for dinner, we all went out of our way to make the occasion a success. He had been a close friend of my Uncle Aldo for many years. Now, after having won several awards from the Academie des Beaux Arts, he was suddenly in the center of the artistic limelight in Paris. His photograph, as well as photographs of his paintings, appeared constantly in the city's newspapers and magazines, along with all the other popular artists of the day.

Adrianus was a frail-looking man close to seventy years old. The still life paintings and landscapes that he painted as a young artist in his native Holland, experimenting with shades and layers of watercolors, were now very popular and he had become recognized as one of the great contemporary artists living and working in Paris.

Three Painters

Thanks to Uncle Aldo, we were occasionally invited to the intimate dinners hosted by Adrianus and his wife. We would join them, often in the company of other great artists living in Paris at the time, including Picasso, Chagall, Matisse, Jean Gabriel Domergue, and others. I admired him as an artist and valued the friendship he extended to me despite my youth, but it was nevertheless with mixed feelings and a great deal of apprehension that I considered his offer to model for him. As my family had never learned of the final episode with Bertrán Masses or the real reason why my modeling for him had come to such a sudden end, they could not understand my reluctance to work for another great painter. In the end, after careful consideration and despite my trepidations, I accepted Adrianus' offer to sit for him.

His atelier, located in the Left Bank of Paris, near the Academie des Beaux Arts, was a quiet and simply furnished room filled with many of his paintings and extra canvases. Dozens of wooden frames of all shapes and sizes were piled high along the walls. He and his wife lived in Paris's Montparnasse District, but their house was situated away from the boisterous heart of the Quartier Latin, in a secluded, semi-isolated street with a little garden in front. Old, sinewy acacia trees helped to shield the house from view. His atelier was located in the back of their house.

My fears of modeling again were soon forgotten, and I truly enjoyed working for him. The painting he wanted me to sit for as a model was a larger than life-size portrait. It was a beautiful painting. It was of a girl who with a little imagination could have been mistaken for me, standing, wearing a black taffeta gown hemmed in bright red silk, wrapped in a long mantilla of Spanish lace. Besides the red hem of my dress, the only other color in the somber-toned painting was provided by the red carnation pinned high on the side of my head, in my black hair. It was a stunning and dramatic painting that I wish I could have been able to keep. It was sold at a Paris gallery and I never saw it again.

When he was commissioned to paint a mural to adorn the villa residence of one of his wealthy clients and he once again asked me to be his model, I gladly accepted. The work had to be done and completed in his studio, the huge panels to be transferred later to the villa where they would be installed along a wall.

Adrianus liked to work in the early hours of the morning and I had to get up at dawn in order to be at his atelier by 7 a.m. It took me well over an hour to get there. It was spring by now, bringing long-awaited blue skies and a bright sun bursting over the city. It felt good to be out in the crisp morning air. I would leave the metro a few blocks from my destination, and stroll across the Pont Saint Michel, glancing below at the Seine River, already at that hour alive and busy with barges and small vessels. I loved the sight of the chestnut trees along the banks of the Seine, in full bloom and thick with new foliage. In front of me and behind me, on both sides of the bridge, the old buildings of Paris reflected their images upon the water of the river. It was a sight I never grew tired of contemplating and I can still see it in my mind if I close my eyes.

In between modeling sessions, Madame Adrianus would often come into the atelier to join us for tea, pushing ahead of her a small cart on which, next to a kettle, would be a tray filled with pastries. In spite of her age, she was still a handsome woman. As a young girl, she had been his model for many of his fine paintings of women, her flawless skin and the flaming red hair of her youth providing him with two striking features which he captured on canvas in extraordinary fashion. She was always very kind to me, and I loved the times we spent drinking tea and eating pastries, the three of us together.

After several weeks, the mural was finished. The scene was a landscape dominated by a lake surrounded by a profusion of trees and greenery, with distant mountains outlined in the background. A lone girl stood in the foreground. Her lone figure, the golden, rosy tones of twilight playing on her skin, complemented and somehow emphasized the peace and serenity that the painting was meant to convey.

Some months later, while attending a dinner at a magnificent villa near Cap d'Antibes, owned by a well-known socialite, as I stepped into the dining room, I came face to face with Adrianus' mural. It had been painted so realistically that looking at it, one got the impression that the shimmering waters on the canvas were being stirred by an invisible breeze. I became a little nervous at being recognized, but relaxed when after casual glances at the painting and a few admiring comments from my friends and the other dinner guests, no one seemed to notice the resemblance between the girl in the painting and me.

The modest fame, or at least recognition of me, that resulted from my modeling for Adrianus resulted in an offer to model for yet another painter. By now, the sour taste of Bertrán Masses' failed and ridiculous attempt to seduce me had faded, and I was happy to be invited to consider another artist for whom to model.

Jean Gabriel Domergue

During those chaotic years in France before the second world war, Jean Gabriel Domergue was one of the most popular painters in Paris. Although he was not considered a Master, his paintings exuded considerable charm, with a freshness and personality all their own. This made them popular, as well as sought after by the art collectors, and they were always in great demand. His particular technique, with its soft, delicate colors, was similar to that of the Impressionists. He specialized in paintings of women and later became known as "the father of the pin-up". The pretty faces of his paintings' girls, with their trademark pert, flowery hats tilted over their eyes and colorful, feathery boas around their necks were seen all over Paris. His models adorned the posters that helped to advertise the Gala Nights at the French Riviera and were constantly seen as well in the advertisement pages of the popular magazines, bringing to the reader's attention the pleasures of drinking an aperitif like Dubonnet, the scent of an expensive new perfume by Guerlain, or the opening of one of his art exhibits.

I worked for Domergue for only a few weeks, but during this short period of time, he painted at least a dozen pictures of me, several of which were used for posters to advertise everything from perfumes to liqueurs to vacation spots. Occasionally, Alma joined me, and we would appear in the painting and the ensuing poster as a matched blonde and brunette, with Alma as the blonde.

He lived alone in a four-story mansion, the well-tended garden closed in behind a high, spiked iron gate, only a couple of blocks away from the Trocadero. I would usually arrive there by mid-morning. After his oriental houseboy had opened the front door for me, I would follow him through an intricate array of salons and corridors until we reached the back of the house where his atelier was located. Minutes later, the butler would appear, summoned as if by magic, walking silently in and carrying a silver tray with a decanter of sherry and an assortment of tiny sandwiches. As soon as the butler left, finding it impossible to resist the temptation,

I would approach the table, pour myself a little sherry from the decanter, and carrying as many of the little sandwiches as my hands could hold, I would go back to sit in my favorite of his armchairs. Once ensconced there, I would sit back and enjoy the food and sip the sherry, daydreaming while surrounded by the luxurious décor.

Domergue would eventually burst into the room, full of energy and enthusiasm. His peculiar way of dressing never ceased to intrigue me. He typically wore a wide Chinese housecoat embroidered with heavy gold thread and buttoned all the way up to the neck, with enormous, billowy sleeves, and a sash of vivid scarlet silk wrapped several times around his waist. Flat, patent leather slippers with dainty bows on them completed the ensemble. He wore a meticulously trimmed beard, which I thought made him look like a modern-day replica of King François I, whose portrait I had recently seen at the Louvre.

He worked incredibly fast, first spreading on the canvas a thick dab of flesh-colored paint straight from the tube. From then on, he moved at a fast pace, working rapidly with brushstrokes all over the canvas until recognizable features began to emerge and take shape. When I posed for him, he began to do a series of portraits which consisted of only my head and my shoulders. He painted my hair in whatever shade struck his fancy on any given day, as a redhead most of the time. Other than the few paintings he did of me with Alma, he only occasionally painted me with my own black hair. The result of this was that very seldom was I recognized by anyone who knew me in the many advertisements that were constantly showing up everywhere with Domergue's signature on them.

The last time that I posed for him was for an advertisement he had been commissioned to do for a new perfume by Houbigant. The new fragrance was called "Quelques Fleurs" ("A Few Flowers"). The advertisement became very successful. When the lovely painting appeared on the perfume package box, it showed a smiling girl kneeling on a field of grass, her head lifted upward, and her arms raised upward as if trying to protect herself from the cascade of flowers descending upon her. He somehow captured the sense that this happy girl had nothing to fear in the whole world and that her whole life would be surrounded by flowers.

Three Painters

My mother had told me several times that she had appeared on a Dubonnet label in the 1930s. I never saw one, despite searching every time I saw a collection of historic posters for sale in Europe or sometimes in North America, though I did find a poster of her and my Aunt Alma in Denver once, advertising of all things the beaches of Belgium. There they were, a blonde and a brunette, each dressed in a modest two-piece bathing suit that probably bordered on being risqué at the time. Then in 1997, when I was working in West Africa, I was sitting in a bar in the middle of nowhere in Equatorial Guinea, well in the hinterland, when I saw behind the bar an old, dust-covered bottle of Dubonnet. I dusted off the label and there, to my shock and surprise, was the undeniable likeness of my mother! Her huge, dark eyes were unmistakable despite how badly the label had faded over the years. I bought the bottle from the barman and couldn't wait to bring it home, but it was confiscated by soldiers at the next checkpoint.

Chapter 6

The Duchess's Palace

Spring 1937

As the summer of 1937 approached, the civil war continued in Spain. Though the Loyalists held on to hope, and some of the bloodiest battles were yet to be fought, the Nationalists' advantage in arms and matériel was granting them an ever-increasing advantage in the struggle. By now, the Soviet Union was sending its propaganda specialists and political officers and military advisers, but they were mostly focused on establishing and maintaining ideological purity within the ranks of the left-wing factions of the Republic. Thus, Republican leadership continued to splinter, while the Nationalists remained united in their purpose. It is lamentable but true that fascism is a more effective ideology for waging war than is democracy.

Although she was by now in her late forties, La Duquesse was still an extremely attractive woman. She wore her long, dark hair tied in a "chignon" at the back of her head. Her hair was a sharp contrast to her pale complexion and complemented her large, languorous brown eyes. She had been born in Spain but had lived in France since her marriage to the Duque de Montpensier, a descendant of one of the oldest aristocratic families in Europe. Alma and Nanita knew her well, for she had been a close friend of their mother's since they attended the same Catholic school together as children. This was my first visit to her palace, and I was fascinated by the richness and sumptuous magnificence of her surroundings.

Alma and I had decided it was time to launch a new career, as Spanish dancers. I had learned to dance Flamenco as a little girl and Alma was a born dancer who could move in perfect rhythm and with a dramatic flair to any music. It started as a fun way for us to pass the time and when Aunt Encarna and my mother, probably as a joke, said, "The two of you look wonderful dancing together! You should make this a professional act", we took them seriously and began practicing and rehearsing in earnest. Modeling opportunities, whether for artists or fashion houses, were difficult to count on for a steady income and we felt we should try to develop a new career.

When Aunt Encarna realized we were indeed serious about our new artistic ambitions, she arranged for La Duquesse to invite us to meet with her. The purpose of our meeting was to discuss the proper time to be formally invited to her salon and presented to French society, where we would debut our dancing talents. She was well aware of my father's affiliation with and support for the Spanish Republic and she knew that he had remained in Spain to fight Franco and his Nationalists. So, in her eyes I was the daughter of a Loyalist, the ranks of the enemy for titled nobility such as herself, and I could sense that she was not entirely comfortable in my presence. On the few occasions that she spoke to me directly, it was in a cold and distant manner, in sharp contrast to the warm and lively conversations she was having with my cousins Alma and Nanita, whose Monarchist father had been by Franco's side since the beginning of the civil war. Nonetheless, she seemed to be greatly enjoying the role she had taken upon herself of playing "fairy godmother" to these refugee children from her native and beloved Spain. She had taken us "under her wings", as she put it, even though it was done somewhat reluctantly as far as I was concerned.

The meeting with her took place on an afternoon. First, we talked over a long lunch, where she carefully inspected our table manners to make sure that we would not embarrass her in front of others, then after lunch, she invited Alma and me to perform for her. We were nervous and somewhat shy in her presence, and it was hard to perform without any accompanying music, but we did the best we could. Alma and I really were a good dance team, able to anticipate each other's moves, and we stayed in perfect rhythm with each other even without audible music. I hummed the tunes to myself and my clicking of the castanets helped us to stay in step.

When we had completed three numbers, we waited anxiously for the verdict.

"You know," La Duquesse said quietly to Aunt Encarna, "They are not so bad. A little rough and rustic, but they do appear to have

"Miss Spain in Exile"

some talent. Even the younger one" (meaning me). "Will they be willing to work hard to perfect their show in time for the Ball?"

I started to open my mouth to say, "Of course! We will work as hard as we can . . . " but a stern glance from La Duquesse made me realize that my opinion was neither being asked for nor was it desired.

"They will work as hard as necessary and will be prepared in time," said my Aunt Encarna.

"Good. They have four weeks to be ready. I shall arrange for their dance act to be a part of the entertainment at the Ball. They will appear at the end of the first set of performances, before the intermission."

The Duchess smiled at Alma and said, "It will be lovely to have you perform." Then turning to me, she said, "You as well. Do not embarrass me."

I felt that she could have shown me a little more encouragement, but still, when our meeting with the Duquesse was over, she had agreed to help us launch our budding artistic career, lending us a helping hand promoting our talent as Spanish dancers. Under her auspices, we would be given a chance to prove ourselves worthy of her sponsorship and support. The "Charity Ball" was the premier event of the social season and it would take place that year in the regal atmosphere of the Montpensier palace, with La Duquesse herself chairing the Ball Committee and in charge of every detail of the proceedings.

Alma and I would have just enough time before the Ball to prepare our costumes and to rehearse and stage a few dance numbers. It was a golden opportunity we had been offered, to be seen not only by the participants of the Ball but also by Paris' theatre critics and the Paris newspapers' social writers, all of whom would attend this annual event.

With the help of José Zamora, an old friend of the family, we began to plan our wardrobe. Zamora was a well-known designer of women's fashion, who had studied and apprenticed under Balenciaga. His sketches were very much in demand by all the haute-couture houses in Paris. More than once, he had been given credit for bringing new and daring ideas into the world of fashion. At present, he was engaged by Lanvin, where he was designing their summer collection. To our amazement, Zamora agreed not only to design our costumes, but to also use his connections to have them sewn and fitted for us at one of the leading ateliers in Paris.

When he showed us the drawings that he was preparing for our costumes, made exclusively for us, we could hardly contain our enthusiasm. Each sketch was more beautiful than the one before. We finally selected a black taffeta gown that looked like it belonged in a painting by Goya, a second costume that imitated the garment worn by peasant brides in the province of Toledo, a third which was an ankle-length gown of embroidered silk, and finally a couple of beautiful Andalucían costumes to complete our collection.

For several weeks, Alma and I had been taking dancing lessons from Maria del Villar, once a famous and respected ballerina who was now retired from performing but still giving lessons. Now we resumed our studies with renewed enthusiasm. Our instructor shared our enthusiasm and promised that she would have us ready in time for our big night. Hour after hour we rehearsed in her studio with her old pianist Mademoiselle Dijon at the piano, playing the lovely Spanish melodies of Albeniz and Granados and the fiery rhythms of de Falla and Turina. Mademoiselle Dijon agreed to be our pianist for our performance at the Ball.

The years of ballet and Spanish dancing lessons that I had taken as a child were now paying off for me. It was easy for me to learn the complicated new steps. Alma was a born dancer and it all came quite easily to her. She would execute the most intricate steps with ease and grace. I had to work a little harder, but I felt myself improving and becoming more confident every day. Señora del Villar was a rigorous and demanding teacher who would not allow us to rest until our steps were perfect and she was completely satisfied with the result. We would practice the same moves over and over and over again until we had it perfect, and then she would make us continue "so that the muscles remember." Our backs and legs would ache for hours after our class with her was over.

We mastered the lively tempo of the "Sevillanas" and the swift turns and rapid movements of the "Soleares". All the while as we practiced, the sound of our castanets and the staccato beat of our "zapateados" (foot tapping) could be heard for blocks. After the strenuous morning lesson, we welcomed the afternoon break, when Alma and I would collapse on her sofa and relax by browsing through her old scrapbooks and photo albums while sipping from tall glasses of lemonade.

"Miss Spain in Exile"

Before resuming our class in the afternoon, Señora del Villar would disappear into the privacy of her bedroom, where she would remain for a long time, talking on the phone. As soon as she was out of sight and we could hear her talking on the telephone, I would sneak on tiptoes into her kitchen and open the cupboard where I knew she kept, inside a large tin, the most delicious spice cake I had ever tasted. Alma and I would each take a generous portion of the cake, trying to finish with the last crumbs before we would hear her bedroom door open and her footsteps in the corridor as she walked back to the studio. The sweet taste and rich aromas of honey, cloves, and cinnamon would linger in our mouths for the rest of the afternoon. She never gave us the slightest hint that she knew about these raids into her kitchen. The tin containing the spice cake was always in the same familiar spot in the cupboard, and somehow the cake was always replenished every day. For as long as our lessons with her lasted, so did the cake.

When we weren't practicing or rehearsing at Señora del Villar's studio, we were discussing our choreography or practicing our steps wherever we were. One evening at the apartment, after dinner, we were in our room and I said to Alma, "I have an idea how to change the transition in the middle of the first piece. Let me show you."

I showed Alma what I had in mind.

"That's okay," she said, "But what if instead you do it this way."

Whereupon, Alma showed me her idea, which I liked and started practicing. Nuria heard the clicking of my heels on the floor and came in with her guitar to provide the guitar accompaniment while Alma sat on her bed and clapped her hands in the gypsy counter-rhythm to my steps. I forgot where I was and began to imagine that I was dancing in front of an audience. As my dancing became livelier and livelier, so did Nuria's guitar playing and Alma's hand clapping and repeated shouts of "Olé! Olé!"

In my enthusiasm, I had failed to notice that the curtains in front of our balcony window were open, as was the window itself. With the lights on in our room, I was perfectly visible to the small crowd that had gathered on the sidewalk across the street, which had a perfect view of me and could hear the guitar music and accompanying clapping and shouting from Alma. When I stopped, I could hear applause and shouts of "Brava! Brava!" and the occasional "Olé" from what sounded like the one Spaniard in the small crowd

The Duchess's Palace

of French people that had gathered to observe the spectacle I was putting on.

For a moment, I was horribly embarrassed, then I walked out onto the balcony, bowed deeply while shouting "Merci! Merci!" to my audience, then, as I imagined a Prima Donna would beckon her co-stars to join her after a performance, as dramatically as I could I invited Nuria and Alma to join me on the balcony to receive the applause of our admirers. When the people began to bore of applauding us, they started drifting away all except the one Spaniard, who must have been homesick as he kept applauding and yelling "Olé!" at the top of his lungs. Alma and Nuria and I went inside, closed the balcony door and the curtains and collapsed onto the bed giggling.

"Too bad they won't be our audience at our debut!" I said. "They liked us!"

"Yes, of course they did!" said Alma. "We are truly phenomenal!" A lack of self-confidence was never an issue for Alma.

"And you are phenomenal with the guitar!" she said to Nuria. "What a shame you will not be on the stage with us. One day you will be!"

In fact, Nuria did perform guitar with us on more than one occasion later.

The weeks of preparation passed quickly, and finally it was the evening of the Charity Ball. Alma and I arrived early for a final rehearsal of our dance numbers with our pianist. At first, we were a bit nervous, as Mademoiselle Dijon had not played on this particular piano before and it took her a little while to become accustomed to its action. Soon, though, she grew used to it and was able to play the pieces with her habitual virtuosity. Alma and I rehearsed our numbers. When we were done rehearsing, we noticed for the first time that La Duquesse herself was standing off to one side, watching us intently. She kept us in suspense for what seemed an eternity, then favored us, me included, with a smile.

"Formidable," she said. "That will do nicely. And you have a future as performers. It is my honor to have arranged your debut!"

With those surprising words, she left us. I almost collapsed in relief. Alma, as usual, contrived an expression of bored nonchalance, but I could tell that she too was relieved at the approval.

We marveled at the sight of the salon, already ablaze with the bright lights of the chandeliers hanging in seemingly endless rows from the tall ceiling. When the evening's ceremonies started, the lackey in charge announced by name each arriving guest, from atop the marble staircase. At the precise moment, flanked by Le Duque and La Duquesse, Alma and I were solemnly presented to the assembled society. We mingled with the crowd as the entertainment started on the makeshift stage that had been erected at one end of the ballroom, then went into the changing room to prepare for our ten-minute act, scheduled for just before the intermission.

"Ready, Alma?" I asked my cousin.

"Ready, Isa!" she replied.

"Nervous?" she asked me.

"Yes!" I answered honestly.

But before we could exchange any more words, we were pushed onto the stage and our music started.

The fifteen minutes of our performance passed as though a blur. I was conscious that there was an audience and that it was watching me, but I was in my own world, seeing no one but Alma and hearing nothing but Mademoiselle Dijon's piano and the click clack of my castanets.

Maria del Villar would certainly have been proud of us if she could only have seen us dance that evening. We had tried to get her an invitation to attend, but her social status as a retired ballet dancer and now teacher was not sufficient for the Parisian society of the day. I was terribly bothered by this, as I wanted her to see us and to be proud of us. Alma and I carried on in time with the music in perfect timing, making all the steps without a flaw. All of this in spite of Mademoiselle Dijon's crazy antics and her somewhat too-spirited accompaniment on the piano. She was rather dazzled by the glamour of the ball and even more dazzled by the bubbling champagne that she had kept sipping through the evening. Her champagne flute, resting at a precarious angle in her hand before the performance and at an even more precarious angle on top of the piano during the performance, was kept constantly filled by the attentive servants. This no doubt had contributed to the ever-increasing ardor and tempo of the playing. Still, our dance performance went off without a single hitch or missed step.

When we were done, there was silence for a moment, and then the assembled audience burst into shouts of "Brava! Brava!" Our audience demanded an encore. We had not anticipated this and had not prepared one, but after a hurried consultation with

The Duchess's Palace

Mademoiselle Dijon, we settled on one of the numbers we had practiced during our lessons but not included for the performance, the stirring "El Baile de Luís Alonzo". This was one of my favorite pieces of music for playing the castanets as well as for dancing, and even though our encore was a bit improvised, to our happiness and with no small sense of relief, it also was met with applause.

The Duchess came to us after our encore and gave us each a hug. For the first time, she was equally warm to me as to Alma.

"My girls," she almost gushed, "You were great. Surely the hit of the evening. I am so proud of you! You were lovely, lovely. There are people in this audience who will take note of your talent. Mark my words, this evening will be remembered as the debut of Alma and Isa. Now, let me have a word with some of my friends here during the intermission and we shall see what we can arrange for your future!"

Off La Duquesse went, in that way she had of hurrying that never appeared rushed or anything but graceful. Alma and I went behind the stage to change out of our stage clothes. Before we did, we thanked Mademoiselle Dijon for her excellent piano accompaniment. She had already managed to have her champagne glass refilled and became very sentimental telling us what an honor it had been to play piano at our debut.

We changed out of our performance clothes into the evening gowns that we had brought and spent the rest of the evening mingling with the crowd. La Duquesse introduced us to several of her friends from the world of the Paris theatre and Alma and I felt very grown up and important. I tried to watch the entertainment that was performing during the second half of the show, after intermission, but it was hard to concentrate. I kept thinking about our future as performers and dreaming of how famous the team "Alma and Isa" would be one day. I also considered perhaps suggesting the possibility that "Isa and Alma" might sound a little better than "Alma and Isa", but I knew my cousin too well to suggest this out loud.

The success of our debut dance recital surpassed by far our wildest expectations. A few days after the Charity Ball, Alma and I found ourselves in the Office of Monsieur Leroy, one of the well-known and important theatrical agents in France, signing an exclusive contract with him. From that point on, offers began to pour in and we were scheduled to open at "La Bagatelle", a new and exclusive night club that was due to open soon. The favorable reviews that we received there helped us a great deal to advance our new theatrical careers. Even Renée Richard, one of the most respected and certainly one of the harshest arts and theatre critics in Paris at that time, wrote a beautiful and somewhat moving article on our behalf.

Those two weeks at La Bagatelle had been highly successful and for us, it was an exhilarating experience. The night club was visited by all sorts of famous personalities, politicians, and people in the arts and the theatre and world of films. Among the regular customers were the Duke and Duchess of Windsor, often accompanied by their entourage.

Our agent Monsieur Leroy could not have been happier, and he was careful to select only the most prestigious bookings for us, the ones that really helped to launch our careers. Before too long, and honestly somewhat to our surprise, Alma and I had become well-known personalities in the artistic and glamorous world of Paris. And somehow the name of the duo "Alma and Isa Reyes" was appearing under the marquée lights! It had been less than a year since our summer vacation in the Sierra de Gredos and the outbreak of the Spanish Civil War. How distant that summer in Pedro Bernardo appeared now!

Now we were getting as many bookings as we wanted. We were particularly excited to be invited to perform at "Le Boeuf Sur Le Toit" (The Ox on the Roof), a nightclub that considered itself avant-garde and prided itself on recognizing new talent and giving it a chance to perform and become better known. In the 1920s and early 1930s more than one jazz ensemble and dance troupe had gotten their break and entrance to fame by performing there. We were the marquée act there for two weeks and after that, even more invitations to perform were coming in.

My Aunt Alma and I became very close years later and I have fond memories of visiting her in Paris when I was young. She never stopped being a colorful character and we used to call her our Auntie Mame, after the 1958 film starring Rosalind Russell. Proving the adage that opposites often attract, she married a very serious and deeply intellectual Russian émigré named Georges, with whom I also became very close during my childhood. I ascribe much of my love of Russian literature and culture to a great extent to the influence of my Uncle Georges. After her husband died, my Aunt Alma reverted to her old ways, and celebrated her 70th birthday on the Italian Riviera wearing a bikini and accompanied by her 55-year old boyfriend of the day. The last time I saw her was in Paris in 1997. We had a lovely time reminiscing about my mother and their adventures together and then we went to dinner at Le Boeuf sur le Toit. This nightclub of the 1930s, off the Champs Elysées, was now a lovely restaurant. It still featured a large photograph of Alma and Isa at the entrance. Without ordering, she was brought her habitual "steak frites" and a bottle of pink champagne. As we were finishing our meal, the actor Jean-Paul Belmondo entered the restaurant and, seeing her, made a beeline to our table to kiss her on both cheeks. Gallantly taking her hand and kissing it, he then told her how beautiful she looked and went off to join his party. My Aunt Alma smiled at me and said, "Oh that Jean-Paul! He is always so fresh!"

Le Boeuf Sur le Toit is still there. Its nightclub days are in the past and it is now a fashionable brasserie with a nice lunch and dinner menu, though they frequently also feature jazz groups in homage to the past. There was a period of a few years, after my Aunt Alma died, that I was doing a lot of business in Paris and I became reasonably well known at the establishment. At first, they didn't believe me when I told them that the girls in the black and white photo by the door were my mother and my aunt. They knew my Aunt Alma, but no one remembered me from the one time I had dined there with her. Finally, on a subsequent trip I brought a photo album with me that had photographs of my mother and Aunt Alma and from then on, they believed me. The recognition was good for a table at the last minute if I had failed to make a reservation or had a business dinner with people I wanted to impress. They also developed the tradition of offering me a glass of champagne on the house when I would arrive. It is the small touches in a city like Paris that can make one feel like a gentleman!

The antipathy within the family that Isa describes between those supporting the Nationalists and those supporting the Loyalists continued well into the next generation. When I was working in Spain in 1976 and 1977, as a geologist with the Spanish Mining Institute and as a Fellow at the Madrid School of Mines, I looked up several of my distant cousins. Those who were affiliated with the Loyalist side invariably greeted me with great warmth and couldn't wait to tell me stories about my family. Those from the Nationalist side were rather more distant and reserved and were somewhat smug about the fact that they had been on the winning side of that internecine conflict. Even in 2014, when I was in Spain looking at some tungsten mining opportunities, I happened to mention at a business lunch that my grandfather had been on the Loyalist side during the civil war. The gentleman with whom I was doing business said, "Oh, so you're a 'Rojo' (a Red, a communist)!" and our relationship was never quite the same after that.

For the rest of her life, the music of El Baile de Luís Alonzo, the piece that was Isa's and Alma's encore performance during their debut, remained one of Isa's favorite pieces of music. Whenever she heard it, if her castanets were nearby, she would slip them into her hands and tap out the accompaniment. If her castanets were not nearby, she would pantomime playing them silently with her fingers against the palms of her hands. As it happened, one of my favorite songs of the Spanish Civil War was "El Quinto Regimiento" (The Fifth Regiment) about the Loyalist militia unit that was formed in Madrid the day after Franco's invasion of Spain. The Fifth Regiment was an elite unit comprised entirely of volunteers which fought heroically at some of the most important battles of the civil war, particularly at the beginning. Like me, my mother was stirred by the words of the song, but she loved it especially because it was to the same tune as El Baile de Luís Alonzo. Whenever I would play it on my guitar and sing it for her, she would play the castanet accompaniment with a big smile on her face and then she would want to reminisce about her debut night in Paris.

CHAPTER 7

On the French Riviera

Summer 1937
In Spain, while Alma and Isa were preparing for their debut, the fighting continued through that spring and into the summer. Things continued to go well for the Nationalists. In May, the ceaseless infighting between various Republican factions in Barcelona became worse and this seriously weakened the defenses of that city. In June, the strategic industrial city of Bilbao, in the North of Spain, fell to Nationalist troops.

In Hitler's Germany at this time, the situation under the Nazi regime continued to deteriorate even more. His police were now routinely imprisoning anyone who was critical of him or the regime. Life for the Jews in Germany was also becoming progressively even more difficult. By then, Jews were excluded from any form of employment, public or private, and so many were left without any way to earn a livelihood. In many towns, Jews could not find any form of lodging that would accept them. It became common to see signs reading "Jews not Admitted" over store entrances, and non-Jews were prohibited from frequenting or buying from Jewish stores.

Meanwhile, Hitler was beginning to foment the trouble in Austria that in less than a year would lead to the Anschluss, or absorption of Austria by Germany. Mussolini continued to give Hitler a free hand for his plans for Austria, in exchange for which Hitler gave Mussolini a free hand for his plans in the Mediterranean.

By now it was the summer of 1937. July would mark one year since the onset of the Spanish Civil War. The bitter fighting continued on several fronts. Britain and France continued their policy of non-intervention in Spain as the Nationalists, with the help of Germany and Italy, continued to gain territory and consolidate their position. In a bitter diplomatic blow to the Republic, in August, the Vatican formally recognized Franco's Nationalists as the legitimate government of Spain.

Europe continued its inexorable slide toward world war, though the inevitability of the world war is seen only in retrospect. At the time, few in the European democracies saw the danger and those who did, including Winston Churchill, were considered alarmists at best and warmongers at worst. A spirit of appeasement still held sway over most of the politicians in power in Britain and France. Hitler took advantage of this apathy to continue his rearming and to continue preparing for his plans to expand the Third Reich. He was preparing for the war that in his mind was inevitable, but which he intended to begin at the time and place that best suited him.

The political turmoil in France recurred that summer. A general strike on May 1 was one in a chain of events that led to the resignation of the left-leaning coalition government led by the Socialist Prime Minister Léon Blum. Although Blum himself was ideologically aligned with the Spanish Republic, he had withheld aid from the Republic, fearing that it would endanger the survival of his coalition government if he sided with the Loyalists. Ironically, it was this refusal to provide aid to the Republic that caused much of his support from the left-wing elements of his coalition, particularly the Communists, to desert him. Blum resigned in July and was replaced by Camille Chautemps, who diluted some of the efforts at reform attempted by his predecessor and who, by agreeing to compromises, was able to remain in power until the return of Blum to the post less than a year later. Chautemps' memory survives as a rather dubious footnote to history. He was one of the first Cabinet ministers in 1940 to suggest an armistice with Nazi Germany. He then served in the collaborationist government of Vichy, under General Pétain, until traveling to the United States on an official mission for the Vichy government, during which he made the decision not to return to France. He spent most of the rest of his life in the United States. After the war, a French court tried him in absentia and convicted him of treason and collaboration with the enemy.

Meanwhile, despite the politics and the rising unemployment and economic conditions that affected the working class, the gay social life of Paris continued, at least among the well-to-do. The restaurants and nightclubs were full nearly every evening. The art shows and exhibits continued to attract large audiences as did the theatres and the Opera. The Exposition Internationale des Arts et

On the French Riviera

Techniques dans la Vie Moderne remained open through the summer and into autumn and attracted crowds of visitors, tourists as well as Parisians. In general, the Parisians paid as much if not more attention to the social stories and gossip pages of the newspapers as they did to political news or to the events elsewhere in Europe.

As summer approached, the residents of Paris began to prepare for their summer vacations, escaping the heat and congestion of the capital for the country or the beach. Those who could afford it prepared to leave the capital for their habitual summer vacations in the playgrounds of Monte Carlo and the French Riviera.

Those early bookings at La Bagatelle and Le Boeuf Sur le Toit, among others, led to more bookings and invitations to audition for more theatres and nightclubs. In the midst of this, we received an invitation to perform at a benefit to raise money to buy medical supplies and provisions for the Spanish Loyalists. Alma herself was not terribly political, but her family did sympathize with the Nationalists, so she declined to participate. I agreed to perform, for the first and last time of my dancing career in Europe, as a solo dance act, with Nuria playing guitar as my musical accompaniment. When I learned that a diplomatic envoy from the Spanish Republic would be attending, I put together a small care package of pipe tobacco and chocolates, together with a letter from me, planning to see if this diplomat could arrange to have the package delivered to my father in Valencia.

I do not remember anything memorable about that evening's performance. Nuria and I were two of perhaps a dozen musicians and dancers who performed, and the audience was much more interested in discussing the situation with the civil war in Spain than in watching the performances. I introduced myself to the envoy of the Spanish Republic and I was delighted when he told me that in fact he knew my father and that he would be returning to Valencia the next day, on his way back to Madrid, and would arrange to have the little package delivered. He promised that he would try to deliver it personally to my father.

Two weeks later, I received a letter from my father in the post. "My dearest Conchita," he began, "Thank you for your kind and loving letter and for the delicious chocolates, which I shared with my men. Thank you also for the tobacco. Next time, if possible, please try to send me Virginia tobacco. I prefer it." I was happy and relieved to see that the civil war had not affected or coarsened my father's refined tastes!

In spite of how busy and hectic our lives had now become, with daily rehearsals and frequent nightly performances, we were still able to find some free time to spend with our family. Nuria and I would ride our bicycles for hours along the lovely tree-lined paths of the Bois de Boulogne, and Mother and I would go shopping together often, enjoying spending quiet afternoons after my rehearsal having tea and pastries at any of the many tea parlors along and in the vicinity of the Champs Elysées.

Monsieur Leroy called us very excited one morning. He had managed to arrange an invitation for us to audition with the director of the Casino de Paris, where Maurice Chevalier was staging one of his spectacular revues. Our audition was scheduled for the next day, which gave us barely time to become nervous about auditioning for such a prestigious audience. Maurice Chevalier himself was there to watch our audition and it was clear that his would be the deciding voice about whether we became part of the show.

Despite the sudden onset of nervousness, at least on my part – Alma seemed immune to these things – our audition went well, and we were signed to appear at the Casino for the next revue. We danced at the Casino de Paris for three evenings, then we were booked at the Bobino Theatre for a few shows, and finally at The Lido, where for the first time we were given star billing. But through all these performances, as we gradually became better known and more in demand, our agent had been working on his surprise for us. He called one afternoon and asked Alma and me to come to his office at 10:00 the following morning.

Monsieur Leroy, we had learned, had no patience with tardiness and was known to cancel an appointment if an artist he was representing had the temerity to arrive even a few minutes late to a scheduled appointment. Alma and I took the metro early and were in his office well before the appointed hour. We sat in his waiting room, nervously wondering what this all might be about, when at the precise stroke of 10:00, he appeared from his inner sanctum and welcomed us into his office. He motioned us to sit on the sofa, instructed his secretary to bring us each a cup of tea and a plate of biscuits, and began.

On the French Riviera

"How would you like to spend this summer on the Riviera?" he asked.

Alma had a big smile on her face, while I in my youthful naïveté asked, "Which Riviera?"

Monsieur Leroy could not tell if I was trying to be funny or really did not understand what he meant, but he did not laugh at me.

"The French Riviera, the Côte d'Azur," he explained patiently. I have you booked for the entire family, first at the Sporting Club in Monte Carlo and then at the Palm Beach in Cannes. It will be wonderful for you! You can take your family with you and it will be a lovely vacation on the beach for you during the days, and in the evenings, you will dance and become even more well-known! Believe me, in the summer, the Riviera is where the best entertainment in France will be performing!"

Alma and I rushed home to share the news with everyone. It was quickly decided that we would take advantage of the opportunity for all of us to spend a summer together on the coast. We were all looking forward to an exciting summer on the French Riviera. Of all of us, Nuria may have been the most excited of all. She kept repeating, "All summer at the beach!" Actually, there was an additional reason that I welcomed the opportunity to spend the summer away from Paris.

An exciting event for me during that busy springtime in Paris was being courted by a glamorous and handsome bachelor, Le Comte de Beauregard, whom I had met one afternoon at the Longchamps horse races. From the day I met him, our apartment was literally inundated with flowers. Bouquet after bouquet of roses would arrive daily. As the friendship grew between the Count and me, so did the interest and curiosity of the public, our visits to the theatre and our dining out together at fashionable restaurants being faithfully reported in the social pages of the Paris press. Amidst endless speculation and with the high hopes of the family, I accepted the Count's invitation to meet his relatives at the family's ancestral chateau. As soon as we had returned to Paris from that weekend, the rumors and gossip started again, with persistent enquiries as to how soon and where the inevitable wedding would take place.

I suddenly realized that I had allowed myself to become entangled in a web from which it would be difficult to escape. I liked Phillipe de Beauregard as a friend, and I had loved the attention he lavished on me, but I was not in love with him. I was very young, and I had never been in love, other than schoolgirl crushes on movie stars and on Don Rafael back in Spain, but I knew I was not in love with Phillipe. Perhaps I should have realized this earlier and not encouraged him, but I was too young to fully understand these things. Once I did realize that I was not in love, I decided I had to end it while I could. I turned a deaf ear to all the suggestions and advice I was being given about taking advantage of this heaven-sent opportunity to become the next Comtesse de Beauregard. This advice came mostly from Alma. My mother understood that I was not in love and encouraged me to wait until I was. My romance with the Count ended as abruptly and rapidly as it had begun. Flowers and unopened letters were sent back to him and I stubbornly refused to meet with him again, despite his stubborn persistence. He would keep a long vigil for hours at a time, pacing back and forth on the sidewalk in front of our apartment. I ignored him, struggling not to feel sorry for him as he carried on his relentless pacing.

So, I certainly welcomed our departure for the Riviera, when the day finally arrived. Although Alma and I would be performing nightly, we viewed it as a family vacation. The six of us were overjoyed at the thought of spending the summer together in the sun and near the sea. As soon as we had stepped into the train station and found out which platform our southbound train would depart from, I began to help Alma load the trunks and suitcases that held not only our normal clothes and beach clothes but also all of our performing outfits. Then I went to join my mother and my sister, and Aunt Encarna and Nanita, who were all waiting on the platform for the arrival of Aunt Marina. She had decided at the last minute to travel with us to the Riviera, but she would go to Nice, near where we would be, where she and Uncle Aldo owned a cottage by the sea.

Aunt Marina arrived on the platform, her presence announced and preceded as always by a heavy fragrance of the Shalimar perfume that she habitually wore. She was dressed in full regalia for the journey. A dazzling array of jewels was on display around her neck and on her arms. Her head was crowned with the biggest hat of her extensive collection, and she carried in one hand a large Spanish fan while gripped in her other hand was the handle of a large wicker basket. We knew from experience that this basket would be filled with all sorts of delicious and dainty delicacies to sustain us during the journey. Uncle Aldo followed dutifully a few paces behind her, struggling to control their little dog Dolly on her leash. Dolly was quite beside herself with the excitement of the station around her and with the anticipation of the train journey, which she seemed to be looking forward to immensely.

Uncle Aldo helped us all to board the train and to finish stowing our luggage, then he went back onto the platform and stationed himself under the window of our compartment. From there he began to recite a litany of instructions and all kinds of recommendations and advice for our trip. He asked us repeatedly whether we were sure we had not forgotten anything. It was only a few seconds before the train began moving and pulling away from the station that Aunt Marina realized she did not have her beloved little Dolly by her side. Uncle Aldo hastily lifted the little dog to the window, where welcoming arms grabbed her and sat her down next to a now-relieved Aunt Marina. Aunt Encarna's little dog Moineau started barking furiously at all this commotion and was clearly not pleased by the presence of Dolly, whom he barked at and tried to bite. Amidst this cacophony in our compartment, our train departed the Gare de Lyon and we embarked on our journey.

Dolly and Moineau were always at hand and took part in all important events that involved the family. Moineau was already fourteen years old and had grown rather senile. He was so incredibly tiny that we travelled with him everywhere we went. He would pass undetected, easily hidden in our handbags or even in the pockets of our coats and jackets. He was a calm and peaceful little dog, and he would remain perfectly still for long periods of time, showering all in the family with affection pouring from his eyes. Aunt Marina's Dolly, on the other hand, was a different story. The Belgian bulldog was mean and ugly and although she was not a large dog by any means, at the slightest provocation she would bare her teeth and growl menacingly. She was ill-tempered and her enormous, bulging eyes tended to convey an expression that was simultaneously sorrowful and contemptuous. The two dogs settled into an uneasy truce in our compartment as the journey continued.

When we reached Marseille, it was almost dawn. Our train made a short stop there and then continued eastward, traveling now parallel to the Mediterranean. The deep blue sea stretched out before us in all its immensity. As the train moved along the coast toward Nice, Nuria and I kept staring at the beautiful sea, our faces practically glued to the window. We passed picturesque beach after picturesque beach, a seemingly endless procession of sun-drenched shores and rocky islands. The distant shores disappeared into the horizon, looking like they had been covered in a dust of gold. It had been so long since Nuria and I had seen the Mediterranean, that beloved sea of our childhood, those waters in which we had learned to swim, and on whose sandy shores we had spent so many hours playing during the carefree days of our youth. My mind was full of memories and images of peaceful times past, really not that many years earlier, when our parents would take us on vacation to the family home on the Costa Brava, north of Barcelona. And then I thought about what was happening in Spain now and I became sad and I couldn't help but wonder if my father was still safe.

Finally, we arrived in Monte Carlo, which would be our base for our performances on the Riviera. Monte Carlo was ensconced among the mountains that rise steeply from the margins of the Mediterranean Sea. We could see its pink, fairytale palace basking under the warm light of early afternoon. In the rosy distance, we could see the breathtaking coastline and the road that led to Nice. We arrived and took a taxi from the train station to the hotel which would be our home for the summer.

We had been booked in a small but comfortable hotel up the hill a little way from the beach. The little hotel had all of its window shutters closed, to keep out the heat and provide shelter from the bright sunlight. Nuria followed me as I climbed the stairs to the room she and I would share with Alma for the summer. We put our things away and lay down to rest a bit after the long train ride, which had left us exhausted. After resting for a couple of hours, we put on our swimsuits and ran all the way down the narrow road to the beach, Moineau following us and barking excitedly at our heels. That was the first of many times that summer that Nuria and I raced each other down that road to the beach

What a glorious summer that was for us! With only one performance to do nightly, at 10 p.m., we had the whole day to ourselves, to enjoy as we pleased. We would usually wake up as the bright summer sunlight pierced the window of our room. We kept the windows and shutters open at night to allow the cool evening air in, then would close them during the day to try to keep the coolness in. After a breakfast of café au lait with croissants and butter and jam, we would go to the beach and spend the morning swimming and sunbathing and reading. Alma, Nanita, Nuria, and I would spend all morning at the beach and only return to the hotel in time to wash and change for lunch. Aunt Marina, inevitably accompanied by Moineau, would come over often from Nice to spend the day with us and then Dolly and Moineau, who continued the somewhat uneasy truce they had established on the train, would be in tow everywhere we went, Moineau exuding love through his eyes at everyone he encountered and Dolly as usual glowering at the world.

We would often have lunch at the hotel. Their daily specialty was usually a large Salade Niçoise, the lovely salad that had been invented in Nice, just down the coast from us, or a bowl of bouillabaisse, the hearty fish stew that, according to legend, was invented in Marseille by fishermen who wanted a hearty meal after they returned from a hard day of work fishing. Or if we wanted something different, we would have a lunch of fresh fish at any one of the informal little restaurants and cafés that were dotted along the coast and that got their fish directly from the local fishermen. The fish we ate at lunch had usually been swimming in the Mediterranean just a few hours earlier.

I could remember for the rest of my life the taste of these fresh fish, particularly the little red mullets or the smelt that would be lightly dusted in flour and then fried in olive oil. I also loved the fresh sardines, prepared the same way. Once we were having lunch at one of those little restaurants with Mother and Nuria, and Mother told the waiter that we wanted sardines, but they must be fresh, very fresh. After a while, our lunch had not arrived yet and Mother asked the waiter, "Where are our sardines?" The waiter pointed at a little fishing boat coming into the harbor and said, "Here they come now! You wanted fresh sardines and you will be served fresh sardines!"

After lunch, we would have a siesta, then usually go back to the beach after our siesta for one more swim. Then we would relax, and Alma and I would have an early and light dinner and set off for our evening's performance. After dinner, Alma and I would briskly walk the half hour to the gates of the Sporting Club, where we would dress in preparation for our performance. By the time we finished our show, it would be midnight, and we would return to our hotel.

Getting back so late, we would go straight to bed so that we could get up the next morning and enjoy the beach.

Our performing venue at Monte Carlo was the Sporting Club de Monte Carlo. It was situated right at the water's edge, with the stage built and elevated in the center of a beautiful garden. The audience sat at tables around three sides of the stage and could see past the stage to the water. The Club's terraces were encircled by marble balustrades that reached all the way to the sea. The view from these terraces was magnificent. Jasmine, laurel, and oleander were in full bloom and their scent permeated the air.

The audience at the Sporting Club was friendly, if not as attentive to our performances as perhaps they could have been. They were there to have a good time and the evening floor show was part of the entertainment. They appreciated our performances, but they were equally focused on their dinners and drinks and conversations with their table companions. Alma and I were able to relax a bit, knowing that we could put on a good show but not be subjected to the same critical scrutiny as we would have been in Paris.

The summer resort towns of the Riviera were booked well in advance for the entire season. The luxurious hotels were filled to capacity by a public eager to spend the day playing in the sun and in the water and in the evening to attend the performances of famous singers and dancers that had been booked by the hotels and casinos. American jazz was becoming increasingly popular and some of the great bands had been brought over from the United States for the summer. Escaping the cities, people from all over Europe were enjoying their summer holidays, leaving behind them all the worries and anxieties that besieged them, leaving behind as best they could thoughts of the turmoil engulfing the world. In all of Europe, the Riviera was perhaps the best place for forgetting, at least for a while, the prospect of war now looming increasingly over Europe. The local newspapers devoted more time and gave more extensive coverage to the local events and the local social life than to political events in Europe or to the impending crises that would bring catastrophe to the continent.

As the middle of summer approached, our booking at the Sporting Club came to an end and we began our second engagement, at the Palm Beach Night Club in Cannes. In order to get to Cannes in time for our performance, we had to leave our hotel by about 7 p.m. every evening. Alma and I would board the little bus that traveled the coast, stopping at all the little towns, until reaching its final stop, the Croisette in Cannes, a couple of hours later. Just after midnight, when our show was done, we would get back the same way, so we seldom got back to our hotel before two o'clock in the morning. From my seat on the bus, half asleep, I would catch glimpses of the glittering sea. Traveling along the narrow road and so close to the water's edge, I could hear the voices of the fishermen as they were getting their boats ready, some lighting the stern lanterns while others were already rowing steadily toward the depths. In the moonlight, the slender shapes of the palm trees and the flowers of the rhododendron bushes were visible against the sky. The air around us was intoxicating, heavily perfumed as it was by the sweet scents of lemon and orange blossoms. Those late-night sights and scents added an enchanting confusion to the fanciful and picturesque sweeps of scenery.

The gala festivals at the Palm Beach attracted people from all over Europe, especially the one held on the 14th of July, Bastille Day, for that was the gayest and fanciest gala of all. Throughout the entire evening, spectacular fireworks lit up the whole bay and crowds of people gathered in all the towns and small villages, waiting for the celebrations and festivities to begin. Dances were held in the middle of the streets all day and night long and an endless row of multi-colored lights illuminated the coastline from one end to the other, their brilliance reflected for kilometer upon kilometer on the surface of the sea.

And it was during the course of that enchanting summer that, suddenly and without at all expecting it, I grew up and became a woman. Perhaps it was the fact that I had fallen in love for the very first time that was causing all the new and strange emotions that I was feeling. These terrified me a bit at first, these odd sensations which although I was aware of them, I did not fully understand. It was a feeling as though I were floating away, waiting in anticipation for all the promises that tomorrow would bring. With the Count Phillipe in Paris just that spring, I had not been in love. Now, I was. And I knew that I was.

His name was Michel. He was a Russian by birth, his parents White Russian emigrés who had been personal friends of the last Tsar, Nicholas II, to whom they were in some distant way related. Michel lived in Paris, where he worked for a brokerage firm on the Paris Bourse (the Paris Stock Exchange). Though young, he was

"Miss Spain in Exile"

obviously brilliant and had been earmarked for rapid promotion in that firm. I met him in Cannes during the Bastille Day celebrations. We had managed to spend every day together since we met. During long walks at midnight along deserted beaches, swimming and sailing from Saint Tropez to the Cap d'Antibes, we had discovered a world of our own. For me, to be in love for the first time in my young life was pure joy, and to be in love for the first time with a handsome and glamorous and somewhat mysterious Russian boy on the French Riviera was a form of heaven!

Those almost six weeks that we had together were glorious. Michel and I spent every minute we could together. To my joy, Michel got along very well with my mother and especially well with my sister Nuria, whom he treated very tenderly, as though she were his little sister. With the dogs, it was a mixed success. Moineau accepted him and adored him, the way he accepted and adored almost everyone. Dolly was a bit more suspicious and Michel's feelings were hurt until we explained that Dolly didn't really accept anyone. We would spend all day together and then Michel would drive Alma and me in his car to Cannes for our evening performance. He would sit in the audience every night, appearing as enthused as the first time he had seen our act, and would make sure that everyone around him applauded equally enthusiastically. Then he would drive us back to Monte Carlo, where he had taken a room in a hotel near ours so that we could spend more time together. In the mornings, he would come to the beach with us, then after lunch, or sometimes before lunch, he and I would leave and go somewhere by ourselves before coming back to pick up Alma and be driven to Cannes for our performance.

Those weeks went by too quickly and I tried to savor every moment. I did not want this fairy tale to end! One afternoon as we were driving back to Monte Carlo, Michel noticed me staring out the window of the car.

"Chérie," he asked, "Why so quiet and pensive? What are you thinking about?"

"Michel," I replied to him, "I do not want this summer to end. I love you. Will you remember me when we are back in Paris?"

He took my hand in his and raised it to his lips to kiss it then said, "I love you too. Of course, I shall remember you when we are back in Paris and we shall continue to see each other. Do not worry. I promise you this on my honor as a Russian!"

I believed him, but I was still a little sad that this lovely time, when we could be together whenever we wanted with almost no thoughts of the outside world, would soon be ending and we would have to return to the real world from the fairy tale of the Riviera.

Finally, the summer was coming to an end. Our engagement at the Palm Beach would soon be over, and we began making preparations for our return to Paris. Michel had already departed for the capital a few days earlier. I was impatient to see him again, feeling lost without him.

When the day to return came, Alma and Nuria and I went to the beach for a last swim, then boarded the afternoon train to Nice and on to Paris. As our train turned northward toward Paris, away from the Mediterranean, I looked at the sea for as long as I could before it disappeared from view.

When our train slowed to a stop back at Paris's Gare de Lyon, I saw Michel right away, despite the huge crowds that filled the station. I leapt out of our compartment and onto the platform and ran into his waiting arms. He gallantly helped Mother and Aunt Encarna with the luggage and piling them in his car, he drove us home. I rested my head on Michel's shoulder as he drove.

Back in Paris, Alma and I resumed our daily routines of rehearsing and learning new dances for our performances. To our utter delight, Antonio Arcaráz, an acclaimed Spanish dancer and choreographer, had agreed to help us choreograph a new dance number. We met him every day at his "Guelma" studio in Montmartre. Antonio was a superb artist who had appeared many times with the Monte Carlo Ballet Company before retiring from dancing to work full-time as a teacher and choreographer. The hours we spent at his studio, although extremely strenuous, were very happy ones. He was handsome and still a graceful dancer and Alma and I learned a great deal from his knowledge and flawless technique. But, as we were soon to find out, he was a perfectionist and not easily pleased. We spent hours in his studio practicing new steps over and over until he was satisfied with our steps. When Michel would come to meet me at the studio, he would be extremely annoyed at having to wait for me for so long until Antonio was satisfied with my progress for the day and would allow me to leave. I could tell that Michel was becoming increasingly impatient and somewhat jealous of my devotion to my dancing. While Alma and I rehearsed with Antonio, he would sit in the farthest corner of the room, looking bored and with such a forlorn and gloomy countenance that we could not help teasing him about it. But Michel's carefree and pleasant personality would quickly return as soon as were outdoors and walking arm in arm toward one of our favorite bistros.

We had not been back in Paris very long at all before Monsieur Leroy had arranged more bookings for us, including a return engagement at Le Boeuf Sur le Toit. With Antonio's help, we continued developing new dances and trying out new choreography and arrangements, so that our performances were always fresh and interesting for our audiences. We continued this way, developing new routines and being booked for several evenings at a time at various venues in Paris. Our popularity seemed to continue to grow.

When we performed in nightclubs, our musical accompaniment was mostly provided by the nightclub band or, in the larger establishments, by their small house orchestras. But we also performed from time to time with Nuria while she played the guitar. This was usually in more intimate settings, sometimes as part of a recital she was performing for a small group, but also occasionally in larger concert halls when Nuria would be invited to perform for a larger audience. We would schedule these performances with Nuria as best we could in between our nightclub appearances. Monsieur Leroy was always very kind about helping us avoid scheduling conflicts so that we could perform frequently with Nuria, though it was not usually a problem. As her performances were usually in the afternoon or earlier in the evening than our nightclub acts, we could usually perform with her and then still make it to our evening performance on time. Occasionally, Nuria would appear in the nightclubs with us too and we would dance part of our show to her guitar accompaniment. This was always popular with audiences, but the nightclubs were not Nuria's preferred venue. She preferred what she considered to be the more serious recital or concert appearance to a nightclub stage.

We were keeping very busy with all these performances until once again, one day, Monsieur Leroy called us back into his office with surprising and exciting news.

We were going to Poland!

On the French Riviera

Years later, in 1963, when I was a young boy, I spent a summer vacation with my family at Cannes. My mother told us all the stories about her summer on the Riviera thirty-five years earlier and we went to Monte Carlo to see the casino and to see where she had danced at the Monte Carlo Sporting Club, which was still there. In fact, the Monte Carlo Sporting Club is still there today, and it still hosts well-known performers for well-to-do audiences. The U.S. Navy's Sixth Fleet made a port call to Cannes to coincide with Bastille Day the summer that I was there with my family. The aircraft from the American carrier put on an air show that afternoon and the ships put on a spectacular firework display from their decks that night. It was one of the few times I was able to watch my mother thoroughly enjoy a firework performance. Usually, the loud noises of fireworks brought back her childhood memories of hiding in a basement bomb shelter during the air raids in Madrid. This would make her shake uncontrollably with fear and tended to make it impossible for her to enjoy any kind of fireworks. On this occasion, though, the fireworks display over the shoreline of Cannes evoked nothing but warm memories for her of that peaceful summer of 1937, that summer when her dancing career continued its meteoric rise. And that summer when she would fall in love for the first time.

1 Isa's father, Ricardo Balcells. Undated photo, *circa*. 1935.

2 Isa's father Ricardo hunting in the Sierra de Gredos during the summer vacation 1936.

3 Isa in gypsy costume on the set of *Les Perles de la Couronne*, preparing to film the scene with the horse that refused to come to the well.

4 Isa in Monte Carlo during the summer on the Riviera, 1937.

5 September 1938, one of the trips from Copenhagen, with the other Miss Europe contestants. Isa is on the far right.

6 Preparing for the final appearance at the Miss Europe pageant.

7 Isa with her dance partner Antonio Arcaráz.

8 Isa with her dance partner Antonio Arcaráz.

I'S AN OLD SPANISH CUSTOM TO BE PRETTY

9 Using a ship's funnel to create a "sombrero effect", Isa appearing in the Society Page of a New York newspaper on the day she arrived in New York on board the *Nea Hellas*.

10 Isa in a publicity photo for her show at the Hotel Nacional, Havana, Cuba.

11 Isa with her sister Nuria. Publicity shot for her show at the Hotel Nacional, Cuba.

12 Isa with George, about the time they were married in Mexico City.

CHAPTER 8

In Poland

Winter 1937–Spring 1938

By late 1937, Hitler had set in motion his plans for the "Anschluss", the unification of Austria with Germany. His agents were fomenting trouble inside Austria to destabilize the country and pave the way for a Nazi takeover. Historically, Italy had always had an interest in the affairs of Austria (with fighting often triggered by disputes over control of the port city of Trieste on the Adriatic), but Mussolini had given Hitler a free hand in Austria in exchange for Hitler's looking the other way with regard to Mussolini's actions in Ethiopia. It was the first of the cynical bargains made by these two dictators, who later referred to themselves as members of the "Pact of Steel".

The events in Austria did not affect my mother directly, but they were the next step in Hitler's plans to dominate Europe and so are significant in setting the context for what was to occur. As the events in Austria unfolded, the rest of Europe in general sat back and watched. Few wanted to risk war over what many viewed as almost an internal matter between two groups of German-speaking people that perhaps should rightly be considered as one nationality after all. Hitler had in fact spelled out his plans and ambitions fairly explicitly in his book Mein Kampf, but there were not many people who took the trouble to heed the warnings. The governments of Czechoslovakia and Poland saw the warning signs for what they were and sought to bolster agreements with Britain and France to protect them from what the more farsighted of the politicians in these countries saw as Hitler's inevitable ambitions to absorb them as well.

Hitler was also very clever in how he managed the public relations of his initial ambitions. He was always careful to couch them as fighting to protect the world from the scourge of communism, or to protect the rights of ethnic minorities, or in the case of

Austria, to protect against the restoration of the Hapsburg monarchy. This created a perception that won him at least the tacit, if not in some cases the overt, support of conservative elements throughout the European democracies.

By the end of 1937, Austria was in the hands of a conservative government. Hitler's National Socialist agents were stirring trouble within the country, in aid of Hitler's plan to use the pretext of preventing a restoration of the Hapsburg monarchy as an excuse to invade. In February 1938, Hitler presented Austria's chancellor, Kurt Schuschnigg, with an ultimatum: include National Socialists in the government or be invaded. Abandoned by Italy and knowing not to expect any help from France or Britain, Schuschnigg adopted a policy of appeasement to Hitler but struggled to keep Austria independent. It appeared that he was giving in to most of Hitler's demands.

Schuschnigg had second thoughts and decided he would stand up to Hitler after all. He announced that Austria "would never surrender its independence" and ended a February speech with a patriotic appeal: "Red, white, red (the colors of the Austrian flag), until we're dead!" As William L. Shirer pointed out in his history of the Anschluss in his book 'The Rise and Fall of the Third Reich', it rhymes in German too: "Rot, weiss, rot, bis wir Sind tot!"

Schuschnigg appealed to Austria's Social Democrats for help and that party agreed to join him in his effort to maintain Austria's independence. In a speech on March 9, Schuschnigg announced that a nation-wide plebiscite would be held on March 13 to determine whether Austrians wanted to remain independent or to unify with the German Reich.

Hitler feared that Austrians would vote against Anschluss and choose independence. The German army massed troops on the Austrian border and Hitler threatened invasion. Schuschnigg resigned and the pro-Hitler lawyer Seyss-Inquart was installed as Austria's new chancellor. The plebiscite was cancelled and on March 11, German troops crossed into Austria without any resistance. Seyss-Inquart announced that he had invited the German troops into Austria in order to prevent a communist uprising – a blatant lie – and Hitler replied with his declaration that he was putting the German army at the service of the Austrian people.

Many Austrians were happy with the turn of events, especially the country's National Socialists. The Austrian Nazis were a minor-

ity in the country but could make a big showing in the streets and at rallies, particularly among Austrian's young, among whom their support was the strongest. The March 13 plebiscite had been cancelled and, on that day, Austria was declared a province of Germany. Seyss-Inquart served as Chancellor for two days and was replaced by a Nazi Gauleiter. On March 14, Hitler returned to his native Austria and was welcomed like a conquering hero in Vienna.

It was Hitler's first acquisition of new territory beyond Germany's frontiers. Without firing a single shot in anger, Hitler occupied and annexed a neighboring country. The western democracies watched and did nothing.

Schuschnigg was arrested and tortured and eventually sent to a concentration camp. He survived to be liberated by the American army in 1945 and emigrated to the United States, where he became a professor of political science at Saint Louis University until 1967. He eventually returned to his native Austria, where he died in 1977.

We had signed a contract to appear at the National Theatre in Warsaw for a period of two months, after which we would tour Poland, visiting other major cities. All in all, we were scheduled to be in Poland for more than four months. Mother would accompany Alma and me for the duration of the trip and I was able to convince Mother to let Nuria take a leave of absence from her school so that she could come too. Michel was not happy that I would be gone for so long, but he understood that this was an important opportunity for my dancing career. We agreed that we would get back together when I returned to Paris, but we also agreed that it would be alright if we saw other people during my absence. Michel seemed almost relieved when I agreed to this.

Our train left the Gare de l'Est bound for Berlin, where we would change trains for Warsaw. The journey was uneventful. The German border guards at the French-German border were stern but polite. Our papers were in order and we had no contraband in our luggage, so we had nothing to fear. Our papers did indicate that we were in transit through Germany and this seemed to make the guards somewhat less interested in us. We noticed that other passengers, who were intending to stay in Germany, received a more diligent inspection and were subjected to more intense questioning. After this inspection, our train proceeded on and we arrived in Berlin without incident.

It did feel strange during our three-hour wait at the Berlin Station to see so many Nazi swastika banners and flags on display everywhere. The station seemed full of soldiers in their uniforms and of what we guessed were Gestapo men in their black leather coats staring at everyone with their cold eyes that seemed to bore into the soul of everyone they looked at. I tried to ignore the fact that these were the people who were supporting the Nationalists that my father was risking his life fighting as I drank my tea and ate my pastry at the station café.

Our train departed Berlin and we sped east toward Warsaw. The border guards at the Polish border were somewhat more diligent in their inspection of our papers and luggage than they had been crossing in from France. It seemed more important to them to check the people leaving Germany than those transiting Germany. We did not attach a great deal of importance to this observation at the time, but it became very significant to us months later when we were trying to return to France. We left the frontier behind and continued across the flat countryside to Warsaw. Nuria and I sat spellbound by the window, looking at the immense, snow-covered fields interspersed with occasional forest. So, this was the magical, mysterious Poland! We felt that we were entering a new world, unlike anything we had ever known.

We arrived in Warsaw on a snowy evening. Accommodation had been arranged for us and we took a taxi from the train station to our new home. Our taxi driver was an amiable, middle-aged Pole who spoke fluent French and asked us about our reasons for coming to his city.

"We are here to dance at the National Theatre," I replied to him, grateful that he spoke this language.

He thought I was trying to be funny and when I managed to convince him that I was not joking, that we were really were there to perform at the National Theatre, he seemed quite impressed by his passengers.

We had been worried about how we would communicate in Poland, as none of us spoke any Polish and it seemed like a difficult language. When I looked at words in Polish, on signs or in newspapers, I could not even begin to imagine how some of the words might be pronounced. It was a relief to learn that almost all educated people in Poland spoke good French and although I managed to learn a few words of Polish, I seemed to pronounce them in ways that were incomprehensible to the Poles, and so in general we used our French to communicate.

We took up residence in an old, not too expensive hotel in the heart of the old, historical part of the city. It was a rather decrepit and dreary building, an ancient palace full of archways and innumerable and seemingly endless dark corridors. It was one of those strange, mysterious places that compel the visitor, as if by instinct, to walk through them with caution, speaking in low tones for fear of awakening the ghosts that surely dwell within the walls. The palace had once belonged to Napoleon's mistress, the beautiful Polish countess Maria Walenska. The main parlor was lavishly furnished, with huge crystal chandeliers hanging from the tall ceiling and thick and intricate tapestries covering every inch of the walls. On top of the mantel of the huge fireplace were two Sèvres vases, the largest and loveliest that I had ever seen.

We had a week of rehearsals to get ready for our performances at the National Theatre. This would be a little different from what Alma and I were used to. Our dance numbers were the same, but we were used to dancing to music played by a solo pianist or occasionally a solo guitarist, or at most the small "combo" at a nightclub or casino. Here, our musical accompaniment was a full symphonic orchestra, playing in a pit while we danced on stage. What this meant for us was that we had to concentrate on the rhythm and gestures of the orchestra's conductor, the only member of the orchestra we could see, rather than making eye contact as needed with the musician when we had to vary the pace to keep our movements synchronized.

To my surprise, it was Alma, usually so confident that she could effortlessly excel at anything that involved dancing, who became frustrated.

"How can they expect us to follow the orders of a conductor like this was the army and he is the sergeant?" she vented in frustration to me during a break one morning.

"I don't know. We have to get used to it," I replied.

"They should have to get used to us, not us to them!" That was the old Alma!

We managed to learn how to work this way, though, and were ready in plenty of time for our opening night. Once we had gotten

In Poland

used to it, we enjoyed dancing to the full orchestra. Where the Spanish melodies we danced to were so pretty and melodic when played by a single instrument, they were powerful and dramatic when played by a full orchestra. Alma and I adjusted our dancing styles just a little to suit the arrangement of the music, adding just a bit more drama to our moves and replacing the somewhat flirty attitude of Flamenco with a more serious demeanor. It was fun and exciting to be trying new styles! Our new style blended well with the classic ballet that made up most of the other acts of the nightly performance at the National Theatre.

Our performances at the National Theatre in Warsaw were a great success. We were well received and got favorable reviews from the critics in the Warsaw newspapers, though we had to have these translated for us. We had all fallen in love with that wintery city and its friendly and cultured people. We spent many delightful afternoons at the luxurious Hotel Europejsky, where would go for afternoon tea, something that especially delighted my sister Nuria. Drinking cup after cup of steaming hot chocolate, it was always hard for her to choose which among the selection of luscious Viennese pastries being offered she wanted that day. But the highlight of the day would be returning to our hotel as it became dark, riding under the moonlight in a "troika" carriage. We would ride through the snowy streets and cross the park on the way back to our hotel, shadows of the tree branches forming lacelike patterns on the ground, with the bells of our carriage ringing merrily as we kept ourselves warm huddling under a thick fur blanket.

We had the days to ourselves to do what we wanted, as long as we would be at the National Theatre by 7 p.m. to dress for our evening performance. On Saturdays, we put on an afternoon performance in addition to the evening show. Sundays there was no performance and we could relax all day.

Nuria had brought her guitar and continued to practice for hours every day. One afternoon, she was overheard practicing by one of the other guests at the hotel, a Hungarian pianist who was touring Poland performing concerts in each major city. He was enthralled by her playing and arranged for her to meet his agent in Warsaw, who in turn arranged for Nuria to perform at several recitals in the city. Nuria was thrilled at the opportunity to perform for an audience. Her recitals were so well received that she continued receiving invitations to play at concerts and recitals for the rest of the time that we were in Poland, both as a solo musician and with orchestra accompaniment.

Darkness comes early to Warsaw on winter days. On most evenings, when heavy snows would blanket Warsaw under a white cloak, the hotel guests would gather in the main parlor to hear the excellent music, much of it lovely pieces by Chopin, played on the grand piano by an old and retired Polish cavalry officer who had been living in that hotel for almost a half century. That old gentleman took a liking to me and would smile and bow gallantly whenever he saw me. As he got to know me, he would always play the pieces that he knew were my favorites. While the delightful melodies filled the room, I would go sit down by one of the many large windows that overlooked the garden, where I would remain, charmed and spellbound by the aged pianist, the timeless music, and the beauty of the snow falling from an opalescent sky. I would sit there, waiting for the magic moment to arrive when the light of the winter sunset would suddenly strike the snow-covered garden and transform that pristine whiteness into hues of red and violet. I never grew tired of waiting for the evening hours to arrive, as I knew that they would be preceded by such wondrous sights. I would sit and enjoy the sights and the music the old gentleman would play until it was time to leave for the theatre.

"You love the music of Poland, don't you, Conchita?" the old officer asked me one evening as I was thanking him for playing my favorite pieces for me that day as I left to go to the theatre.

"Oui, monsieur, je l'aime beaucoup," I replied in the French that was our common language for communication.

"That is because the Spanish people and the Polish people understand each other," he said as he stood and took my hand to kiss it in his gallant, old-school way. "We are both a romantic and a cultured people who understand chivalry and appreciate the beautiful things in life. I hope our people will prove adequate for the modern age, which I fear does not attach so much importance to these things."

His remarks haunted me later as I looked back on them and thought about the terrible events that would overtake Poland and all of Europe and wondered what had happened to my friend the old officer. He was a relic of an older time, when chivalry and gallantry still mattered. And he was right in what he said. People like him were not suited to survive the new wave of barbarism that

In Poland

would soon take over throughout Europe. Indeed, it was his comrades from the Polish cavalry who, so the legend went, tried to stop Hitler's tanks with their horse-mounted cavalry less than two years later when Blitzkrieg war was waged on Poland. They never stood a chance.

From the very start of our engagement at the National Theatre, Alma and I had become close friends with the group of boys and girls that made up the Warsaw Ballet Company, and who were appearing on the same program with us. We met with them outdoors after each nightly performance and we would ride together in horse-drawn sleighs, racing along snowy streets. Konrad, the young star of the ballet, would follow us on horseback, riding "Cossack-style" at fast pace and singing old Polish songs at the top of his lungs. He would make all of us laugh with his crazy antics. He was a handsome and vivacious boy, his artistic career already ensured and with a wonderful future ahead of him.

I do not recall the exact occasion when we first became aware of our mutual attraction, but we both discovered it at the same time. Once we realized that neither he nor I was completely happy unless we were together, we rarely left each other's sight for very long. We managed to get away often from the rest of the group, taking long walks along the banks of the Vistula River, staring at its frozen surface, which reflected like a mirror the colors of the sky. I felt somewhat guilty about enjoying my time with Konrad so much when Michel was waiting for me in Paris. But the feelings of guilt would depart whenever I was in Konrad's presence and then I would remember that Michel had never actually proposed to me and that we had agreed we could see other people while I was away from Paris.

During a holiday, with no performances scheduled at the theatre, I traveled with Konrad to Zakopane, a beautiful ski resort in the south of Poland, to spend a weekend with him and his parents at their cabin. Zakopane was a little town high in a forest in the Tatra Mountains. We traveled by car across the immense flat plain of Poland, the monotony of the landscape broken, every once in a while, by thick enclaves of woods in which we could see deer and foxes roaming among the fir and pine trees. Eventually we reached the foot of the Tatras Mountains and our car climbed steadily upward until the magical little town of Zakopane appeared before our eyes.

For several days, we were lost to the world. Konrad tried to teach me to ski but gave up after seeing me fall flat on my rear for the hundredth time. But I was more than happy to stay indoors in the company of Konrad's parents. In the afternoons, I would follow Konrad's mother into the kitchen to help her prepare dinner. Dinner was usually the Polish dumplings called pierogis, which I had come to love, especially when they were smothered in sour cream. Afterward, we would join Konrad's father in the parlor, where the three of us would sit next to the fireplace, drinking tea while we waited for Konrad to return from the slopes. Konrad's father occasionally insisted on spiking our tea with Polish vodka. "It will get the blood cells chasing each other and keep you warm!" he would say.

The holiday was fun and remained a treasured memory for me.

"Do we have to go back to Warsaw, Konrad?" I asked him the afternoon of our last day there. "This is like living in a fairy tale. Can't we just stay here?"

Konrad took my hands in his eyes and locked his big, gentle eyes onto mine. "Conchita, you know we must go back. We are professionals and we have careers. But we will come back here together one day!"

We returned to Warsaw and resumed our nightly performances at the National Theatre. Our engagement there was coming to an end, though, and soon we would be leaving Warsaw.

On the evening of our last performance at the National Theatre, the staff of the theatre held a farewell party for the entire company. We danced and sang until dawn, a bittersweet and somewhat melancholy mood pervading the air through the party in spite of the merriment and gaiety at the thought of Konrad and I saying taking leave of each other. He was accompanying the Polish ballet company to Budapest. Alma and I were leaving for Łodz, the second city of our Polish tour. Konrad and I bid a tearful goodbye to each other and solemnly promised that we would find a way to be together again as soon as we could.

After performing at Łodz and then Katowice, our next stop was at Krakow. We arrived in Krakow after dark. The sky was clear when we arrived, but snow had been falling on this beautiful city all day. Of all the Polish cities I saw, Krakow was the most enchanting. It was a fairytale place, like the ones that exist solely in our imagination, a vision-like image that enters our minds while reading or

In Poland

listening to children's stories, evoking fantasies of strange, dream-like creatures and magical castles. It was very late when our train arrived at the station and the old city seemed to be deserted, the maze of cobblestone streets glowing under a full moon, while the slender needles of the city's many church towers seemed to be piercing the sky above them. All around the city square, the old wrought iron lamps faintly illuminated the centuries-old buildings with their haloes of yellowish light.

As the end of our Polish tour was approaching, we found ourselves back in Warsaw. The international situation was once again becoming tense and we were advised by our manager to have all our papers in order in case we would have to leave Poland and return to Paris on short notice. But April had arrived, bringing with it the perfume and aromas of the thousands of wildflowers that grew in the parks of Warsaw and in the surrounding fields. A few patches of snow remained here and there, but spring had taken over the land, the trees bursting with new, tender leaves and interminable rows of bright red poppies and tall yellow sunflowers growing everywhere. The Vistula River, its water at last free from the ice that had imprisoned it all through the winter, flowed gently through the city, its banks crowded with people enjoying the long-awaited blessings of warmth and sunshine.

When we met with Konrad and the rest of the national ballet company, they greeted us with the wonderful news that they too were going to be in Paris in the near future, as they were scheduled to appear at the Paris Opera House in August. Konrad's hair was streaked with gold threads and his skin tanned from the short vacation that he had just taken with his family on the shores of the Baltic Sea. We hardly left each other's sight during those few precious days left to us in Warsaw before going our separate ways. When the day came to say goodbye to each other, Konrad accompanied us to the train station. In spite of the fact that we were planning to meet in Paris not long afterward, as I looked into Konrad's eyes, I could not fail to notice that they now bore a new and unfamiliar sadness, his usually merry expression all but banished from his face. His easy smile, so dear to me, had faded completely away. For the last time, he kissed my hand, still holding it tightly and only letting go when the train started to move forward, pulling us apart. I remained alone at the rear of the train, clutching in my hand the small bouquet of flowers that he had given me a few minutes earlier. As the train slowly gathered speed, I lost sight of him.

On leaving Poland, my soul was filled with sorrow. Looking back, I see that I must have had a grim foreboding of the chaos and tragic events that would soon engulf us. Hitler's demonic plans continued to evolve, and it was only a matter of time before Poland fell victim to his aggressions. The Polish Ballet never did reach Paris and I would never see Konrad again.

Our train crossed Germany and sped toward the French border. As we were getting closer to the border, my mother's nervousness became more and more apparent. Alma, Nuria, and I knew only too well the reason for her nervousness. Mother's, Nuria's, and my Spanish passports had long expired and anyway, passports of the Spanish Republic were not universally recognized, especially by Germany. We had been traveling all over Europe with the police permits issued to us by the French authorities in Paris, to use as temporary identification and travel documents until such time as we could receive valid passports from our own country. Our police permits had expired while we were in Poland and there had been no way to renew them. We had thought we would be able to renew them while in Poland, but the French consuls first in Warsaw and later in Krakow had been uncooperative. This was all a part of the French government's continuing confusion and ambivalence as to how to deal with the Spanish Civil War. No one on the diplomatic staff wanted to take a chance of getting in trouble for helping a handful of refugees from the Spanish Republic and we were left with expired and therefore useless identity papers.

When the time came to return to Paris, no alternative was left for us to be able to cross the border back into France other than to forge new dates on our permits. The evening of our last day in Warsaw, having once again that afternoon been unable to get us new and properly dated papers from the French consulate, my mother had patiently and carefully erased the expired dates in our identity papers. She then, using her eyeliner pencil, had painstakingly and meticulously written in new dates that would appear to be valid. Our documents had received only a cursory glance from the officials as we entered Germany from Poland, as our train tickets indicated that we were transit passengers en route to Paris. But we knew from previous experience that the scrutiny of our documents leaving Nazi Germany would be more intense. We were terribly

In Poland

concerned and in great fear that the guards at the border would detect the forgery. We could not even begin to imagine what catastrophic consequences might result to us as refugees from the Spanish Republic being caught in Nazi Germany with forged papers. I was nervous and afraid in a way that I had never experienced before, even during all the hours of hiding in a bomb shelter during the air raids in Madrid.

At the French border, the train stopped and to our horror, not only did the German border police come on board but also the dreaded Gestapo, looking sinister in their habitual black leather coats. We could see the frontier with France less than twenty-five meters away and it was tempting to jump off the train and simply make a run for it. The four of us could barely breathe as we heard the opening and closing of doors in the other compartments as they approached ours to check our papers. Alma's papers of course were valid, as she had been living in Paris for years. Mother tried to convince her to sit in another compartment so that if we were caught, she would not be implicated. Bravely, Alma refused to leave our sides. She insisted that she would stay with us and help us to implement our plan.

On the way across Germany, Mother had instructed us, "Flirt with the police when they come in and try to distract them!" As the unsmiling men in uniform and the cold-eyed Gestapo men in their black leather coats entered our compartment, Alma and I, motivated by sheer fright, started putting to use all the guile and charm we could muster, batting our eyelashes and smiling and flirting, hoping we could distract them so that they would not peer too closely at our forged documents. I babbled incessantly in French and Spanish while Alma kept repeating the few phrases of German that she had picked up, with such a strong French accent that the words were clearly unintelligible to the Germans. Nuria all the while kept offering the men chocolates from an open box, placing them right under the noses of the by now completely bewildered officials. Mother, with great willpower, managed to fake an attitude of utter nonchalance and boredom as she handed over our documents, hardly daring to look up from the novel she was holding in her hands as our papers were examined and then stamped with exit visas. With a final "Heil Hitler", the soldiers and Gestapo left, closing the door behind them. The four of us collapsed into the seats of our compartment, taking a deep breath and looking at each other as we breathed huge sighs of relief. We could hardly believe that our stratagem had worked so well.

In later years, my mother would laugh as she recounted this episode, especially when she would talk about the "Spanish señorita antics". Though she took great delight in how they had managed to confuse and bewilder the Gestapo and the soldiers, the episode shook her badly. Years later, in 1974, I came home from college for a Christmas break wearing my new knee-length black leather coat, a gift from a girlfriend. I arrived at my parents' house after dark and my mother opened the door and for a split second before she recognized me, she just saw a large man in a black leather coat standing in the shadows, backlit by a streetlamp. It evoked a visceral memory of that confrontation with the Gestapo and how horribly that could have ended. She started to shake in remembered fear until she got hold of herself after she recognized me. I never wore the coat around her again. Eventually, I gave it away.

Poland made a deep impression on Isa that she never got over. She loved the piano music of Chopin for the rest of her life. In addition to loving the music for its own sake, she also loved hearing it for the memories it evoked of that trip to Poland during her youth and of the friends she made there, including her friend the gallant old cavalry officer. She would often talk about how much she had loved Poland and the Polish people whom she had met, considering them a very intelligent, cultured, and polite people who had made a tremendous impact on the cultural history of the world. She became very emotional the day she told me the story of how when Poland was invaded by the Nazis, less than two years after her trip there, and Warsaw was besieged and under constant aerial bombardment, Radio Warsaw would broadcast Chopin's Military Polonaise *continuously to let the world know that the city was still alive and fighting. Then one day at the end of September 1939, the music was replaced briefly by Chopin's* Funeral March *before Radio Warsaw went silent. Warsaw had fallen.*

Decades later, I was doing geologic work in Slovakia and Poland and made several trips to the Tatras Mountains, where Isa and Konrad had taken their skiing vacation. Although I never made it to Zakopane specifically, I did see several towns and villages that were

In Poland

near it and must have been just like it. That corner of the world is indeed a fairy tale land, particularly in the winter. I could see why my mother had such fond memories of it and why she remembered it with such warm affection.

I also was able to spend some time in Krakow when I worked in southern Poland. It was easy to understand why my mother found the city so lovely and enchanting. I remembered her describing a park near the medieval wall where she would go for walks. I found what I thought was the park she had described and went for a walk around it in her memory. It was the last time that I visited Krakow when I had one of the most strange and inexplicable experiences of my life. I left Krakow and drove west toward the coal-mining town of Lignice, where I had meetings the next morning. There was a point during the drive that I felt a very strange sensation in the pit of my stomach. It was as though a chill had gone through me and turned the water in my gut into ice water. It made no sense to me at the time. Looking at a map of my journey that evening, I realized that this sensation had affected me as I was passing within less than fifteen kilometers of Auschwitz.

Chapter 9

Miss Spain

May 1938
Europe was thrown into turmoil during the summer of 1938 by the crisis in Czechoslovakia's Sudetenland. Hitler precipitated the crisis in February by demanding self-determination, including the right for their territories to be assimilated into the Reich, for the ethnic Germans living in Austria and in the Sudeten Province of Czechoslovakia, the west side of which bordered Germany. The issue had been resolved for Austrian Germans by the Anschluss. It was clear to many that Hitler now wanted to accomplish the same thing with Czechoslovakia, at least with the Sudetenland and possibly with the entire country.

Ethnic Germans accounted for a bit under a third of the population of this part of Czechoslovakia and had organized several years earlier into a political party, the Sudeten Germans People's Party, led by a supporter of Hitler, which advocated a split from Czechoslovakia and union with Germany. The government of Czechoslovakia refused to recognize this party and disagreed vehemently with their advocacy of splitting away. Aside from the question of what other revolts this might foment among other ethnic minorities within Czechoslovakia, there were two additional reasons why the Prague government was opposed to giving away the province. First, it was a region rich in natural resources, including lignite and coal. Second, the area was vital to Czechoslovakia's defense, as it was hilly and steep, forming a natural barrier to invading forces, and contained many of Czechoslovakia's border fortifications.

In the early summer of 1938, Hitler ordered his generals to begin planning for war with Czechoslovakia. He continued giving money and support to the Sudeten German People's Party and encouraged them to make trouble within the Sudetenland, hoping to create a chaotic situation which would justify sending in troops to restore order and protect the ethnic German population. His plan was risky. The Czechoslovakian army was strong and professional. The terrain and fortifications of the Sudetenland would have given a tremendous advantage to the defending army. France had signed a mutual defense treaty with Czechoslovakia, promising support if the country were attacked. Britain's Prime Minister Neville Chamberlain hinted that a German invasion of Czechoslovakia might "possibly involve other countries". However, Hitler bet that in 1938, the still war-weary French and British would not come rushing to Czechoslovakia's aid. The Soviet Union had also signed a mutual defense treaty with Czechoslovakia but was beset with internal problems and Hitler also doubted the Soviets would come rushing to aid the Prague government. Still, Hitler's generals could not guarantee him victory in the Sudetenland.

Hitler bided his time and waited during the summer for the Sudeten crisis to ripen. Meanwhile, he continued in his speeches to demand justice and fair treatment for the ethnic Germans living in Czechoslovakia. German newsreels continued to show "evidence" of Czech atrocities being committed against innocent German families living in the Sudetenland and with each new propaganda film thus produced, Hitler would repeat his public threats to use military force if required to support and protect the Sudeten Germans.

As these events unfolded, a sense of building unease began to settle over much of the population of western Europe. But other than statements of support which in the end were meaningless, the western democracies watched but did nothing. The mood of appeasement is summed up well by an excerpt from a speech British Prime Minister Neville Chamberlain gave to Parliament some months later, in September 1938, when the Czechoslovakian situation had turned into a full-blown crisis, ending with Nazi Germany being given the Sudetenland and eventually all of Czechoslovakia, again without Hitler having to fire a single shot. Chamberlain's words: "How horrible, fantastic, incredible it is that we should be digging trenches and trying on gas masks here because of a quarrel in a far-away country between people of whom we know nothing."

In Spain, meanwhile, as the civil war went on, the situation for the Republic continued to worsen. By April 1938, Nationalist forces *had split the Republic in two: one part centered in Madrid, the other in Barcelona and Valencia on the east coast. The intervening ground, including La Mancha, was now firmly in the hands of Franco and his Nationalists. By May, Franco felt sufficiently confident in his ultimate victory that he announced that the only terms he would consider for a truce would be the unconditional surrender of the Republic.*

We had been back in Paris for a few weeks and Alma and I were taking a break from our dance performances after the hectic schedule of our Poland tour. I was doing some modeling for Guerlain to bring in some money for us, but not working terribly hard and enjoying some needed relaxation. Michel and I had reunited. I told him about Konrad, and he told me about the several French (and one Hungarian) girls with whom he had spent some time while I was away. We still enjoyed each other's company immensely and soon were spending almost all of our free time together again.

One afternoon as I returned to our neighborhood from the Faubourg de Saint Honoré, my sister Nuria was waiting for me outside the entrance to the Metro station. As soon as she saw me climbing up the stairs, she started shouting at me, waving a large envelope in her hand.

"Conchi," she yelled excitedly, "You won't believe what this is! You might be Miss Spain!"

I started to become angry with her and was about to ask her what she thought gave her the right to open an envelope that clearly had been addressed to me, when her words finally registered.

"Miss Spain? Are you crazy? What in the world are you talking about?"

"Read this. It's all explained in the letter."

My initial anger with my younger sister for invading my privacy was immediately replaced by excitement and a feeling of incredulity.

The envelope, which had arrived that morning and which she and Mother had opened, contained an invitation from the Paris newspaper *Le Monde*, asking me to fill out the enclosed application if I wished to appear as a contestant for the upcoming Miss Spain competition. The competition was being sponsored by the newspaper and would be held in Paris due to the war in Spain. There were written instructions about where and when to appear in person in front of a select panel of judges for interviews before I could be formally accepted as a contestant for the title. The winner of the Miss Spain title would be eligible to appear at the pageant for the Miss Europe contest, to be held in Copenhagen in September.

The letter and its invitation created quite a turmoil in our household, with my entire family whole-heartedly backing my decision to enter the competition. Alma of course appointed herself as my coach and began lecturing me on how to behave during the interview. I filled in the application form and mailed it back to *Le Monde*. Within a week, my invitation for the formal interview had arrived by return mail. As the day of the interview approached, I became increasingly nervous. We all tried to guess what sorts of questions would be asked and as we did not have a clue what these might be, we focused on my practicing looking composed and on comporting myself as though I deserved the title Miss Spain.

On the day of the interview, I asked my mother to come with me for moral support. When we entered the reception at *Le Monde* headquarters, we saw a dozen or so other girls waiting for their chance to be interviewed. Like myself, they were all Spanish refugees, now living in Paris or in other parts of France until the war in Spain would be over and depending on which side won, they could either return home or possibly face permanent exile. I was the last to be called and by the time they did call me in I was quite nervous.

In I went to the interview room where I was asked to walk up and down the room a few times by the panel of six judges. I could feel their eyes examining me with every step that I took, and this only added to my nervousness. Then they invited me to sit and the six of them took turns asking me a series of questions. By the time I was through answering all their questions, most of which I thought were quite silly, I was exhausted and anxious to get it all over with and go home.

"Well?" asked my mother anxiously as we walked toward the Metro to go home.

"I don't know. I don't think I did very well. I'm sorry, Mamá." I was more worried about disappointing my family than I was about the outcome of the interview. By then, I had convinced myself that the whole thing was silly, and I didn't really care about the outcome.

"Don't worry, Conchi," said Mother in her gentle way as she took my hand. "I'm sure you did very well and if those stupid judges are too blind and idiotic to choose you, then that is their problem!"

When we got home and I told Alma how I thought that I had not done very well, despite all her coaching, she said something similar to Mother's comments, but in true Alma-style, also added some colorful comments about what she felt was the ancestry of the judges.

Less than a week later, to my great surprise, I was notified by telegram that I had been selected as Miss Spain 1938.

Alma and Mother and everyone else announced that they had known all along that I would be selected. All of a sudden, it all did not seem so silly any longer. I was quite proud of myself!

As soon as the official photograph was released to the press, I began to receive far more requests for advertising jobs than I could possibly handle. Following the advice of my theatrical agent, I turned them all down to focus on my performing career rather than on becoming an advertising model. Then all kinds of gifts started to pour in as well. I received daily a variety of items from a number of the Parisian houses of haute couture, including jackets and coats from Lanvin, suits and dresses from Patou, and a couple of long evening gowns from Schiaparelli. When I went to Cartier at their invitation to select my gift of a gold wristwatch, the whole scene was faithfully recorded and then presented on the front page of the magazine *Paris-Soir*. Diamond earrings from Van Clef and Arpels as well as two beautiful silk scarves and a matched set of luggage from Hermès and finally a huge bottle of perfume from Guerlain were among the many gifts I received. It was all advertising for these houses, but for me the gifts seemed lavish!

The Spanish newspaper *ABC*, firmly Nationalist in its orientation, ran my photograph in their editorial page under a caption that essentially said, "It is a pity that the new Miss Spain is not representing Franco's Spain. She is pretty enough to capture the heart of any young Fascist." That I was not representing either political side of my country was true. Spain, still torn by civil war, was mentioned constantly in the French press. Every article about the Miss Europe competition mentioned that I appeared not to be representing either side. I wanted to represent Republican Spain, but the sponsors of the Miss Europe contest, *Le Monde*, had discouraged me from stating this because of the controversy that might raise within France. I refused to be seen as representing Fascist Spain as long as my father was still fighting the fascists.

So, in the end I decided not to represent either side. To *Le Monde*'s credit, and to that of the other promoters of the contest, they respected my wishes to remain neutral. Following the advice of the newspaper staff, it was agreed that for photographs and publicity appearances, I would carry neither the red, white, purple tricolor of the Republic nor the red and yellow flag of the Nationalists. Instead, I would simply carry a white banner with the word España written on it. Perhaps this accounted for the big ovations and applause I would receive later, during the Miss Europe contest, when I would step on the stage along with the other girls, all wearing the flags of their respective countries. The obvious omission of the Spanish flag reminded everyone of the tragedy that was still unfolding on the other side of the Pyrenees.

That silly comment in *ABC* about "capturing the heart of any young Fascist" upset me more than it should. I hoped my father had seen the news and would be proud of me, but I couldn't stand the thought that he might think I could represent the Spain of the Nationalists whom he was risking his life fighting.

"Papá knows I would never allow myself to represent those Fascists, doesn't he?" I asked my mother the morning after I had seen the article.

"Of course, Conchita," she replied. "Don't worry. Papá knows you would never betray him."

Now that I was "Miss Spain in Exile", as the Parisian press called me, the offers to dance continued to pour in and Alma and I had our choice of bookings. Alma teased me one day, saying, "You know, now that you are Miss España, perhaps we should become the Isa and Alma duo!"

"Really?" I asked innocently.

"No, of course not!" said Alma.

And so still as Alma and Isa Reyes, we continued to appear through the summer, now more often than not with star billing, in nightclubs and theatres all over Paris. When we performed on theatre stages, it was often with Nuria playing guitar for at least a portion of the performance. The Miss Europe contest was several months away, and as exciting as I thought was the idea of possibly being awarded that title, I did not let myself become too worried about it. It still seemed somewhat unbelievable to me that I was Miss Spain! The Miss Europe pageant would come soon enough. In the meantime, Alma and Isa Reyes continued to perform and to hope for the best.

CHAPTER 10

Sharing a Hotel with the Russians

Summer–Autumn 1938
Through the rest of that summer, the crisis in the Sudetenland continued to escalate without resolution. Hitler continued his blustering and his propaganda campaigns seeking to lay the groundwork that would justify an eventual German intervention in Czechoslovakia. As it became evident that rather than satisfy Hitler's territorial ambitions, the Anschluss with Austria had merely whetted those ambitions, waves of tension swept over Europe during the summer. Meanwhile, the barbaric persecution of minorities, especially Jews, which Hitler had put in place in Germany was now being implemented in Austria. If anything, the persecution of Jews in Austria was even more ruthless and barbaric than that in Germany.

Through that summer of 1938, the tensions between Germany and Czechoslovakia continued to mount as Hitler mounted a war of nerves against the smaller country. As summer approached its end, it finally became evident to Britain and France that Hitler was determined to annex at least the Sudetenland, if not indeed all of Czechoslovakia, and his bellicose posturing convinced the democracies that he was willing to risk a general war in order to do so.

In Spain late that July, the long and bloody Battle of the Ebro began. It would last for more than three months, ending with defeat for the Republican forces in mid-November. With that defeat began the slow, final collapse of the Republic and its army as the Nationalists continued to win victories and consolidate their territory. The foreign volunteers of the International Brigades continued to fight valiantly on the side of the Loyalists, but their hopes for ultimate victory were growing dimmer.

Shortly after I was selected to be Miss Spain, we had to move out of Aunt Encarna's apartment. The owner from whom she had been leasing it was Jewish and had been living in Venice. Now, she was finding Mussolini's Italy an increasingly uncomfortable place to live and we received a telegram from her one day that she would be returning to Paris in two weeks and needed her apartment back.

We began looking for a new place to live. Fortunately, Alma and I were bringing in enough fees that we could look in reasonable neighborhoods, although we did not want to spend money unnecessarily just to have a fashionable address. We did not know how long we would be able to continue getting as many bookings as we wanted, and with the uncertainty that was falling over all of Europe, we did not know how long our money might have to last us or under what circumstances we might have to go somewhere new. Mother in particular could not get over the memory of having sold her last piece of jewelry less than a year earlier and was terrified of once again being short of money to survive. She was insistent that we not spend too much on rent unnecessarily. Aunt Encarna felt the same way. Although she was still receiving the monthly funds from her ex-husband, she could never be sure that this would last forever.

For ten days, we looked all over Paris, but the places we saw were either too small for the six of us, too expensive, or in neighborhoods that we did not feel safe in. We were beginning to despair and wonder where we could go when, just in time before the widow's return, we found a new place to live.

Michel called excitedly one afternoon to tell us that a Russian family that was friends with his father had suddenly managed to obtain their visas to emigrate to America and would be vacating their apartment in a residential hotel in two days. If we wanted it, it was ours!

Of course, we told him that we would go to look at it. Michel came to pick us up and drove us to the hotel, and it was perfect for us. The rent was well within our budget and the current occupants were in fact leaving in two days, having only suddenly and much to their surprise not only been granted their visas but, miraculously it appeared, they had also been able to book passage on a ship leaving Cherbourg for New York in two days. The apartment was large enough for the six of us to live comfortably, although not quite as large as our current dwelling. We were so happy to have found a place to live that we did not care at all if our new home was a

Sharing a Hotel with the Russians

little smaller! The apartment was ours if we would just agree to take over the rent payments. On the spot, we agreed and with Michel's help, we quickly took care of the necessary paperwork and two days later, we moved into our new home.

Our new dwelling was a spacious and airy three-bedroom apartment on the top floor of a residential hotel off the Rue Daru, in the heart of the White Russian emigré population of Paris, in the 8th Arrondissement. The building was just down the street from Paris' Russian Orthodox cathedral, the Alexander Nevsky Cathedral. Perhaps because of the nearby cathedral, this neighborhood had become home to a large number of the White Russians living in Paris. Paris had become a magnet for the White Russians, the refugees from the Russian Revolution of 1917 and the ensuing Russian civil war between the Bolsheviks and the supporters of the Tsar. Indeed, our building was inhabited principally by White Russian emigrés, many of them aristocrats and even nobles, a duke or two among them. Refugees from the old, doomed regime of the late Tsar, they had moved to Paris to escape the turmoil, and for many of them the certainty of imprisonment and likely execution, in their country. They were now forced to make a living and subsist by working as doormen and waiters for the deluxe hotels and restaurants of Paris, or as taxi drivers. Many of them had come to live in this area, on and near the Rue Daru.

As before, we settled in two to a room, with Encarna and Nanita sharing one room, Mother and Nuria the second, and Alma and I in the third. And also, as before, Alma's and my room was the smallest but had the best view. If we looked out our window, we could catch a glimpse of the Russian cathedral's spires and their golden onion dome tops. There was a small living room and as the hotel had a dining room in which we could take our meals, there was no need for either a dining room or kitchen. Best of all for us, the apartment was fully furnished with furniture and all the necessities, and so we were able to move straight in.

Our new neighborhood was ideal for Alma and me and for our careers. We were near most of the nightclubs and theatres in which we performed and equally near the fashionable streets of Boulevard Haussmann and Rue de Faubourg Saint Honoré where we still had the occasional booking as fashion models. We were also very near the lovely Parc Monceau, where we would all often go for walks when the weather was nice. Nuria especially liked going to this little park during those long summer days. She would take her guitar and sit on a bench to practice, soon attracting a small crowd of admirers.

About once a month, the habitual peace and quiet of our hotel was disturbed by our aristocratic neighbors, when they would invite their compatriots to their quarters for one of their periodic reunions. For several hours, all hell would seem to break loose, their habitual polished good manners and impeccable behavior now forgotten. The party generally would last all night, the deafening noise echoing through the entire building as the music and conversation got progressively louder and louder, keeping the other residents awake until the early hours of the morning. Wine and vodka glasses were thrown against the walls and sent crashing to the floor, accompanied by the boisterous arguments and loud singing we could all hear and that we knew was a prelude to what was coming next. Empty vodka bottles would be thrown down the stairwell. Soon, we would hear the furious tapping and pounding of feet, engaged in the lively dances that were now taking place, accompanied by much clapping of hands, shouts, and a continuous uproar, while the music from the balalaikas played nonstop for hours. Then, they would insist on doing Cossack dances, which inevitably resulted in the smashing of some furniture as the dances became overexuberant. The party would continue, getting louder and louder and more and more raucous, until the early hours of the morning. At some point, usually around 3 in the morning, they would finally have drunk the last drop of vodka, and the festive atmosphere would be replaced by a deep melancholy. Then they would all fall asleep and in the resulting quiet, we could finally go to sleep, too.

Inevitably, the next day the impeccable manners and graciousness of their noble upbringing would return to our neighbors and they would apologize profusely for any inconvenience their party may have caused. They would insist on buying us tea and giving us little pastries in apology for the mayhem they had caused the night before. And just as inevitably, it would all recur just a few weeks later.

In the attic of the hotel, occupying a small room under the mansard roof of the building, lived an old Frenchman, a penniless man who was an exact lookalike of Victor Hugo. He had a terrible and mean disposition that scared the wits out of us every time we chanced to run into him in the building. Whenever this occurred, usually when going up or down the stairs, his terrifying and piercing stare would land on us like that of an avenging prophet, his eyes seeming to radiate sparks of fire at the mere sight of us. Apparently, the presence of us six females, plus Aunt Encarna's ridiculous little dog Moineau, exasperated him beyond his endurance to bear. Whenever he would hear us climbing the stairs, he would suddenly appear outside the door to his room, his gigantic frame almost touching the ceiling, his long, white beard half covering his face. With his right arm outstretched in front of him, he somewhat resembled Michelangelo's God as he yelled at us in his thundering bass of a voice: "Go back to Spain! Go back! In the name of God, go back!" For a few seconds, while in his presence, we would be seized by terror and simply freeze, but once we were back in our rooms, with the door securely locked behind us, we would look at each other and laugh hysterically for a long time.

Soon it was officially announced that the King and Queen of England would be visiting Paris. The royal visit was at first scheduled for June 1937 but eventually took place in July. The French police, with their customary display of zeal in these situations, immediately sprang into action, inspecting and searching every hotel in the city, including ours, for hidden anarchists and revolutionaries who could pose a security threat to the upcoming royal visit. These police raids began to take place frequently, and generally at the least convenient time, usually between midnight and dawn. This never failed to stir a deep sense of outrage in the hotel tenants. It was a nuisance, to say the least, to have to get up from bed and assemble with the other residents in the main parlor and wait there for the police inspectors to examine our papers. Wearing our nightgowns or pajamas, as the case might be, shivering in the night chill, we could hear the noise and uproar taking place in the building, with the gendarmes running up and down the stairs, noisily opening and closing doors in pursuit of some hidden clue that would justify their being there and so rudely interfering in our lives.

Our concierge, Madame LeFevre, wearing her chenille robe and night bonnet, would sullenly follow at the heels of the gendarmes, muttering the word "merde" ever so softly while keeping a watchful eye on all the proceedings. "It is a shameful thing," she would say, "that my hotel has to comply with so much scrutiny and so much nonsense." After passports, or in our case police permits, had been carefully examined and all their questions answered to their satisfaction, the police would depart. On their departure, Madame LeFevre would lead us all into the dining room, where huge bowls of steaming café au lait and plates of warm croissants had been placed on the table. While we ate and talked excitedly, we would all curse the French police in our native tongues, Nuria meanwhile trying to calm down the furious Moineau, who could not stop barking at the indignities that had been inflicted upon us.

The presence of the Russians seemed to lead the gendarmes to search our building a bit more frequently and with a bit more zeal than they would search others. Or so it appeared to us, anyway.

"Why do you think they search us so often?" I asked Mother after one particularly intrusive search.

"It is because of the Russians," she replied. "They are famous for organizing conspiracies and for harboring anarchists. Perhaps we should move to another building?"

But we stayed. Despite their occasionally raucous behavior, we liked the Russians and they had adopted us as family. They were well-educated and cultured people, despite the menial jobs that they now held as a result of life's circumstances. They all spoke an excellent and literary French and could discuss with equal ease the classics of French and Russian literature. They loved poetry and introduced me, in translation, to some of the beautiful poetry of Alexander Pushkin. Nuria, with her love of words and literature and poetry, would spend hours with them in deep discussion of books and poems.

I, on the other hand, bonded with the Russians more over music. They had a phonograph and a huge selection of records of Russian classical music. I loved the music of Tchaikovsky and Rimsky-Korsakov and Mussorgsky and would spend hours with them listening to this beautiful music, which often made them so homesick for Russia that they would have tears in their eyes. In return, I introduced them to the beautiful music of my country, the music of Albeniz and Granados and Manuel de Falla. Sometimes we would listen to the Spanish music on one of the few phonograph records that we had. Other times, Nuria would play it for them on her guitar.

We also all bonded with them over our shared love of dance. Like all Russians, they loved ballet and when a group of them came one evening to watch our performance at Le Boeuf Sur le Toit, their applause and cheering was the most enthusiastic in the entire audience. When we came back to the hotel at the end of the evening, they were all waiting for us and presented us with the huge bouquets of flowers that they had bought for us on their way home.

"You should both be dancing at the Bolshoi Theatre!" one of them said to us, as his companions nodded in agreement. "When the madness in Russia – the Union of Soviet Socialist Republics, as the heathens in power now deign call it – has ended, we shall take you back to Russia and introduce you the directors of the Bolshoi and you will dance in front of a Moscow audience that will truly appreciate your talents!"

One evening, during one of their drunken revelries, which coincided with a night off for Alma and me, they enticed us to perform our dance for their friends while Nuria played her guitar as accompaniment. They all loved our performance, but how much was because of our talent and how much was because of the bottles of vodka they had consumed, it was impossible to tell. After we had danced for them, they tried to teach us to do the Cossack dances that they loved. To this day, I do not comprehend how these men, most of them at least middle-aged, managed to perform such athletic feats of strength and grace! After ten minutes of attempting to follow their moves, I was afraid my knees would never work properly again, and I insisted on stopping before I hurt myself. Alma, gamely, tried it a little bit longer, but then she too gave up.

To everyone's surprise, the constant surveillance and tenacity of the police finally paid off one night, when after another raid on our hotel, they walked out of our building carrying away with them a man who had been living there quietly and unobtrusively for months. He was so quiet and appeared so timid that no one ever suspected his true identity. He was a revolutionary and anarchist, with a whole arsenal of weapons that was discovered hidden in his room. He was a quiet, polite man with whom we had only exchanged the occasional "bonjour" without paying too much attention to him. Now, as he was being led away, he was certainly not a quiet man any longer, shouting terrible profanities and threats at the gendarmes who held him tightly by the arms. I rushed downstairs to join the people gathered there watching the spectacle, standing next to Madame LeFevre, who was clearly in a state of shock and ready to pass out any minute. Before being hustled into the waiting police van, the arrested man turned toward us and bowed in a most chivalrous gesture of farewell and with his handcuffed hands he waved goodbye to everyone present. We never saw him again or learned what had happened to him or even his true identity. We thought it best not to ask too many questions, lest we create the impression that we were somehow associated with him.

The hotel was run, if not too efficiently, by our landlady, the owner of the hotel, Madame Louise de Menard. She was originally from Alsace and still spoke French with a heavy Alsatian accent which was sometimes hard for us to understand. Her own living quarters occupied the entire second floor of the building, with balconies and huge windows on every side. She was of undefined age, a widow of a French army officer who, she liked to boast, had served heroically during several of the key battles of World War One. She kept his military medals and ribbons on display in a glass-fronted case off the small reception alcove on the ground floor. She was extremely proud of these and never missed an opportunity to describe the meaning and significance of each one to anyone who seemed interested. She seemed to make a comfortable living, between her late husband's military pension and whatever income she managed to make from the hotel. We guessed this because her passion was going to the horse races at every opportunity and placing bets on the horses, which we knew was not an activity for the poor. We were used to seeing her occasionally outside the hotel door, on her way to the races at the Hippodrome Longchamps. On these occasions she would be all dressed up in her best outfits, white gloves up to her elbows, and, when the weather allowed it, carrying a parasol with an ivory handle.

She was aided in the task of running the hotel by the concierge, Madame LeFevre, a good-humored and patient woman who seemed to be obsessed with the shining and polishing of the brass railing of the staircase. She was constantly wiping this with a cloth until it shone brightly. Madame LeFevre was not alone handling the care and maintenance of the hotel. Two of her sons lived there and helped her, as did one daughter-in-law and one grandson, "Le Petit Monsieur Philippe." Le Petit Monsieur Philippe was five or six years old and his job was to watch the activities until he became bored or hungry, at which time all other activities would cease until his wants had been attended to.

Madame LeFevre was a kind and gentle soul, who seemed to feel a special affection for the guests at "her" hotel (she really did consider it hers, and probably for good reason given all the effort she devoted to its upkeep) because we were mostly refugees, mostly from Russia but now us Spanish refugees as well. She would pretend to lose her temper with the Russians after their monthly parties, but they would kiss her hand and treat her with elaborate courtesy, then begging her forgiveness, which she would quickly grant them. Since most of the Russian residents, despite their noble upbringing, worked mostly menial jobs in Paris to make ends meet, Madame LeFevre felt that they were on an equal footing socially and that made her somewhat more tolerant of their behavior.

"They must miss their home country," I overheard her saying to Mother and Aunt Encarna one day. "It is understandable that they would want to get together with their friends to have drinks frequently."

She was especially kind to Nuria and me. After she overheard me telling Nuria one day that I missed our traditional Madrid afternoon merienda (snack) of hot chocolate and churros or almond cookies, Madame LeFevre started surprising us some afternoons with two cups of hot chocolate and a croissant or a brioche left over from breakfast or, if we were lucky and she had gone to the patisserie that afternoon, she would have a little plate of madeleines or financiers or, my favorite, petits fours.

"I do not know how to find churros in Paris," she would say to us with a smile. "The financier is our Parisian almond cake, even nicer than your Madrid almond cookie!" We were always touched by her kind-hearted efforts to ease our homesickness.

The staff also included three maids, young girls from the country, who cleaned the rooms daily, a gardener to tend the small garden in the courtyard behind the hotel and the house plants and flowers that decorated every room, a full-time cook, and an octogenarian janitor who seemed to have simply been with the building since its construction. It was never really clear to us quite what the janitor did, but he seemed to be as much of a fixture at the hotel as the wall hangings and furniture. Sometimes, he even seemed to be as covered in dust as was the furniture.

I should also mention Fifi, the old, toothless, overfed dog of Madame LeFevre, who was forever keeping a somnolent watch on everything that took place in the hotel, growling unhappily once in a while when someone or something annoyed her. After a fractious beginning, Fifi and Moineau had reached a truce and tolerated each other, if warily. The one time that Dolly came to visit, however, it was a different story and Aunt Marina was informed in no uncertain terms that she herself was free to visit whenever she wished, but "that barbarian of a little dog" was not!

The cook, Monsieur Alain, ruled the domain of his basement kitchen. When he was in a good mood, which unfortunately was not too often, he would allow us to visit him there, watching him prepare meals and letting us sample small tastes of the succulent dishes he was preparing. In between making omelettes and cooking poulets rôtis, or while stirring sauces with one of his huge wooden spoons, he would constantly drink straight from the bottle of red wine that he always kept within reach on the top of the stove. We never saw him without an open bottle of wine within reach and he clearly considered wine glasses an unnecessary complication to the important business of drinking wine. Nonetheless, Monsieur Alain's culinary talents were spectacular. He would throw together an "omelette aux fines herbes" or a plate of "truite amandine" or cook an absolutely perfectly roasted herbed chicken with what seemed to be no effort at all, and the results were always perfect and delicious. In deference to the Russian residents, he had learned to prepare a few Russian dishes. These included a version of beef Stroganoff which he had modified to be somewhat Bourguignon-inspired and, if he could find enough beets, a form of Borscht soup. This last he would make for the Russians, but he considered it somewhat barbaric and complained that it stained his best wooden spoon a permanent deep red color. After that, he kept a special spoon solely for use in stirring the Borscht.

Usually, the meals that Monsieur Alain put together were fairly simple but always delicious. Every once in a while, though, he would feel inspired and would take pains to fully apply his culinary skills. On these occasions, the results were always spectacular. We never were able to tell if these moods hit him on days that he had drunk more or less wine than usual, but whatever the reason, we would all feel especially fortunate on those occasions. If we were lucky enough to have invited a friend over for dinner on that day, our guest would leave enchanted and convinced that Monsieur Alain's cuisine with his marvelous soufflés and velvety sauces, could compete successfully with the best in Paris. Even our Uncle Aldo was impressed the day he was able to experience one of these special meals with us.

Sharing a Hotel with the Russians

Michel and I continued to see each other frequently. If I was dancing in a theatre, he would wait for me by the performers' entrance until my performance was done. Sometimes, though, he would come in and walk around backstage, always looking rather amused and curious at all the goings-on that took place behind the stage. Then he would take me out for a coffee and dessert and, if the weather was pleasant, a long walk to help me to unwind after the evening's performance. During the weekend, we would go to the Bois de Boulogne for a picnic and a walk and sometimes a game of boule, which he played in a somewhat more aggressive style than did most of the French. He would often invite Nuria to come with us. She was delighted to accompany us and would bring her guitar and play for us as we had our picnics.

Michel was now a lieutenant in the French army reserves and had already been mobilized twice by the French government, only to be abruptly relieved from active army duties a few days afterward. These sudden mobilizations were nerve-wracking, but as with everything else in his life, Michel stayed calm and in a philosophical mood about them.

"There is no reason to be concerned, Conchita," he would say to me. "They call me up, I put on my uniform, I issue a few orders to the sergeants who are old enough to be my father, the sergeants pretend to follow them, in the evenings I drink some wine with the other officers in our mess, and two days later they send me home. We shall see what happens, but I do not think there will be war any time soon."

Although he remained in the reserves, and with his intelligence and natural leadership qualities was soon promoted to captain, and although he knew he could be called up again at any time if war did break out, Michel continued with his job at the Paris Bourse. He was very successful in his job there and had continued to advance rapidly. He loved the good things in life, spending money like there was no tomorrow and talking to me constantly about his dreams of becoming a millionaire.

"With your good looks," I used to tease him, "I will not be at all surprised if one day you will meet a rich woman, marry her, and live in luxury for the rest of your life!" My half-joking prediction for Michel turned out to be prescient. He survived the war and managed to get to America afterward. Years afterward, we met by chance at a mutual friend's home in New York and he introduced me to his American wife. Michel had married the heir to the Schrafft chocolate empire.

Michel and I were close friends and we loved each other, but I was not at all sure he was the man I wanted to marry and spend my life with. He did not ask me to marry him that summer, so we continued to enjoy each other's company without worrying too much about plans for the future.

Throughout that summer, Alma and I continued our dance performances. We had been introduced some time earlier to a well-known Spanish dancer and choreographer living and performing in Paris, named Antonio Arcaráz. Antonio owned the Guelma Studio, where he gave lessons in Spanish dance. We contacted him and asked him if we would be willing to help us choreograph some new numbers and give us lessons as needed to learn the new steps. Somewhat to our surprise, he agreed enthusiastically and invited us to start coming to his studio in the afternoons for lessons and rehearsals.

We would regularly go back to see Antonio Arcaráz at his Guelma Studio to ask him for ideas for what we could add to our repertoire or how we could improve our performances. He was always very generous with his time and his ideas, and he helped us perfect several new dances. We would occasionally dance with him in his studio as a trio, and then he would say half-jokingly, "You know, we really should become a trio! With your good looks and talent and my experience, we could really become something!"

Eventually, we would become the Trio Arcaráz, but for the time being, we remained the duo Alma y Isa Reyes. We had as many bookings as we wanted, usually with star billing, and rarely for more than a week at a time. This kept us from becoming bored with our performances.

If we weren't rehearsing with Antonio or working on developing new acts with him, our days were free. Nuria and I continued to go for long walks in the Parc Monceau and sometimes we would go back to the Bois de Boulogne, which we loved so much. Occasionally during the days, I would still do a bit of fashion modeling on the Faubourg de Saint Honoré, more for the extra cash it would bring in and to not lose my contacts there in case my dancing career ever came to a sudden end than for love of modeling.

CHAPTER 11

The Miss Europe Contest

August–September 1938
These intermittent mobilizations of the French army that affected Michel were due to tensions arising from the ongoing Sudeten crisis. Hitler's posturing and demands had not ceased over the summer, and the French government would occasionally mobilize its forces in a show of strength, with the impression that these demonstrations of resolve would scare Hitler and prevent him from doing anything rash and starting a war. Little did they realize that Hitler was continuing to march along on his planned timetable, judging, rightly as it turned out, that he could obtain what he wanted at this stage without war. In Hitler's mind, the inevitable war would come when and where he wanted it, at the time and place that most suited him.

By September, the Sudeten crisis was nearing a climax as Hitler remained inexorable in his demands upon Czechoslovakia. Europe began to prepare for the possibility of war.

Despite the growing unrest and rising fears of war, the 1938 Miss Europe pageant went on as scheduled. It was the last such pageant to be held before World War Two and would not be held again until 1948, several years after the war had ended. The first Miss Europe contest had been held in 1929 and had been founded by a senior French journalist, Maurice de Waleffe, who nine years earlier, in 1920, had established what became the Miss France pageant. The annual pre-war pageants were organized by major European newspapers and as a result received a great deal of publicity throughout the European press. Miss Spain had last won in 1935 and Isa was hopeful that she could regain the title for her native country, albeit in an apolitical context given that the civil war that was still being fought in Spain, the sponsoring newspapers' would not allow her to represent Republican Spain, and she continued to adamantly refuse to represent Fascist Spain.

"Miss Spain in Exile"

The summer had passed quietly and quickly for us in Paris. Alma and I continued to have as many bookings as we wanted. We performed for five or six evenings most weeks, so that we could have one or two nights off each week. I had gone back to part-time modeling as well, just to bring in some extra money for us. With my Miss Spain title still fresh in people's minds, I had as much modeling work as I wished for, working for the fashion houses on Paris' Faubourg de Saint Honoré. In addition to my work for Guerlain, now both Givenchy and Chanel had taken me on as a model for their summer and autumn collections. Domergue continued to paint posters as advertisements for various products and destinations and I was still one of his favorite models. Alma joined me sometimes and we would pose together for Domergue, Alma as a blonde and I as a brunette, advertising everything from perfumes to beach vacations on the Belgian coast.

Finally, in late August, it was time to start preparing for the journey to Copenhagen for the Miss Europe competition. The competition itself would be in Copenhagen on September 10, but there would be a few days of publicity events in Paris first and then a week or so of publicity events and charity appearances in Denmark before the actual competition. We learned that Maurice de Waleffe, a senior journalist from *Le Monde* and one of the original founders of the Miss Europe contest, as well as his wife, and two press attachés from the French diplomatic corps would accompany us to Denmark. Except for the girls representing the Scandinavian countries, most of the European contestants had already arrived in Paris to take part in the pre-pageant publicity events before we would all travel to Copenhagen for the contest. The Scandinavian girls would just meet us in Copenhagen.

Together in Paris, we all attended lectures where the rules and regulations we were expected to follow during the contest were explained to us in great detail and where we were assigned our carefully selected chaperones. The rules seemed so complicated to me that I was afraid I might not be able to follow them all! I was delighted that Mother was accepted as a suitable chaperone for me as we were looking forward to the ten-day trip together. This time, Nuria would not come along. She was busy with her upcoming school examinations as well as with her classes at the Paris Music Conservatory, where she was continuing to study classical guitar. Her playing had progressed to the point that she was now getting

The Miss Europe Contest

even more frequent offers to perform at concerts and recitals throughout Paris.

The night before our departure for Copenhagen, a special dinner party was held for us contestants at Maxim's restaurant. By then I had made two good friends among the other contestants, Miss Belgium, a pretty, green-eyed girl, and Miss Russia, a lovely, tall girl who was modeling at Schiaparelli. The three of us had become inseparable. We attended all the publicity events together and we sat together at the dinner at Maxim's.

We arrived in Copenhagen in the afternoon after the long train journey from Paris. It was a beautiful, late summer day and we were immediately enchanted by this beautiful and clean city, situated on a beautiful harbor. We were all given rooms in one of the newer hotels in the city, which of course we shared with our chaperones. The publicity events started that first evening, with a dinner at one of the restaurants in the Tivoli Gardens. The Scandinavian contestants had arrived in Copenhagen and once they joined us, there were twenty-five of us in all. Right after that first dinner, all of the contestants participated in the opening ceremonies of the Miss Europe contest at Copenhagen's concert hall. Due to the ongoing crisis in Czechoslovakia, contestants representing Germany, Austria, Poland, and Czechoslovakia were conspicuously absent from the contest.

We attended ceremony after ceremony, traveling all over Denmark to appear at dozens of social events, several each day. We were exhausted much of the time, from the sheer amount of travel and number of events that we had to attend, but the country was stunningly beautiful, the people were charming, and we were flattered by the constant attention that we received wherever we went. The weather was beautiful, with warm and sunny days and cool evenings, usually with a gentle breeze off the sea. The food we were served was always delightful, with at least one meal each day featuring a Danish Smorgasbord of hot and cold food served "buffet style". My favorite at these was always the little open-faced sandwiches served on buttered bread. At these meals, I would always think about how much my sister Nuria would have enjoyed being with us and then I would think about my father and how much his refined and gourmet tastes would have enjoyed the Danish butter and ham and other delicacies that would be offered to us at every meal.

"Miss Spain in Exile"

Whenever I thought about my father, I would become worried and sad. Communications from him were so infrequent, due to the civil war still raging in Spain, that it was always a huge relief when we would receive the occasional letter from him to find out that he was still alive. We had not heard from him for almost two weeks before we left Paris for Copenhagen. There was no way we could telephone him. All we could hope and pray for was that he was alive. We would simply have wait to receive the next reassuring letter from him. As I would eat all this delicious food, which I knew he would have enjoyed so much, I would think of him and pray that he was still safe and alive and hope that he had good food to eat despite the privations of the war in our Spain.

We traveled by ferry boat from island to island and on land, we traveled from town to town in the comfortable and deluxe bus that had been assigned to us. When we traveled by ferry boat, we would pass harbor after harbor, surrounded by little towns and fishing villages with brightly colored houses reflecting off the sparkling waters of that northern sea, so different from the Mediterranean Sea that I was used to! Those little villages looked like they were out of a fairy tale and the houses they contained looked like they should have been made out of gingerbread. When I tried to convince my friends Miss Belgium and Miss Russia that we should go for a swim in that beautiful, clean water, they both looked at me like I had lost my mind. They asked me if I had put my hand in the water to test its temperature. When I did as they suggested and put my hand in the water and realized how icy cold it was, I understood why they had looked at me that way.

When we traveled by land, we would pass through endless fields of farmland, with grass greener than I thought was possible. Harvest time was approaching, and the farmers were busy at work. Whole families appeared to be working together to gather the crops and to take care of the farm animals, the fat and sleek cows that made Denmark so famous for its butter and other dairy products, and the pigs that were the source of the world-famous Danish hams that were so delicious and that my father had loved so much.

We were taken to Odense, the birthplace of Hans Christian Andersen, whose stories had enthralled me so much when I was a child. It felt like being in one of his fairy tales to be there. Really, my whole life felt like a fairy tale during that entire trip to Denmark! Here I was, somehow Miss Spain (although "in exile") surrounded by my fellow beauty pageant contestants in a lovely and peaceful country, surrounded by beauty and by happy people, everything looking so calm and gentle. The civil war in Spain seemed very far away. Even my working life in Paris, glamorous though it could feel to be to be a dancer and model, seemed very distant and far away. The news of the deteriorating situation in Europe, which we could not help but hear being discussed around us, seemed terribly far removed from our little bubble of the Miss Europe pageant.

One of the next stops after Odense was Elsinore, site of the famous castle, where we were told Hamlet's ghost remained in residence. Our guide told us that he could be heard every night, wandering the halls of the castle. That certainly seemed and sounded believable to us!

I loved the entire time we spent in Denmark and I did not want my little fairy tale to end. I would always love the Danish country and its charming and gentle people, and I would keep nothing but very warm and fond memories of my time there.

Then came the final evening, September 10, when Miss Europe was to be selected. The gala dinner was held at the royal palace, with the king and queen of Denmark presiding as hosts. After the dinner, we were taken to the Royal Ballet Theatre, where we were deluged by photographers taking hundreds of pictures and following us all over the place. Then we all appeared on stage, each girl wearing her national costume and carrying the flag of her country, except for me, still holding in my right hand the white banner with the word España written on it. I received a loud ovation because of the crowd's sympathy for the plight of my country and perhaps also because I must have looked somewhat sad and forlorn as the only girl on the stage without a flag to carry proudly.

At the end of the evening, the panel of judges, which included Monsieur de Waleffe, selected Miss Finland to be Miss Europe 1938. I was awarded second place as Miss Spain, with Miss Hungary and Miss Italy completing the list of finalists. My friends Miss Belgium and Miss Russia came running to congratulate me and we all hugged. Finally, the whole group moved to the ballroom of our hotel, where the party continued.

It had been an exciting and fun-filled ten days, but we were all happy and somewhat relieved that it was over. We were eager to return to our homes and our normal lives. I was tired and I slipped

"Miss Spain in Exile"

away from the party to go the room Mother and I shared to try to relax a little bit. I wanted to call Michel and give him the exciting news that I had come in second place in the Miss Europe pageant. On the way to my room, I was told that I had a message, that a Mister Konrad from Poland had been trying to telephone me.

Back at my room, while the party and the dancing were still taking place downstairs, I asked the hotel operator to place a telephone call to Warsaw for me. I waited what for what felt like an interminable time for the call to come through. Finally, Konrad was on the line. But instead of hearing him talk in the jovial tone of voice that was so familiar to me, he now sounded distressed and somewhat listless.

"Things are going to be very difficult for us here in Poland," he said. "You know, Isa, our contract with the Opera House in Paris has been cancelled. I want to say goodbye to you, because I don't know if I will ever see you again."

That was the last time I would hear Konrad's voice and those were the last words that I ever heard him speak to me. I started to ask him what he meant when he said, "Things are going to be very difficult for us here in Poland", when the phone connection was suddenly lost and all I could hear was crackling and static over the phone line. The hotel operator was not able to reestablish the connection although I asked her several times to keep trying. She finally gave up after more than thirty minutes of futile attempts, after which she told me that it would be impossible to reconnect. I was never able to speak with Konrad again. I learned later that he left Warsaw shortly after that telephone call and I was never able to find a way to contact him after that.

I felt so disturbed and such a deep anguish from Konrad's words that I ignored the repeated calls from the other girls, asking me to come back down and rejoin the party. Preferring to be left alone with my sadness, I shut myself in the room and went to bed. But I could not sleep. Konrad's words were ringing in my ears all through the night.

The next morning, we all said goodbye to each other, and Mother and I boarded the train to return to Paris. Before we left the hotel, I asked the hotel operator one more time to try to place the call to Warsaw for me. She was not able to get through.

A year and a few months later, after the Danzig crisis and the invasion of Poland by the Nazis, after Warsaw had fallen, a letter from Konrad's mother reached me in Athens. It had been posted in London where, as I recalled, Konrad's married older sister lived with her British husband. Konrad's mother had been able, with the help of friends and family, to flee Warsaw and reach safety in London, just in time. Her husband and Konrad, their only son, had not been so fortunate. As I read her letter, I learned of their tragic fate. They had joined the Polish Resistance after Warsaw fell and had been captured, imprisoned, and tortured by the Nazis. Ultimately, they had met their deaths by firing squad at the hands of the occupiers. They were among the first of the Polish Resistance fighters to be shot by the Germans. She included a small photograph of Konrad with her letter. The photograph had been taken about the time when I knew him in Warsaw, during his days with the Polish ballet. As I looked at the image of Konrad, with his engaging smile and lively eyes, my own eyes blurred with tears, my mind full of fond memories of him, of that young and beautiful boy, so full of life and joy, that I would never see again.

Despite how it ended with that sad telephone call from Konrad, Isa loved to reminisce about her time in Denmark during the Miss Europe pageant. She liked to tell the story of how during the Nazi occupation, the king of Denmark replied to the Nazi demand that Jews wear the yellow Star of David in order to be identified as Jews by wearing such stars in public himself. To her, this symbolic and courageous act typified what she knew about and felt toward the Danish people.

It turns out that that story about the king wearing the Star of David like that is apocryphal. Nonetheless, the Danish king was a visible symbol of the Danish resistance to the Nazis throughout the occupation and was greatly loved and admired by his people. With the support of their king, the Danes did demonstrate remarkable courage in protecting their Jewish population from the Nazis. In October, the occupying Nazis ordered the Danish Jews to be rounded up for deportation. After the order had been given by the occupiers, Danish civil servants did indeed start identifying and contacting the Jews . . . in order to warn them to go into hiding! Then, over several nights in October, ordinary Danes, aided by the Danish Resistance, evacuated all of Denmark's remaining Jews, those who had not managed to get out earlier, or who had not been captured earlier, taking them in boats across the Baltic Sea and to safety in neutral Sweden. About 7,200 Jewish lives were saved by this evacuation. After that rescue, the Danish government, led by the King and Queen, who had insisted on staying in Denmark with their subjects rather than being evacuated, as they could have been, continued to intercede with the Nazi authorities on behalf of the 500 or so Danish Jews confined in the Theresienstadt concentration camp outside of Prague, and almost all of these were saved. The moral and physical courage demonstrated by the Danes resulting in the saving of approximately 99 percent of the Jewish population of Denmark from the Holocaust.

During that September 1938, while Isa was in Copenhagen and then back in Paris, the tensions around the Sudetenland crisis continued to escalate. Europe continued its inexorable slide toward war, although Britain and France continued to hold on to the hope, or the illusion, that war could be avoided if only Hitler could be sufficiently placated. Hitler gambled on Britain's and France's reluctance to go to war over Czechoslovakia, despite both countries having made guarantees to Czechoslovakia, and he continued his blustering and his threats against that country. He continued to couch the language of his demands in the guise of seeking only self-determination and justice for the ethnic Germans who were unfortunate enough to be living in other lands. This lie helped to provide a rationalization for Britain and the appeasers.

In Britain, official policy by now had come to be clearly defined by the appeasement of Hitler, almost whatever the cost. This policy stemmed from a desire to do anything required to avert war and to believe Hitler when he would state that each of his demands would be his last, that he was only seeking to rectify one last historical wrong. Britain, under the leadership of Prime Minister Neville Chamberlain, chose to try to negotiate with Hitler. On September 13, Chamberlain asked Hitler for a personal meeting to try to find a solution to the Sudetenland crisis that would avert war. Hitler agreed to see him, and Chamberlain departed immediately for Germany.

The first of what would be three meetings between Chamberlain and Hitler in September 1936 took place at Berchtesgaden, near Munich, on September 15. Hitler demanded that the Sudetenland be handed over to Germany. Without consulting the Czechs, Chamberlain agreed that any areas containing more than 50%

ethnic German population should be handed over to Czechoslovakia. Returning to London, Chamberlain managed to get the Czechs and the French to agree to this proposal.

On September 18, Mussolini gave a speech in Trieste in which he stated unequivocally Italy's support for Hitler's Germany in any disputes with Prague.

Then on September 22, Chamberlain departed again for Germany, this time to meet with Hitler in Bad Godesberg in order to work out the details of the peace plan. Hitler arranged for Chamberlain to be welcomed lavishly on landing in Cologne, complete with a military band playing "God Save the King". Chamberlain began the meeting by informing Hitler that Britain would not object to Germany annexing all of the Sudetenland, calculating that this would placate Nazi demands. When Hitler asked for clarification, saying through his translator, "Does this mean that the Allies have agreed with Prague's approval for the transfer of the Sudetenland to Germany?" Chamberlain replied, "Yes, precisely."

Now, Hitler shook his head and, stating that this was no longer sufficient, he made new demands that took Chamberlain by surprise. He now insisted that Czechoslovakia be dissolved, its territory to be split between Germany, Hungary, and Poland. Chamberlain refused to accede to this and, shaken, returned to his hotel. Afraid he may have gone too far, Hitler later that evening telephoned Chamberlain's hotel, saying that he would accept annexation of only the Sudetenland with no further territorial demands, provided that Prague began the evacuation of ethnic Czechoslovakians from German-majority areas immediately. Hitler then agreed to extend this ultimatum to October 1 and further promised that upon completion of the annexation of the Sudetenland, Germany would have no further territorial claims on Czechoslovakia and would enter into an agreement guaranteeing the borders and territorial integrity of Czechoslovakia.

With the situation unresolved, Chamberlain returned to London and both Britain and France began to mobilize their military and reluctantly prepare for the increasing likelihood of war.

On September 26, Chamberlain had a letter hand-delivered to Hitler in which he again stated his desire to find a peaceful solution to the crisis. Hitler's reply was a speech given that evening at the Sportpalast in Berlin and broadcast on the radio, in which he stated that the Sudetenland was "the last territorial demand I have to make in Europe."

Mussolini then suggested one more meeting to try to resolve the crisis and avert war, this one to be a four-power conference including Germany, Britain, France, and Italy to decide the fate of Czechoslovakia. Czechoslovakia was not invited to participate in this meeting or take part in the discussions! Her fate would be decided by the others and she would be informed of the decision after the fact. This third meeting began in Munich on September 29. Britain and France were motivated by a desperate desire to avoid war and, without consulting the Czechs, this time they agreed to all of the demands Hitler presented. The four powers agreed that all of the Sudetenland would be handed over to Germany immediately. German troops would be permitted to occupy the entire Sudetenland immediately and, further, land containing majority ethnic Poles and Magyars would be returned respectively to Poland and Hungary. Although recognizing that this would leave a rump Czechoslovakia, stripped of her natural defenses as well as much of her natural resources and armaments industries, both Britain and France acceded to these demands, believing Hitler when he assured them that these would be his last territorial demands in Europe.

After the British and the French had accepted these demands, they then made it abundantly clear to the Czechs that if they resisted this, then they would have to fight Nazi Germany on their own. The final agreement was reached and signed on September 30. The next day, October 1, Czech border guards were instructed to abandon their posts and the Wehrmacht marched in. Within days, Polish and Hungarian soldiers had occupied the ethnically Polish and Magyar parts of Czechoslovakia.

The Munich Accord, or Munich Betrayal, as it became known, was in fact a betrayal of epic proportions. The country of Czechoslovakia, created at the Versailles Conference and by the Treaty of Paris after World War One, to a great extent due to the idealistic dreams of U.S. President Woodrow Wilson and his dreams of redrawing the boundaries of Central Europe along just lines, was abandoned by her supposed allies and left defenseless and doomed. Once again, Hitler won a major victory without firing a shot.

My father had spent a lot of time in Czechoslovakia during the years prior to Munich and had grown to love the country and its *people. He happened to be in Prague on the day that the Munich Accord was signed and for the rest of his life, he never got over the emotional impact of being there that day. He could describe in vivid detail the sight of grown men crying in the streets as they learned the news of how they had been betrayed by the western democracies that they had trusted and came to the realization that the dream of a free and independent Czechoslovakia was coming to an end.*

Neville Chamberlain returned to Britain from Munich confident he had secured "peace in our time." As he deplaned at Croydon Airport, near London, he proudly waved to the welcoming crowd his piece of paper, signed by Hitler and himself, and declared success at averting the outbreak of a major war. Hitler later referred to it as "a scrap of paper."

CHAPTER 12

A Christmas Holiday

October 1938–January 1939

As is now known, the betrayal of Czechoslovakia at Munich did not prevent World War Two, it only delayed its onset. After Nazi German troops had occupied the Sudetenland in October, an uneasy peace settled over Europe, but as events continued to unfold, the political situation in Europe continued to deteriorate.

What was left of a dismembered Czechoslovakia, the so-called "rump state", stripped of natural defenses and a significant percentage of her industry, including her not-insignificant armaments factories, and her natural resources, would be easy prey to the Nazis later.

On the night of November 9 – 10, Nazi-led mobs, with the tacit if not the outright explicit support of the authorities and police, engaged in a night of terror against Germany's and Austria's Jewish population. More than 1,000 shops and synagogues were burned or otherwise destroyed, over 30,000 Jews were arrested, and at least 40 were killed by the mobs of rampaging Nazis. The sidewalks of German and Austrian cities were covered with so much broken glass from smashed shop windows, that the infamous night has become known as Kristallnacht. By the end of the year, nearly 320,000 of the total population of German Jews, 500,000, had fled the country. Due to restrictions on what they could take with them, in general they left with only what they could carry in their pockets or in a suitcase, with severe punishment of anyone trying to smuggle out more than a token amount of cash or anything of value. They had long-since been forced to sell homes and businesses for pennies to the Nazi insiders.

One of the few bright spots in Europe during that winter was the event which became known to history as the "Kindertransport", or Children's' Transport, in which 10,000 unaccompanied Jewish children from central Europe were allowed to be transported by train to Britain. These children from Germany, Austria, Czechoslovakia, Poland, and the Free City of Danzig in Poland were allowed to find refuge in Britain, but their parents had to stay behind, and most were never heard from again.

Meanwhile, in Spain, the civil war was nearing its inevitable end after two and a half years of bitter fighting. In October, the International Brigades left Spain. There are not reliable estimates of how many casualties they had suffered, but their casualty rates were high, the result of inadequate training, poor equipment, and their common utilization as shock troops. Many of the Brigade members were originally from fascist countries, including Germany and Italy, and these men could not safely return home. Most of these were given Spanish citizenship and incorporated into regular army units of the Republic for the duration of the civil war. Others were repatriated to their home countries although some, like those from Belgium and Holland, had been stripped of their citizenship for fighting in a foreign army. Some of the Brigade members found refuge in the Soviet Union, but many of these became victims of the ongoing Stalinist purges and were never heard from again. Most of the Americans of the Lincoln Battalion were repatriated home to the United States. Years later, these men became victims of the McCarthy-era anti-communist hysteria. Many were investigated by the FBI and hounded from their jobs. The International Brigade was given a farewell parade down the main boulevards of Barcelona on their way out of Spain, the Loyalists demonstrating their gratitude to these idealistic volunteers from all over the world who came to fight the fascists on Spanish soil. After that parade, in general those volunteers who returned to their homes did so to a thankless homecoming.

At the time that the members of the International Brigade were leaving Spain, the Nationalists had approximately 50,000 "volunteers" from Italy and Germany fighting on their side. These men eventually returned to a hero's welcome in their home countries. In addition, there were approximately 30,000 Moors from Morocco fighting as mercenaries on Franco's side, who were free to return home to North Africa when the fighting eventually ended.

By January 1939, Barcelona had fallen to the Nationalists. What remained of the Spanish Republic was essentially two enclaves, one centered in Madrid and the other in Valencia. No one held out hope that either could survive for much longer.

We had not heard from Father in over three weeks when a letter from him arrived, addressed to our mother but clearly meant for all of us.

"Dear Concepción," his letter began. "I am sure you are hearing the news that the situation for the Loyalists here in Spain is not improving. The Nationalists continue to take the advantage at almost every battle, and it is becoming increasingly difficult for us to hold on. I am afraid that soon we will lose Barcelona. It is already impossible to communicate with Madrid and I am afraid that General Franco and his fellow traitors are simply waiting for the rest of the Republic to surrender or be captured so that his prize, Madrid, will fall into his hands like a ripe plum.

"I am still in Valencia, doing what I can to help with preparing for the defense of this city. I am also working with the Diplomatic Corps to help prepare for what will now almost certainly soon be a government in exile. When I have done all that I can, when the end appears near, I shall come to join you in Paris. Conchita and Nuria, be good girls and help your mother and know that soon we shall all be together again."

It was heartbreaking to hear the tone of defeat in Father's words, but this sadness was tempered by the joy in learning that he was still alive and that we might see him soon! After she read the letter out loud to us, Mother sat quietly gazing out the window. I knew she was thinking about how our lives had changed and she must have been wondering what the future would hold for our family when she would reunite with her husband.

It was early October now. We had been back from Copenhagen for three weeks. The weather in Paris was gorgeous, with nice warm and sunny days and cool evenings. We were trying to enjoy this nice weather as much as we could before the grey skies and rains of a Parisian winter set in. The leaves on the trees were just beginning to turn their autumn colors and we spent as many afternoons as we could walking in the parks.

Alma and I had gone back to our routine of dancing five or six nights each week and doing a little bit of fashion modeling as well, to bring in supplemental cash. We appeared regularly at Le Boeuf sur le Toit through October and November and became known as one of the more frequently returning acts there. Because we were appearing in that one venue so often, we were careful to meet with Antonio at his Guelma Studio often to get his advice on new dances we could work into our performance, to avoid becoming stale. As always, Antonio was kind and generous with his time and ideas and helped us as much as he could. He was never short of new ideas for us and it was always exciting to go see him and learn from him.

We would also update our dance costumes regularly, to add to the impression that our act was not just the same thing over and over. By then, as a result of our modeling work, Alma and I had good friends among the couturiers and designers of the Parisian fashion world, and so we could usually get help designing and sewing our new costumes. They were all based on traditional Spanish dresses and Flamenco outfits, so it didn't involve a great deal of original designing. A small change here and there in our dresses and we would feel like we were in a new costume. I continued to wear a flower pinned in my hair for every performance, and I would try to vary the color of the flower to add additional variety to my appearance.

By late November, winter was beginning to settle in on Paris. The skies were just a bit greyer and darker every day and there began to be as many or more rainy days than sunny days during the week.

Our booking agent was still the same Monsieur Leroy who had been so responsible for helping to launch our careers. He had told us that he was working on an engagement for us over the upcoming Christmas holidays, but would not tell us what it was.

"I am hoping for the Riviera again, or maybe Italy!" I said to Alma. "I am tired of this grey weather!"

Monsieur Leroy called one afternoon in early December and told us that he had booked Alma and me on a three-week tour in northern Europe over the Christmas holidays. That was a bit of a letdown after dreaming of a return to the Riviera and an escape from the cold and rainy weather that is Paris in winter, but Alma and I quickly decided we would make the best of it and at least enjoy seeing someplace new together.

Then came the less welcome news that Alma and I would travel alone. I had never spent a Christmas away from my mother and

I was not happy to do this for the first time in a new place where I would not know anyone.

We had received one more letter from Father two weeks earlier. In that letter, he hinted that he might be leaving Spain to join us in Paris sooner than we might have realized. He had to write somewhat cryptically because of the military censors that read every letter going out of or coming into Spain by then, and he did not want to be accused of defeatism for wanting to leave Spain to be with his family. I asked Mother about this.

"Why is Father afraid? Will they accuse him of being a traitor?"

"No, Conchi", replied my mother in that patient tone she always had when I was upset or afraid. "The days of the Republic are almost finished. Your father will do what he can to help with the defenses of Valencia, but he is trying to tell us that he will leave before it is too late to get out safely so that he can be with us."

"So that is why you will not come with us on this trip?"

"Yes, that is why. Your father may not be able to get word to us and I don't want him to arrive in France and not know where we are or how to reach us."

Mother did not tell me the real reason then, knowing how much it would have upset me. The French by then were aware that when the Spanish civil war ended, there would likely be a mass influx of refugees into France. Given the ambivalent attitude of France's Third Republic to the Spanish Republic, no one was too sure how these refugees would be treated until the French government had decided what to do with them. Mother had heard rumors about this from friends of Father's who were still in the Diplomatic Corps of the Spanish Republic and she wanted to make sure that if he could make it into France, he would be able to find her and seek her help getting to Paris. And if Father had stayed in Spain after the Nationalists won, his fate would be even more certain. The Nationalists would at the very least imprison him for a long time but more likely would simply shoot him.

"Then, Mamá," I said, "Let's forget about this tour. I don't want to be away from you and Nuria and I want to be here if Papá comes. What if he can't stay for very long? What if he has to leave again soon and I don't see him?"

I was distraught and beside myself with anxiety now.

"Don't worry yourself, Conchi," replied my mother, taking my hand in hers and smoothing my hair gently with her other hand.

"I promise, if he comes while you are away, I will send you a telegram and you can come back to Paris that very same day. You should go on the tour with Alma. We don't know what our future will be, and you need to keep your jobs. You cannot disappoint Monsieur Leroy or let him down after all that he has done for you. Go and do your work and try to have fun and we will be here when you return."

"And you promise you will let us know if Papá comes or even if you hear anything from him?"

"Of course, I promise. Do not worry yourself."

A few days later, Alma and I boarded our train for the north coast of France. Our first stop was Normandy.

Performing in the casinos and resorts of northern Europe was a much different experience for us. The audience was less attentive than we were used to. More than once, we found ourselves dancing in front of an indifferent audience, more concerned with the conversation among themselves and with enjoying the sumptuous meals being placed in front of them than in what we were doing on the stage. It was the first time we had experienced this kind of apathy while we were performing, and it was something of a letdown for us.

This was especially the case in Deauville, a seaside resort in Normandy where Alma and I stayed for about ten days, performing every evening. All the time that we were in Deauville, the weather was cold and wet and miserable – as only Normandy can be in December! – and Alma and I felt lonely and unhappy. We spent most of the days shut in our hotel room, watching the cold and misty rain that never let up and which contributed nothing toward lifting our spirits. The indifference of our nightly audience did not help ease the gloom that enveloped us.

From Deauville, we continued on to Saint-Malo, Trouville, and then Dinard in Brittany. We travelled mostly by sea, on the ferries that serviced the seaside resort towns of northern France and the Low Countries. The weather did not improve, but we enjoyed those short sea voyages immensely, despite the rough waters of the northern seas, which made the ocean churn with waves larger and more menacing than we had ever seen. Those little boats we were on gave the impression that they might capsize at any moment, but we were too mesmerized by the dramatic sights of the ocean and the coastline to feel fear. The coasts of Normandy and Brittany were a fantastic sight, so different from the shores of the Mediterranean to which we were accustomed. Gigantic cliffs rose abruptly from the ocean's edge and between the sheer cliffs, enormous, sandy beaches stretched as far as the eye could see. Vast as the beaches were, they would disappear from view altogether when the tide came in, leaving hundreds of seagulls flying aimlessly, their wings grazing the crests of the incoming waves.

We left Dinard by boat and approached Saint-Malo just after dark. The little port was shining in the distance, glittering in the darkness like a jewel, with its picturesque harbor protecting the dozens of vessels and fishing boats anchored next to each other on the water. The whole town was lit behind the port, with Christmas decorations up everywhere. We stayed in Saint-Malo several days performing every evening, and would spend our days exploring the town, which had so many historical buildings and sights within it. We especially loved exploring the old cathedral in the center of the old town. We spent hours walking on and around the tall granite walls that surrounded the old town. How enchanting it was, despite the weather, to walk under and through the ancient ramparts of the old citadel! Then we would climb to the top of the highest turret and from that vantage point gaze down at the mighty ocean below us, its green and swelling waters turning to silver whenever the faint rays of sunshine, filtered through the constant cloud cover, would hit its surface.

It remained bitterly cold, but as we approached Dinard on the first of the three days we would spend performing there, we were greeted by sunshine. The ocean seemed calmer and the grey sky that had been so menacing began to show patches of blue, the first blue sky we had seen since leaving Paris. We stayed in an old Inn in Dinard, not far from the beach and near the famous casino, where we would be performing in the evenings. Dinard at that time was a favorite vacation resort for the English and as we entered the Inn's dining room, the place was full of English tourists enjoying their afternoon tea.

Alma and I spent many hours walking along the length of Dinard's magnificent beach, its white sand so powdery that our feet would sink into it, almost to our ankles. Darting in and out between the fierce splashes of the gigantic waves that sent tons of foamy water crashing down against the shore, we roamed among the crags and crevices of the shoreline, searching for tiny mussels and sea urchins. We would harvest as many as we could and then take them back to the privacy of our room and eat them by the dozen. Whenever the weather allowed it, we would stay on the seashore well past sunset, collecting our delicacies as well as all kinds of seashells, reluctant to walk away from the glorious scenery to go back indoors.

We spent Christmas in Dinard. Because it was Christmas day, we had no show to perform that evening. Without the performance to keep us occupied, it was a lonely day and an even lonelier evening for us. We were able to call Mother and Nuria by telephone to wish each other a Merry Christmas, but hearing their voices only made me feel even more lonesome.

"Is there any news about Papá?" I asked my mother on the telephone.

"No, Conchita. We haven't heard anything from him since the last letter that you saw."

I continued to worry about my father. I could not help but wonder, was he even still alive? Would he be able to get out in time? I had no illusions about how he would be treated by the Nationalists if they were able to capture him, after they had won.

After the performances at Dinard, we continued traveling along the northern coast of Europe. Alma and I laughed at the thought that not so long ago, we had posed for Domergue to paint a poster advertising the coastline of the Belgian Riviera, and now here we finally were! He had painted us in our two-piece swimsuits standing on a sandy beach bathed in sunshine and now we were on this coast on cold and grey days, subjected to almost constant rain and a ceaseless cold and blustery wind. The last activity that these days inspired was swimming or even being outdoors if we did not need to be. Every day that passed without news about my father made me more and more anxious. The weather remained dismal and this did nothing to elevate my mood or spirits.

We were booked to perform as part of a New Year's Eve show at a nightclub near the Hotel Metropole in Brussels. Brussels seemed like a beautiful city, with its Grande Place all lit up and decorated for the holidays, but we were there less than 24 hours and I simply didn't have the chance to get to know it very well. The audience for our New Year's Eve performance was entirely focused on their drinks and their festivities and I'm not sure whether they paid any attention at all to our performance. I was not terribly upset about this, but it bothered Alma, who felt that she was wasting her talents for such a boorish and inattentive audience. We had to be in Amsterdam by the next afternoon, so we left for the train station as soon as we had finished our performance, not staying to see the rest of the show or to celebrate the arrival of the new year. By the time we stopped at our hotel to pick up our baggage and found a taxi still operating on New Year's Eve, we were running late and were worried we might miss our train.

New Year's morning found us feeling stranded in a small railroad station near Antwerp, waiting for the train to take us to Amsterdam. We had missed the last express train with direct service to Amsterdam from Brussels and according to the ticket agent in Brussels, our only option to arrive in Amsterdam on time was to make this connection with the Amsterdam-bound train coming from Antwerp. At this late hour on New Year's Eve, we were almost alone at the station. The only other people there were an extremely forlorn-looking English couple and one very angry-looking Belgian man. Alma and I joined our traveling companions, sitting on the single wooden bench in the waiting room. The English couple gave us a tired smile, while the apparently very angry Belgian scowled at us, then got up and walked away from the bench, lighting a cigarette and muttering inaudibly as he did so. It was well past midnight when we finally boarded the train. The café at the station had been closed and we were tired and hungry. By the time we finally boarded the train to Amsterdam, Alma and I were feeling so lonely and unhappy that we kept on promising each other that we would never again spend another Christmas or New Year holiday away from family and friends.

We arrived in Amsterdam the next morning, the first day of 1939. It was a beautiful and sunny day, although cold, and everything was closed because of the holiday. We took a taxi to the little hotel where we had been booked and on the way there, we saw how beautiful a city it was, with its canals and beautiful architecture. Amsterdam was the second to last stop of our tour and we were scheduled to be there for five days, performing in a nightclub every night. We went to the nightclub that same afternoon, as had been agreed, to make sure the orchestra was familiar with our pieces and to get used to the stage. We did our first performance that night. The audience was relatively small and quiet, as might be expected the day after the New Year's Eve celebrations, but still more attentive and pleasant than the Brussels audience had been twenty-four hours earlier.

Our five days in Amsterdam passed quickly. The weather was pleasant while we were there and we spent our days exploring the city, walking along the canals, and visiting the art museums. It was a beautiful and delightful city, but we were lonely and missed our family.

All in all, except for the few pleasant days at Saint-Malo and Dinard, this had been an unhappy trip and a miserable way to spend the holiday. One afternoon, to my surprise, Michel telephoned me from Paris and when I told him about our experiences, he immediately suggested that he join us for the last stop of our tour, at The Hague. He met us there and after our two nights of performing there, he took us back to Paris in his car. We drove across the flat plain of Holland on roads that never strayed too far from the sea, traversing pretty little towns until we reached Belgium. I remember the drive across Belgium as a progression of beautiful countryside dotted with toy-like villages that appeared to have come straight out of fairy tales. On the last leg of the journey back to Paris, we stopped at Saint Michel and marveled at its dream-like beauty, at the centuries-old monastery, and at the sight of its beautiful abbey, rising phantom-like, it appeared, from the middle of the ocean. It was an unforgettable experience.

Back in Paris, Alma and I took a few days off to recover from the journey and then resumed our routine of performing five nights each week, back in the same nightclubs as before, and doing a little bit of modeling work during the days.

We still had not received any word from Father since his last letter. During those next few months, the situation in Spain continued to worsen for the Republic and nobody really felt any longer that the Republic had any chance of surviving. Every week, several officials of the Republic would arrive in Paris, having decided to get out before it was too late to escape with their lives. Many of these of course had known Father and worked with him. These men would always call us to let us know that they were in Paris, but when Mother would ask if they had any word of what had happened to Father, they would shake their heads and say no. We began to fear the worst.

"Miss Spain in Exile"

Isa's mother was right to be worried about the possibility of her husband being interned in a camp in the Pyrenees. The French established several such camps, which had an infamous history in the time preceding and then during World War Two. Little was known about them at the time, but conditions in them were scarcely better than in many of the German concentration camps. The conditions were brutal, particularly during winter. Starvation and freezing to death were common. By early 1939 these camps, including the infamous Le Vernet, were being used to intern refugees from Spain. Within short years afterward, they were being used as holding camps to detain French Jews on their way to the killing camps of Eastern Europe. Over 500,000 refugees from Spain crossed the Pyrenees into France that winter, many of whom were confined in these brutal camps. Among the detainees were the writer Arthur Koestler, who had stayed in Spain fighting the fascists even after the rest of the International Brigades had left, and a young surgeon named Carlos Parés. Koestler of course went on to great fame as a writer, particularly well known for his classic novel Darkness at Noon. He wrote about his experiences in a French internment camp in his book Scum of the Earth. The surgeon escaped France and eventually married Isa's sister Nuria. I knew him as my Uncle Carlos.

Although this trip over Christmas was not in general a particularly fond memory for Isa, she did remember for the rest of her life the stark beauty of the coasts of Normandy and Brittany in winter. Years later, I was in Paris with my mother and father. I must have been about ten years old at the time. My father and I had gone for our habitual morning walk, and passing an art gallery on the Rue Marbeuf, off the Champs Elysées, we stopped to admire the paintings on display in the window. One in particular caught my father's eye. It was an oil painting of a beach scene, looking like Normandy or perhaps Brittany, with a grey sky and low, dark clouds. On the immense beach was a lone rowboat, looking tiny in comparison to the immensity of the beach and the ocean and looking abandoned.

"Your mother will like this painting," my father said to me. "Let's surprise your mother and buy it for her."

The art gallery had not opened yet, but it was open later when we passed by it again on our way back to our hotel. We went in and my father bought the painting and arranged to have it delivered to our hotel later that day. As he had predicted, my mother loved *the painting and was excited to have it to take home. She began telling us how much it reminded her of that Christmas tour at the end of 1938. That evening, Aunt Alma came to have dinner with us and before we went out to dinner, she came to see the painting. It reminded her as well of that holiday trip and both of them spent dinner reminiscing about that Christmas holiday and that tour of performances in northern Europe that they had made.*

Chapter 13

Father is Alive!

February–March 1939

In Spain by now, the civil war was all but over. In February 1939, the governments of Britain and France recognized Franco's government as the legitimate government of Spain. France named Marshall Philippe Petain, hero of World War One and later head of the collaborationist Vichy French government, as its ambassador to Franco's Spain. With the Republican cause now all but lost, what was left of the Republican government tried to negotiate a peace with Franco. Franco refused, reiterating his demand for an unconditional surrender. On March 28, the victorious Nationalists entered Madrid in triumph and the civil war ended. The last city to fall was Valencia, on March 30. With that, in the first days of April, the Republic formally surrendered unconditionally to the Nationalists. The Spanish Civil War was over. Over half a million lives had been lost in the tragic conflict, the most devastating in Spanish history.

As winter continued to sit over Paris, most of the days gray and cold and often wet and rainy, Alma and I continued our lives dancing most evenings wherever in Paris we had been booked. I did a little bit of fashion modeling as well during the afternoons, but, as before, that was only to bring in a little bit of extra cash.

We had not heard from Father since we had received the last letter from him several months earlier. None of his friends that came to see us or that we could contact had any news about what may have happened to him or even whether he was still alive. My mother would become silent for long periods of time, staring at the few photos of him that she had managed to bring when we left Spain with the belongings we could carry. That had now been less than

Father is Alive!

three years earlier, but it felt like a lifetime ago! Nuria and I knew that during those periods of silence, Mother was preparing herself for the worst while still praying that her husband was alive.

The Spanish Civil War was ending. It was clear that it would end with the inevitable victory of Franco and his Nationalists despite three years of valiant and heroic efforts by the defenders of the Republic. Madrid and Valencia, the last two holdouts of the Republic, were surrounded and surely could not last very much longer. Had Father been able to get out? Or was he still there, and if he was, what would happen to him when the victorious Nationalists got their hands on him?

Then, one afternoon in February, when we least expected it, we received the joyous news that Father was alive!

The good news came via a friend of Father's, Felipe Revuelta, one of the diplomatic envoys from the Spanish Republic to France. He came to our apartment in the hotel one afternoon to give us the good news in person. When he knocked on the door and my mother opened it and saw him standing there, she turned ashen.

"My God, what has happened to Ricardo"? she screamed. Seeing him, she had assumed that he had come in person to deliver sad news.

"No, no, Concepción, don't worry yourself. Ricardo is fine. He is already in France and will be in Paris by tomorrow, the day after tomorrow at the latest. I wanted to give you the good news to your face. He is already on his way to Paris!"

At these words, Mother sighed and almost fainted with relief. Nuria and I were beside ourselves with joy and excitement and we couldn't stop asking questions.

"What happened to him? Is he alright? How did he get out of Spain? When will he be here?"

"Quiet, quiet, all of you. Ricardo is fine. Let me tell you what has happened."

Señor Revuelta went on to explain what had happened and how my grandfather had gotten out.

In the final days, as it became clear that Valencia could not survive the siege of the Nationalists that now encircled the city, my father together with two of his friends had organized and implemented a dangerous and desperate plan. With forged permits to transit Nationalist territory in their hands, purportedly (albeit illegibly) signed by a high-ranking Nationalist officer, they had left

Valencia in a fishing boat one night. Landing on the coast north of Valencia, behind Nationalist lines, they had been met by a car that had been arranged to come from Barcelona and was waiting for them. They drove until dawn, then hid in a village near Girona during the day. Driving through the next night, they managed to reach the French border in the Pyrenees, two days after leaving Valencia. Twice, when confronted by Nationalist soldiers during their journey, they had blustered and shown their forged permits to travel across Nationalist territory, and in the confusion that had overtaken Spain as the civil war was ending, that had been sufficient to get them as far as the French frontier. They exited the car a few kilometers from the border post and hid by the side of the road until the sun had come up, not knowing if the border crossing would be open during the night and not wanting to risk being caught trying to sneak across at night if the crossing was closed.

As it became daylight, they walked toward the border. The guards on the Spanish side let them through without questioning their right to leave Spain or inspecting their papers too closely. The forged permits worked as well as they had before.

But now came another, more dangerous moment as they tried to enter France. The French were not particularly sympathetic to Republican refugees and were in fact already interning many of them in the notorious internment camps of the Pyrenees. As they walked to the French border post, they hid the forged Nationalist travel documents in their heavy winter overcoats, dropping the papers through slits they had cut in the linings of the pockets. Thanks to work he had been doing with the Diplomatic Corps of the Spanish Republic, in addition to his duties with the militia, my grandfather had not just a normal passport, but a diplomatic passport of the Republic. This diplomatic passport, together with his talent for bluffing and a small bribe, convinced the French border guards to let him in. The same ploy worked for his friend.

Don Felipe continued with his explanation.

"Once they were in France, they were able to send me a cable at the consulate from a post office. They did not want to linger long near the border in case the guards at the border had a change of heart, or to let someone at the post office know your address in case the gendarmes made problems after all, so they asked me to come tell you the news. He is on his way even now to Paris by train. I am sure he will be here by tomorrow. The next day at the latest, if he

Father is Alive!

cannot get on an express train. His companion is on his way to Marseille."

We had all sat on the edge of our seats, hanging onto every word of this story. As Don Felipe finished telling the story of Father's remarkable and almost miraculous escape, Mother finally relaxed and with a huge sigh of relief, she sat back on the sofa where she had been sitting.

"How can I thank you for bringing us this good news?" she asked Don Felipe.

Felipe smiled and said, "Don't worry yourself, please. It gave me such great pleasure to be able to give you this joyous news. The looks on your faces, that is all the thanks that I need. Now, I will leave you to prepare for Ricardo's return. I shall see you soon."

With that, he took my mother's hand and kissed it, bowed to all of us, and left.

When our bearer of good news had left, we sat silently for a few minutes before we all burst into tears of joy and relief. I was happy that Alma and I did not have to perform that night. It would have been impossible for me to perform my dances in front of an audience when I had just learned that Father was alive! We shared the news with Aunt Encarna and Alma and Nanita when they returned from their afternoon of shopping and they shared our joy and relief.

As the evening went on, we could scarcely talk about anything other than the fact that Father was alive and how joyous it would be to be reunited soon. I could still picture his kind and gentle face and the sad look in his eyes when he had said goodbye to me at the train station in Madrid, what seemed like a lifetime ago. The news that Father had survived the war could not help but be mixed with the realization that the fact that he had left Spain meant that those fascist Nationalists had in fact won, or were about to win, the civil war. But our sadness and bitterness at the fascist victory was more than compensated by the news that Father had survived and that we would see him.

We were so excited that we barely slept that night. The next morning, we had our usual breakfast of café au lait with croissants and then took vigil by the front door of our building to wait for him.

Mother, Nuria, and I could hardly wait for the joyous reunion, but when it came, our joy was tinged with sadness at the changes in Father's appearance. He was a broken man, physically as well as spiritually, one more political refugee facing an uncertain future.

"Miss Spain in Exile"

His large, brown eyes, always so bright and full of joy and curiosity, now looked sad, as though they had witnessed too much brutality to smile the way they used to. But still, how happy we all were to see him and how much we enjoyed what in the end was only his short stay with us in Paris!

We knew right away that his visit would be a short one. On his first day with us, he explained that due to the French reluctance to welcome Republican refugees from Spain and even having entered France on a diplomatic passport of the Spanish Republic, he had only been able to get a visa to stay in France for ten days. Despite his efforts to get a visa for a longer stay as he entered, he had not been able to do so and in fact, had been lucky to get even a ten-day visa.

We discussed as a family whether we should all stay together in Paris and take our chances with renewing Father's visa or obtaining another passport, but he convinced us that it was too dangerous to risk being caught in Paris without valid papers. Father also believed that with the possibility of war in Europe imminent, it was madness to risk remaining on that continent, and he convinced us of this logic as well. It was agreed that he would go to the New World, like so many of our ancestors had done in the past, where he would try to carve out a future for himself and his family, and he would send for us as soon as he had established himself in a new country.

Once again, if only for a few days, we were a united and happy family, the four of us going for long walks together all over the city. It especially delighted us to go for long walks in the Bois de Boulogne and in the gardens of the Tuileries. The weather improved as spring gave hints of a possible early arrival. Nuria and I, walking or sitting next to our father and mother, were again the two happy little girls of that long-ago time, back in that familiar world of our own that was now lost forever. How far away and long ago that peaceful and familiar world seemed to us now! Father would smoke his pipe and say very little but would devote all his attention to our incessant chatter, never taking his eyes off of us.

One night, he and Mother came to Le Boeuf Sur le Toit to watch Alma and Isa Reyes perform. He was delighted at our show and it was lovely to see him sitting in the audience with my mother, with a bottle of champagne at their table, his pipe as always in his mouth, and hints of his old smile on his mouth and in his eyes.

Father is Alive!

The consulate of the Spanish Republic was still functioning in Paris, though it would not be for very much longer. My father had friends there and they were working as hard as they could to find him passage to the New World. It was agreed that if they could not succeed, they would at least try to get him to England where he could wait for a spot to be available on one of the trans-Atlantic ships that traveled regularly to America.

The Consul himself called one afternoon with the news that as the result of a cancellation, there would be a cabin available on the *Queen Mary*, sailing from Cherbourg to New York in two days' time. And, by the way, the cabin was a first-class accommodation, all that was available. Father agreed to take it.

We saw a hint of Father's old sense of humor returning on our last evening together when he said to all of us, "Well, I may be a refugee, and my country may not exist for very much longer, but at least I shall travel into my exile in a First-Class cabin on the *Queen Mary*! I suppose it could be worse!"

We all laughed with him, though the laughter was tinged with sadness that we would be saying goodbye to him again soon. And again, we did not know for how long it would be until we were all together again.

Father saw me looking sad. He took my hand in his and said, "Look at me, Conchita. Look into my eyes."

I did as he asked, and for the first time in a long time, since those days so long ago in Pedro Bernardo before the horrible war had started, his eyes were the eyes that I remembered. Gone was the bitterness and even most of the sadness. His eyes were full of warmth and sparkled with love as he looked into my eyes.

"Now listen to me, Conchita. I promise you. As soon as I land in the New World, I will be working on ways to have all of you come to join me. Our family will be together again soon. Do you trust me and believe me, little angel?"

"Yes, Papá," I answered him. "Of course, I trust you and believe you."

"Then don't look so sad! Promise me you will not be sad."

I promised him and we all sat down to have our last dinner together before once again having to say goodbye.

The next day, Mother and Nuria and I drove with him to Cherbourg, where he would board the *Queen Mary* to cross the Atlantic Ocean. With tears streaming down our cheeks, we stood amidst all the commotion on the pier as the passengers all filed on board. We watched as the ship's crew completed the final preparations for the voyage. Father stayed with us on the pier for as long as he could and so he was one of the last passengers to board the ship. When he was on board, he immediately made his way to the railing on the deck so we could see him. From the pier below him, huddled close together, we kept on waving and smiling back at him until the moment when the huge ship began to pull itself loose and away from the dock. Just at that moment, the ship's horn blew a long blast which echoed over the widening gap of water between the dock and the ship.

For me to this day, no other sound in the world seems to carry more sadness and melancholy than the bass sound of an ocean liner's horn announcing that the ship is about to sail away to distant lands. For some it may be the sound of going on an exotic vacation or of beginning an exciting adventure. For me it is the tear-laden sound of a forced farewell and a reminder of being at the mercy of world forces beyond my control.

Standing together amidst the noise and the uproar and huddling even closer against the chill breeze that had suddenly kicked up, we were very much aware that this new separation from Father represented yet another potentially traumatic change in our lives. What would he find for himself, and for us, in the New World? When would he send for us? Would we be able to escape Europe before another war engulfed us and forced us to once again change all of our plans? We dimly suspected that although we could not identify them, a series of events was now in the making over which we had no control, and which would determine the course of our lives.

My father arrived in New York, but it took him only a short time there to determine that he would be unable to extend his visa to stay in United States. This visa, which he so desperately sought, was simply unavailable to him. He wrote us a letter explaining this and telling us that he had decided to sail on to Cuba to see what opportunities he might find there. A few weeks had passed before we received a second letter, this one posted in Havana, telling us that he had decided to settle down there.

It was a long letter telling Mother about his ambition and hope to find a way to make a living there. "Soon," he wrote, "I will find work and I will send for you to join me on this peaceful, sun-drenched island in the Caribbean."

Father is Alive!

In fact, he had a few jobs there before landing the job he would keep for most of his years in Cuba, that of being the news announcer for Radio Havana. His deep, sonorous, and Castilian-accented voice leant an air of authority to the news broadcasts and he was very popular in that role. Later, we used to joke that my father had become the "Walter Cronkite" of Cuba during those years. Among the news broadcasts he read over the air for Radio Havana was the one on December 7, 1941 in which he told about the Japanese bombing Pearl Harbor.

Not knowing how long it would take him to find work, or when he would have a sufficiently stable life there to send for us, we continued with our lives in Paris. Alma and I continued dancing, which brought in enough money to live, decently if not in luxury, and we decided to continue as best we could until Father knew what his future was, and where. Our agent was trying to get us bookings in places like the Savoy in London and our future looked promising enough, if only we could erase from our minds the ever-present thoughts and fear of war. These thoughts and fears by now seemed to have taken a permanent grip on our existence. We knew we were not alone in this, though. All of Europe and much of the world at large prayed and waited nervously to see what would come next.

They did not have to wait for very long.

On March 15, 1939, Hitler invaded Czechoslovakia. It is more accurate to state that he invaded what was left of Czechoslovakia, the rump state without natural defenses that was left as a result of the Munich Accord, or Betrayal, of the previous September. This was a blatant breaking of all of the promises that Hitler had made to Neville Chamberlain, as well as publicly, renouncing any further territorial ambitions in Europe after he was given the Sudetenland. Hitler presented Czechoslovakia with an ultimatum, threatening it with total destruction if it did not open its borders to the German army. Having been left essentially defenseless after Munich, Czechoslovakia had had no choice but to accede. The German army occupied Czechoslovakia without meeting any resistance and by the next evening, Hitler and several of his high-ranking Nazis were in Prague.

Two days later, Prime Minister Neville Chamberlain gave a speech in Birmingham condemning Hitler's aggression in

Czechoslovakia and stating that Britain would resist any further attempts at territorial expansion by Nazi Germany, with armed force if necessary. Notwithstanding Chamberlain's warning, by the end of March, Hitler had begun a propaganda campaign alleging Polish mistreatment of German nationals inside Poland. To many, the campaign was eerily reminiscent of the propaganda campaign that presaged the Sudeten crisis. Meanwhile, Mussolini issued an ultimatum to Albania, insisting that Albania become a protectorate of Italy, with Italy having the right to station troops within Albania.

Neville Chamberlain pledged Anglo-French support to Poland if Polish independence was threatened by Hitler's Germany. Both Britain and France, along with most of the rest of Europe, now began to see a European war as likely inevitable.

Chapter 14

Two Weeks in Venice

March 1939

By 1939, Benito Mussolini, "Il Duce", had been in power in Italy for seventeen years. He ruled as Prime Minister from 1922 until he was deposed in 1943. At the beginning, he presided over a constitutional government. In 1925, however, he dropped any pretense of democracy or constitutional rule and established a fascist dictatorship with him at its head. His movement can be credited with originating the term fascist or fascism, though it may have been one of his followers who first actually used the word. The origin of the word fascist is the Italian word "fasces", meaning literally a bundle of sticks. The meaning or symbolism is that while it may be easy to break one single stick, it is nearly impossible to break a bundle of sticks. By analogy then, a single person or citizen might be broken, but a group standing together would be impossible to break. Thus, the word fascism was originally a call for national unity, but it translated quickly and easily into a demand for single-minded devotion to the national leader.

In 1919, Mussolini had founded the Fasci Italiani di Combattimento in Milan. Two years later this became the Partito Nazionale Fascista (the National Fascist Party). In 1922, he led a march of his followers, the "Blackshirts" on Rome and was installed as Prime Minister shortly thereafter. During the next few years, he managed to remove or neutralize his opposition with the help of a ruthless secret police and a series of laws that transformed Italy into a one-party dictatorship, with himself as the unquestioned leader, "Il Duce". His model of authoritarian and totalitarian rule and his notion of fascism as an unquestioning loyalty to the state and its leader were an inspiration for other dictators of the Twentieth Century, including Hitler and Franco.

Mussolini's foreign policy had the ambition of expanding the sphere of influence of Italian fascism and, to some extent, of restoring the glories of the Roman Empire. In 1923, Italian troops initiated the "pacification" of Libya and in that same year, Mussolini ordered the bombing of the Greek island of Corfu, which had once been a Venetian colony. Years later, in 1935, he invaded Abyssinia (present-day Ethiopia), where his mechanized and modern army and air force committed countless atrocities against the defending primitive forces. The League of Nations condemned the Italian invasion of Abyssinia but was powerless to do anything about it and stood by impotently as the ruthless and vicious conquest of Abyssinia was completed, ending in 1936 with the creation of Italian East Africa, which comprised Abyssinia, Somalia, and Eritrea.

Between 1936 and 1939, Mussolini, together with Hitler, was an overt supporter of Franco's Nationalist insurrection in Spain, sending arms and munitions as well as tens of thousands of "volunteer" soldiers to fight on the side of his fellow fascists in Spain. In 1939, following an ultimatum not unlike the one that Hitler had presented to Czechoslovakia, Mussolini's fascist legions invaded and occupied Albania.

The ideological and political brotherhood between Mussolini and Hitler was formalized by their "Pact of Steel", signed in May 1939. This pact, formally named the Pact of Friendship and Alliance between Germany and Italy, was a complete military and political alliance between the two fascist powers, including provisions for mutual defense should one of the two member countries be attacked.

With Father gone, and now on his way to the New World, we all settled back into the routine of Paris life. Alma and I danced most evenings of each week and Nuria continued her classical and flamenco guitar studies and continued performing frequently in concerts and recitals, as well as still sometimes playing guitar as the musical accompaniment to the Alma and Isa Reyes dance duet. We were sad that we had said goodbye to Father, but optimistic that he would soon get settled in his new life and we knew that he would send for us as soon as he could.

To our joy and surprise one day, our agent, Monsieur Leroy, informed us that he had booked Alma and me for two weeks in Venice, at the Venice Casino. I was overjoyed because I had always wanted to see this beautiful city, with its beautiful canals and fascinating history. Once again, Mother and Nuria stayed in Paris and Alma and I went by ourselves, but this time it was because Nuria had been booked to perform several guitar concerts and she did not want to miss these opportunities to continue performing in front of larger audiences.

We traveled to Venice by train and arrived on a beautiful spring afternoon. The sky was bright blue and reflected off the gorgeous Adriatic Sea. A motorboat had been arranged to transport us by canal to our hotel in the historic center and as we rode into the city, we were amazed at the sights and at the beauty of Venice. The canals reminded us of Amsterdam, but the feel of the city was totally different. I was enchanted with Venice from the moment we arrived.

We checked into our hotel and then went for a long walk to explore the city. We had dinner at a little restaurant near the Rialto Bridge and then, tired from the train journey, we retired for the evening.

The next morning, we went early to the casino and had a full day of rehearsals with the orchestra to prepare for our act. The orchestra was very good and very professional but was not used to the rhythms of Spanish music and it took most of the day practicing and rehearsing until we were all comfortable. We had been booked for two weeks as one of the top-billed acts of the floorshow at the Venice Casino and after our day of rehearsals, we settled into our routine of nightly performances. The Venice Casino was a beautiful and historic building, the oldest still active casino in Europe, having opened in the year 1638. It was a lovely place to perform and it felt glamorous to be performing at such a historic site.

Venice was everything I had hoped and expected it to be. We were staying in a small hotel near the Casino and spent our days lazily exploring the sights and museums of the city, indulging in an occasional ride in a gondola, then having a delicious dinner of seafood before going to the Casino to change into our costumes and prepare for the evening's performance.

I fell in love with Venice! The weather was beautiful when we were there, with bright and sunny days and just a little bit of a cool breeze off the Adriatic Sea in the evenings. I never tired of walking across St. Mark's Plaza, stopping for a coffee at any one of the outdoor cafés that encircled it. There I could sit for hours, watching the people walk across and laughing at the crazy antics of the pigeons who seemed to consider the plaza theirs and seemed to resent the people who intruded on their domain. I would go into the lovely St. Mark's Cathedral and look at all the beautiful art it contained and then walk along the Grand Canal to the Bridge of Sighs and all the way back around, stopping whenever I wanted for another coffee or to look into the shops and admire all the exquisite Italian goods, especially the beautiful leather products for which Italy was so famous. I treated myself one day to a beautiful leather handbag and bought two little purses to take back to Mother and Nuria as gifts.

The only disconcerting aspect of Venice for me was the profusion of fascist banners and flags, constant reminders that I was in a fascist regime. The odious symbol of the bunch of sticks held in a clenched fist was everywhere, as was the Italian fascist flag, the traditional Italian tricolor of green, red, and white, but now with a fierce and warlike eagle in the middle of it, its talons gripping the bunched sticks of the fasces. Also, everywhere, scrawled on walls or on the sides of trucks, the endless repetition of the word "Duce!" Wherever I walked were the black-clad security police and stern-faced men that I was sure were members of the secret police. They were such a sharp contrast to the jovial Venetians that it was hard to reconcile the images.

Without exception, all of the Italian people I met were friendly and polite and loved talking to me when they found out I was Spanish. It was occasionally awkward, since their government had openly supported Franco and his Nationalists, and so most Italians just assumed that a "good Spaniard" would be on the same side. As long as we avoided Spanish politics, though, everything was alright. I found to my surprise that speaking Spanish as I did, it was easy to understand Italian and to make myself understood. My Italian improved a little bit every day and by the end of our stay there, I could have a reasonable conversation in Italian, without too much rolling of eyes at my grammar or my frequent use of a Spanish word, but pronounced with what I imagined would be the correct Italian intonation. My guesses at Italian pronunciation were usually based on my lifetime love of the operas of Puccini.

My main impression of the Italian people was that they were a kind and fun-loving people who loved to laugh and have fun and who worshipped art and artists and lived for the good things in life.

It was difficult for me to reconcile this impression that I had formed with their obviously fanatical support for their fascist Duce, Benito Mussolini, or with their army's actions in Spain, or earlier in Abyssinia. In both places, I knew, Italian soldiers had behaved with a ruthless barbarism.

I had become friends with the old Italian gentleman who was the manager and concierge of the little hotel where Alma and I were staying. He had recognized me from photos he had seen in the newspapers of the Miss Europe contest and he had asked me one afternoon while we were having a coffee together why I was the only girl in those photos not carrying the flag of her country, only my banner with the word España written on it. This had clearly stuck in his memory. Signor Lorenzo was such a kind and courteous gentleman that I felt comfortable telling him the truth.

"My father was fighting for the Republic in Spain during the Miss Europe pageant," I explained to him in my half-Spanish and half-Italian. "But they would not let me wear the flag of the Republic."

With some hesitation, not knowing how Signor Lorenzo would react, I added, "And I did not want to wear the flag of Fascist Spain."

To my relief, he took my hand in his and kissed it like the old-fashioned Italian gentleman that he was. "You are a brave girl," he said. "It took courage to honor your father like that in these times."

I asked him what he meant, and his reply helped me understand a little bit what I was seeing around me and what had been occurring in Spain and Abyssinia.

"Conchita," he said, "We Italians support Mussolini, but some are more fanatical in their support of him than others. He helped save us from communism and if we did not have Mussolini, maybe we wouldn't even be a country by now. We Italians are not like the Germans, we are not by nature a disciplined people. The Germans like their Hitler and worship him because he tells them what they want to be told. We Italians like our Mussolini, but we worship him because he tells us what we need to be told. He tells us that we need to believe in Italy and that we need to work together for our common future

"I am not proud of what our armies did in Abyssinia. What civilized man can support dropping bombs from airplanes on a people who try to fight back with spears? But too many of my countrymen view it only as a return of the days of glory of the Roman Empire. Every Italian yearns for those days of glory and longs for

Italy to be taken seriously and have a seat at the world's table. That is why Mussolini has embarked on his adventures in Abyssinia and in Spain, to show the world that Italy is to be taken seriously. And that is why the Italian people support him.

"What can we do? If we say anything against Mussolini, the secret police, the OVRA, hear of it and we soon wish we had kept our mouths shut. So, we go along with it, we follow it, we even occasionally become fanatical about it. Mussolini knows how to play to our sense of drama. But we are not true believers the way the Germans are. We Italians will follow Mussolini as long as it benefits us to do so. Some of us hope that it will not be forever. Myself, I am afraid that that madman Hitler will get us all into a war from which there will be no escaping."

That was the one and only conversation about world politics that this kind old gentleman and I had. He seemed afraid to ever bring up the topic again. I never heard from Signor Lorenzo after we left Venice and I used to wonder what had ever happened to him. Years later when I returned to Venice, I went back to our little hotel and asked, but no one knew.

The secret police in Italy during that period were the Organizziazone per la Vigilanza e la Represione dell' Antifascismo, the Organization for the Vigilance and Repression of Anti-Fascism, or the OVRA. They had been founded in 1927 and were used by Hitler, Himmler, and Goering as the model for Nazi's Geheime Staatspolizei, the Secret State Police, or Gestapo. The OVRA had a well-deserved reputation for ruthlessness and was instrumental in stifling any descent and helping to keep Mussolini firmly ensconced in power, though they never achieved the notoriety of the Gestapo.

Signor Lorenzo was right in his prediction. The Italians, despite having worshipped Mussolini for years, turned on him when Italy began to lose the war. In the end, he was shot by Italian partisans on April 28, 1945, his body hung by its heels from a gas station in Milan after being kicked and spat upon by crowds. His hanging corpse was stoned by spectators.

In addition to its incredible, almost unbelievable beauty and its fascinating history, Venice was an important cultural city. The oldest film festival in the world, the biennial Venice Film Festival, had begun there in 1932. The city remained a magnet for artists and for collectors of fine contemporary art as well. Unfortunately, though, there was in addition to this a dark side to the city's recent history. Hitler and Mussolini had first met face to face in Venice in 1934, laying the foundation for what would become their evil pact and eventually their collaboration on the Fascist side in the Spanish Civil War.

One evening, Alma and I lost track of the time and were running a bit late arriving to the Casino. By the time we got there, it was almost curtain time for the floorshow. Lucia, the fat, good-natured woman who helped us backstage with our costumes, was in an uncharacteristically foul mood. In fact, she was fuming. "How could you have forgotten what a special night this is? Are your brains no bigger than those of a butterfly?" she shouted. "Farfalla, farfalla! (Butterfly, butterfly!)" she kept shouting at us as she followed us into our dressing room. We had to admit that she was right to be upset with us for being so late. The main salon was already ablaze with its thousand lights and customers were pouring in through the main doors in an endless procession. Alma and I had to hurry to change into our costumes, pin the tortoise-shell combs that held the "mantillas" on our heads, and try to find the earrings and carnations that completed our attire amidst the usual clutter of our dressing room table. We heard the orchestra playing the final notes of the "Merry Widow Waltz", our cue to let us know that we were due on stage in about two minutes. Alma and I rushed out of the room but were surprised to hear the orchestra switch from the delicate rhythms of the waltz to the martial tempo of a military march. They had not done this on previous evenings, and we wondered what was going on.

The repeated exclamations of "Mamma Mia" from Lucia and the rest of the backstage crew were almost lost in the commotion we could hear from the casino's floor. From behind the stage, through a crack in the curtain, we watched Il Duce, Signor Benito Mussolini himself, the fascist dictator of Italy, making his grand entrance. He strode in slowly and pompously, with a great sense of drama, jutting his chin forward the way he always did for photographs and newsreels, as he greeted the adoring crowd, his right arm outstretched in front of him in a fascist salute. Amidst the thunderous applause, he walked through the center aisle and sat down at his reserved table in the middle of the front, very near the stage. He was followed by a dozen or so men, mostly in uniform, escorting a group of women elegantly clad in evening clothes.

"Miss Spain in Exile"

It felt very strange to realize that I was about to perform in front of this dictator, who among other things, had been so instrumental in helping Franco and his Nationalists, whom my father had risked his life trying to defeat, and who now had won the civil war in Spain. I wasn't sure I wanted to go out on stage now. As Lucia had reminded us, we had been told that tonight would be a special night with a special audience, but I suppose it had not really sunk into my head who that audience would be. Stage managers and agents were always telling us, "This is a special audience, you must be at your best tonight!" I had not realized that I would have to perform in front of Mussolini himself!

Alma immediately caught my mood and took me by the arm and said, "It's just politics and politicians, Conchita. Don't worry yourself. Just dance and perform like they were anyone."

I almost said, "That's easy for you to say! You and your mother support the fascists!" but Alma and I had never argued or fought over political issues and I did not want to start now, especially just minutes before a performance.

"You're right," I said. "Let's get on with the performance."

I told myself there was nothing I could do about it and I might as well just go on stage and perform. I calmed down and went to the edge of the stage to peek out at the audience. My gaze fell upon an attractive-looking man who, although he had come in walking next to Mussolini, had detached himself from the group and was now seated at a nearby table, to the left of Mussolini's but still very close to the stage. "Who is that man in the white uniform?" I asked Lucia out of curiosity. She answered me, shocked that I did not recognize him, "That is Count Ciano, Mussolini's son-in-law."

Galeazzo Ciano, Count Ciano, was, in fact, Benito Mussolini's son-in-law and also served as Foreign Minister in Mussolini's government. He was an Italian diplomat and politician who had married Mussolini's daughter Edda in 1930. Despite this marriage to Il Duce's daughter, Count Ciano was well known as a womanizer. He was a man with a lust for power and a lack of scruples, combined with an intelligence that had gotten him to the heart of the Italian fascist regime. He was widely seen as the second most powerful man in Italy, and for a long time was being groomed by Mussolini to be his successor.

Ciano had served as a bomber squadron commander during the Italian invasion of Abyssinia in 1935. Mussolini appointed him

Foreign Minister in 1936 when he returned from Abyssinia as a highly trumpeted hero. As Foreign Minister, Ciano was instrumental in orchestrating the Italian intervention in the Spanish Civil War, the alliance with Hitler's Nazi Germany, the Munich Accord which led to the dismemberment of Czechoslovakia, and the subsequent invasions of Albania and Greece.

An insight into Ciano's view of the world, and of history, can be learned from this entry he made in his diary while in Warsaw in 1939, not long before the Nazi army invaded Poland: "Too many painters, sculptors and architects have represented Italy in Poland in the past. They love in us the poetry of the pen rather than the strength of our arms, in which they still do not completely believe. We must work hard to correct the bad name they have given us for centuries." Like his father-in-law, Ciano also faced an ignoble death when the tides of the war changed. He turned against Mussolini at the end and, and as a result, was accused of treason and imprisoned. He was shot by a firing squad on January 11, 1944.

When the acclamation for their adored Duce had subsided, the crowd quieted, and the house lights dimmed in preparation for our performance. The orchestra began playing the lively musical arrangement of Bizet's opera "Carmen". Our audiences always enjoyed our carefully choreographed dancing to that beautiful and lively music. As we appeared on the stage wearing our black lace costumes, the crowd greeted us with applause in anticipation of our number. We began our performance, based on one of the traditional Flamenco dances that Carmen performs in the opera, and we could feel the energy of the audience enjoying our act. I don't know what impulse prompted me on that particular occasion to remove the carnation from my hair and throw it toward the audience. Perhaps it was because we were feeling so much enthusiasm from the crowd. Perhaps it was because I had been feeling so distraught and nervous at the sight of Benito Mussolini before our performance that I felt a huge relief at actually being able to dance on the stage and this led to my impulsive act.

For whatever reason, I threw my carnation toward the audience, and with totally unintentional aim, it flew straight toward the table where Count Ciano and his companions were dining. To my horror, I saw it land right in the center of his dinner plate. With Alma frowning at me, obviously disapproving of the whole incident,

I managed to regain my composure and finish the dance. From a corner of my eye, I could see Ciano wiping food off the flower with a corner of his napkin. I only dared to look back toward him when the music stopped. I gasped as I realized that he had started to walk toward the stage. He stopped when he was standing right in front of me and then, to the cheers and applause of an amused audience, including Il Duce, he bowed and handed me back my flower. I smiled and curtsied while trying to pin the carnation back in my hair before leaving the stage. I was so flustered, I wasn't able to affix the carnation back in my hair and, now horribly embarrassed, I ran off the stage and went to our dressing room.

It was not long afterward that we heard a knock on our dressing room door. When I opened the door, two bellboys from the casino rushed in, carrying bundles of dozens of roses. In a matter of moments, our dressing room was filled with flowers. I did not have to look at the attached card to know who had sent the flowers. Two large C's were written in black ink on the card.

We went back on the stage to perform the second half of our act and I managed to finish my performance without any incidents. Count Ciano seemed preoccupied with his dinner companions and scarcely looked up at me during my act. To my relief, there were no more flowers or messages from him after the performance. Alma and I went back to our hotel and I tried to erase the memory of Il Duce, Ciano, and their fawning entourage from my mind.

Mussolini departed from Venice the next day, but Ciano stayed behind. I ran into him by chance one evening when Alma and I were dining with friends in a Venice restaurant. After exchanging greetings, he sat down next to me. I could scarcely conceal my embarrassment and the sense of guilt I was feeling just from being in his company. I could not erase from my mind that this was the second most powerful ranking official in fascist Italy, whose government had sided with Franco against the Spanish Republic and helped him win the war, the war in which my father had fought against the Fascists. Count Ciano had the reputation of being a "Don Juan" par excellence. I could now attest to this, as in spite of the company around us, the man was actively trying to seduce me. Because I was a guest at a friend's table, I had to put up a polite and civilized front through the course of the dinner, but I managed to keep my distance from him, barely paying any attention to his conversation and flirtatious comments. My aloofness did seem to disconcert him a bit, and this was a source of some small satisfaction to me.

I could not believe that he would be so persistent, but the following morning the concierge of the little hotel where Alma and I were staying, my friend Signor Lorenzo, came rushing up to our room to tell me that I had an important visitor waiting for me downstairs.

"Signorina Isa," he said, almost breathless with excitement and from running up the stairs to our room, "You will not believe this! It is Count Ciano himself, come to see you!"

"What?" I exclaimed. "What are you talking about? Why would Count Ciano be here. Are you trying to make a joke? Who is here to see me?"

"Signorina, look yourself if you do not believe me."

Signor Lorenzo took my arm and led to the window of our room. I looked out the window and sure enough, there downstairs, next to a shiny new Alfa Romeo sports car was Count Ciano, pacing impatiently by the front door of the hotel. Now I was nervous and not sure how best to behave. The last thing I wanted was to see Count Ciano or have to deal with him in any way.

"Signor Lorenzo," I said as coldly and formally as I could in my distraught condition, "Please go downstairs and tell Count Ciano that I cannot receive him. In fact, tell him I do not wish to receive him."

"Signorina Isa, please! I cannot insult Count Ciano!" Signor Lorenzo implored me, a look of great nervousness now appearing on his face.

"You are not the one insulting him. I am!"

"Please, Signorina, do not ask me to do this. At least come downstairs and receive him."

"No, Signor Lorenzo," I insisted. "I will not come downstairs to see him. But I understand. Please then tell him I am indisposed and cannot see him, that I am not feeling well."

The poor man finally agreed to act as my messenger and returned downstairs to tell Ciano that I could not receive him. When this failed to dissuade him, I sent down a sleepy and by now thoroughly annoyed Alma, who was finally successful in conveying my wishes to be left alone.

"Well?" I asked when she came back upstairs. "Did you ask him to leave me alone?"

"Yes, he will leave you alone now", Alma replied.

"What did you tell him?"

"I told him that you were secretly the mistress of a high-ranking Nationalist official in Spain and that if he were to discover that you were having an affair with Count Ciano, there would be serious diplomatic consequences!"

"Oh no, Alma! You didn't say that!"

"Yes, I did. I'm quite sure he will leave you alone now!"

And then we both burst out giggling and fell on our beds, laughing at the absurdity of the situation. Later, I went downstairs and thanked Signor Lorenzo for his help as my messenger and assured him that Count Ciano would not be returning and that there would be no repercussions.

What amuses now, when I think back on this episode, is how different and perhaps more simple life was in those days. Here was the Secretary of State of Italy, the son in law of the dictator, courting a young Spanish girl whose background was obviously totally unknown to him. Was I just another potential conquest? Would he have sat down at the table with me and pursued me so ardently had he known I was the daughter of a well-known anti-Fascist? Somehow, I doubted it.

For the rest of her life, Venice was one of Isa's favorite cities. Other than the encounter with Mussolini and what she viewed as the absurdity of Count Ciano trying to seduce her, she had nothing but warm memories of the time she and my Aunt Alma spent there. Much later, after the war, she visited Venice often with my father and that became one of their standard destinations for a romantic vacation. She always looked forward to returning to Venice with him, when they would habitually stay at the Hotel Danieli with its lovely views of the Grand Canal and the island of San Giorgio Maggiore. They would go at least once on each trip to the Venice Casino to play baccarat and roulette at the place where my mother had danced during those two weeks.

Chapter 15

Berlin

April 1939
The buildup to World War Two had continued during April. The latest crisis to affect Europe was the Danzig Crisis, centering around that port city on the north coast of Poland, now known as Gdansk. Danzig had formerly been a Prussian city and its population at the time was predominantly ethnically German. After World War One, the Treaty of Versailles had established Danzig as a quasi-independent city-state. It was an enclave within the newly recreated independent country of Poland, the territory of which, until the Treaty of Versailles, had been partitioned between the Kingdom of Prussia (later to be Germany), Russia, and Austria (later to be the Austrian-Hungarian Empire) since 1795. Danzig was to be governed by a local parliament overseen by a High Commissioner appointed by the League of Nations. The city's extensive port facilities were open to both German and Polish use. Danzig was entirely surrounded by Polish territory and the Baltic Sea and had no direct land connection to Germany.

By 1933, over 35% of the Danzig parliament was made up of German Nazi Party members and a significant percentage of the population wished to become part of Germany. In the ensuing years, the anomaly of the Danzig enclave festered with Germany and Poland, with the status quo remaining unsatisfactory for both countries. By the spring of 1939, Hitler had seized upon this as his next cause. The subsequent events became known as the Danzig Crisis.

Hitler's methods and tactics had gradually evolved during the last few years. As he seized more land and as his military grew in size and power, he became more and more willing to risk war. Indeed, by the summer of 1939, he wanted war, but he continued to insist that he would be the one to decide on the timing and location of its outbreak. He had reoccupied the Rhineland and annexed Austria without firing a single shot. It was by now recognized that his military had been unprepared for war at that time, but the western democracies did not call his bluffs. By the time of the Czechoslovakia Crisis, Hitler was still unprepared for war, and his generals advised him not to go to war yet. Nonetheless, he was prepared to risk it if he had to, rather than to be seen as backing down. After Czechoslovakia it was different. He now had access to the significant arms factories of the Czechs, and he had had more time to prepare his forces. Not insignificantly, the battlefields of Spain had of course given his Luftwaffe a chance to learn and perfect the new methods of air warfare, both in air support of ground forces during what came to be known as Blitzkrieg campaigns and in the terror bombing of civilian populations.

Hitler did not want a diplomatic solution for Danzig. He wanted an excuse for war with Poland. The German press maintained a campaign of propaganda about how badly ethnic Germans were treated in Danzig. Through the spring and summer of 1939, he made a series of demands on Poland, calculated to be more than the Poles would be willing to accept, including demanding that Danzig be formally acknowledged as being part of Germany, that a German highway and railway be built to Danzig, this route to comprise a "Danzig Corridor" over which Germany would have rights, and that Poland join the Anti-Comintern Pact with Germany and Italy. Hitler cleverly kept his demands well out of Polish reach, yet close enough to keep negotiations alive. Hitler wanted war, but not just yet, not until he had finished preparing.

On April 28, using Polish intransigence on the Danzig question as an excuse, Hitler announced that he would no longer honor the nonaggression pact that Nazi Germany had signed with Poland in 1934. A few days later, Poland reiterated its staunch refusal to capitulate to Hitler's demands to annex Danzig and the Danzig Corridor. After Hitler's occupation of Czechoslovakia in March, France and Britain had extended a Guarantee of Independence and Mutual Assistance to Poland. Both governments reiterated this support for Poland in the face of likely Nazi aggression during the Danzig Crisis. By now, scarcely seven months after the infamous Munich Accord, Hitler's promise that he would seek no more European territory after the Sudetenland was but a distant memory in the minds of the appeasers.

Berlin

By the time that Alma and I had returned to Paris from Venice, it was almost spring. We did not want our show to become stale and we started thinking about what we could change or add to introduce some variety. We decided also to select a new wardrobe to wear for our new numbers. We went back to see Antonio Arcaráz at his Guelma Studio to ask him if he would help us once again. To our joy, he was as enthusiastic as ever and we started going to see him in the afternoons for lessons to learn new steps and to work on new routines and to rehearse them with him.

That spring in Paris, the last one before the Second World War, was the balmiest and most beautiful that anyone could remember. Along the boulevards, the acacia trees were in bloom and the parks and gardens all over the charming city looked like gigantic mosaics with the abundance of multicolored flowers everywhere. Michel and I took advantage of the lovely weather to take day trips to the country at every opportunity. With the top of his convertible down and a picnic basket on the back seat, we would drive for hours feeling the warmth of the sun and our faces and the spring air enveloping us gently under the blue sky. Driving along tree-lined roads, we would reach Versailles, Fontainebleau, or my favorite, the forest of Vincennes by early afternoon and find a quiet spot to enjoy our picnic lunch. With no one in sight, the kilometers of open country surrounding us seemed to belong exclusively to us. After eating our lunch, we would lounge lazily under the shade of a tree and wait for sunset. As the sky darkened, we would amuse ourselves by counting one by one the tiny stars that would begin appearing in the firmament.

It was during an afternoon at the Guelma Studio that Antonio asked us to wait for him after our lesson because he had important news to discuss with us. As he explained to us, his manager had been working on a deal for him to appear at the Wintergarten Theatre in Berlin. Antonio was proposing to us that we join him to form a trio with him. He suggested that as a trio, we could perform not only in Berlin, but after Berlin in other European capitals as well.

Alma and I discussed the opportunity. On the one hand, the thought of going to Nazi Germany was horrifying. It had been bad enough to simply transit the country the year earlier on our way to and from Poland. We still remembered how horrifying had been that search of our papers on the way back to France, when my mother had forged the date on them with her eyeliner pencil. On the other hand, a partnership with Antonio could be the springboard our dancing careers needed to really launch us into international success. Certainly, there would be great advantages in partnering with Antonio. He was a well-known and highly respected dancer, several notches above Alma and me in fame and prestige. He was always in great demand throughout the theatrical world and was far better equipped than Alma or I to deal with agents and negotiate details like salaries, working conditions, and so on, which Alma and I had to confront every time we signed a contract. As young girls, we knew we were often taken advantage of in these commercial matters, but there was little we could do about it.

After a few days, perhaps inevitably, Alma and I agreed to accept his offer. Within a week, the duo "Alma and Isa Reyes" had become the "Trio Arcaráz". We began rehearsing in earnest, as Antonio explained that we had to be ready to perform in Berlin by a certain date in the third week of April.

My relationship with Antonio, first as his student and now as his dancing partner, had always been excellent. The same could not be said about his relationship with Alma. Their relationship when she was his student had been as smooth as mine had been. Now that we were partners, she was less willing to listen to any criticism and would take personally any suggestions he offered her on how to improve her performance. Worse, she began to offer him suggestions on how to improve the choreography, a domain which he considered absolutely to be his own.

The two of them were now always arguing and would become furious with each other over the merest trifle. When their arguments became overheated, I would simply walk away and sit with our pianist, an elderly Spaniard of impeccable manners and calm disposition. He would offer me one of his cigarettes, which I would smoke in silence as I sat with him, the two of us waiting for the storm to pass so we could resume our rehearsal. They would stop fighting, rehearsal would resume, and then at some point, amidst the clacking of the castanets, they would renew their quarrel and start throwing insults at each other again. If we had already resumed dancing when their argument inevitably renewed, they would continue their verbal assaults on each other while continuing to tap their feet without missing a step or losing the tempo of the dance. In spite of this bellicose and somewhat disconcerting atmosphere, the three of us managed to prepare for our debut as a trio, our dance numbers choreographed to the last detail and practiced until we had polished them perfectly.

Antonio had marvelous taste in selecting our new dance numbers as well as the music to accompany them. He also had exquisite taste in choosing our new costumes. He bought these for us himself, spending a small fortune to make sure our costumes were perfect, with beautiful long dresses and the matching shoes and accessories all made to order. Antonio was gay, but one would never have guessed this from his dancing. On stage or during rehearsals, he would appear to be lusting after his female dance partners with a fiery hunger and passion that he articulated almost erotically with his flamenco steps. When dancing with Alma and me at the same time, he would appear to be lusting after both of us simultaneously and manage to convey the impression that even the two of us would not be enough to satisfy him!

One morning, we were asked to attend a meeting at Antonio's manager's office. As we entered the room, we sensed that this was to do with something important. He carefully closed the door behind him, sat back down at his desk, and nervously rubbed his hands together for several seconds before saying anything. When we heard him explain the reason that we had to be in Berlin and ready to perform by a specific date, we were shocked and astounded at the reason. In my case, I was greatly disturbed as well. There was going to be a gala performance at the Wintergarten Theatre as a part of and as the culmination of the festivities that were going to be held in Berlin during the third week of April. The occasion? Adolph Hitler's fiftieth birthday celebration!

I was aghast at this news and announced that there was absolutely no way that I would agree to perform for that monster on the occasion of his birthday. It had been bad enough to perform for Mussolini in Venice! This would be horribly worse!

I was terribly upset, especially as it dawned on me what the symbolism of a performance of Spanish dancers at this event would be. It was meant to demonstrate solidarity between the Nazi regime of Hitler and the Spanish Nationalist forces of Franco, and this shortly after my father had left Spain for exile, defeated after risking his life fighting against the fascists. It was like a kick in the stomach for me. In tears, I left the office and collapsed into a chair in the waiting room.

Alma had somewhat less political consciousness than I did and really had always been more sympathetic to the Nationalist cause anyway, although she was always careful not to say this too much in my presence. She could only view this as a tremendous career opportunity for us and it was inconceivable to her that I would consider not taking advantage of it. For the next two hours, she and Antonio tried to persuade me to accompany them, but I obstinately refused. Finally, Antonio gently reminded me that I had signed a contract to be part of the Trio Arcaráz and that this meant accepting all the bookings. I tried to be released from the contract, but to no avail. In the end, emotionally exhausted and drained of resistance, I agreed, and I too signed my name at the bottom of the booking agreement prepared by Antonio's manager.

When Michel learned about the whole situation, he was as distressed as I was. During our last evening together before I left for Berlin, he tried his best to cheer me up. Darling Michel, I must have looked terribly unhappy to him, for he proposed to marry me immediately and have him stay with him and forget about going to Berlin. "Don't worry about the contract, mon amour," he said. "We shall hire a lawyer and extricate you from this horrible commitment." I am sure he felt greatly relieved, though, when I did not accept his offer. Michel and I loved each other, but we had known for a long time we were destined to be friends more than husband and wife. "You know we shouldn't marry, Michel. We will talk about this all when I come back," I promised him.

On a sunny April Paris morning, the Trio Arcaráz, accompanied by a small mountain of luggage and trunks containing our multiple changes of costumes arrived at the Gare de l'Est and boarded the express train to Berlin. For Alma, this would be her first and last tour with Antonio and me on the stage. Now that the civil war had ended, with Franco and his Nationalists the victors, Alma was growing increasingly anxious to join her mother and her sister Nanita, who had just returned to Spain to live in Madrid. Antonio agreed to let her out of her contract provided she honored the commitment at the Wintergarten in Berlin. After our planned two weeks in Germany, Alma planned to return to Spain to continue her career as a solo dancer there. That was why it was so important for her to get the publicity that the Berlin performances were expected to generate for us. For me, of course, it was a different story. With my father now in exile, I had to erase from my mind any thought of returning to Spain any time soon. Antonio and I would continue as a duo after Berlin. I agreed to this, as long as after those two weeks, we would not stay in Germany.

Our train sped its way across France. The three of us were uncharacteristically silent for most of the journey, each of us preoccupied as we were with our thoughts. On reaching the French–German frontier, we were assailed by the familiar fear and apprehension that we had felt on previous occasions, although this time our travel documents were in order with valid dates. Our fears were heightened by the sight of so many Gestapo officials and German border guards boarding the train and staring at all the passengers with their hard and cold eyes while they demanded to inspect papers and searched luggage. We went through the anguish of answering dozens of questions from these hard men and resisted the temptation to say something like, "How dare you hold us up or question us, we are here to provide the birthday entertainment for your precious Fuhrer!" Finally, they stamped our documents and allowed us to continue our journey, exiting our cabin with a loud "Heil Hitler" at which we nodded because we were afraid to do otherwise.

As we continued our journey, now in Germany, I repeatedly called Antonio's attention to join me at the window, pointing out to him the seemingly endless rows of military equipment lined along the fields next to the train tracks. Between each pair of towns, we could see masses of heavy equipment, including what looked like tanks and cannons, covered by canvas, as well as different types of aircraft parked in neat rows at the several airfields that looked like they had been recently built near the tracks.

"I am telling you, Isa, it is a good thing that apparently the war has been averted for now," Antonio said to me. "Imagine what the Germans could do with all that arsenal!"

When we reached Cologne, we stepped off the train and into the station to stretch our legs and buy some food, hardly able to make our way through the crowded platform. Returning back to our compartment, we were distressed to see that it had been practically taken over by German soldiers. By now, there were hardly any civilians on board, and we had the eerie feeling that we had somehow boarded a military transport by mistake. The soldiers in our compartment were coldly polite, in an arrogant sort of way, as they made room for us to sit and then continued their conversation in a guttural German that was utterly incomprehensible to me.

Arriving finally at the German capital, we were met at the train station by one of the Wintergarten Theatre's artistic directors, who led us outside to a waiting limousine. We realized that we really were being given the full "star" or VIP treatment. This was confirmed when our host informed us that rooms had been booked for us at the luxurious Hotel Adlon, a center of Berlin social life and a favorite of the Nazi elite. Our rooms were indeed luxurious and from the large windows we could see the nearby Brandenburg Gate and the lovely Tiergarten park nearby.

We rose early the following morning to attend our first rehearsal at the Wintergarten. It took Antonio forever to convince the chauffeur sent to fetch us that we would rather walk the short distance from the hotel to the theatre than ride in the car. It seemed that he finally understood when he stepped aside to let us go. It was a beautiful sunny morning and it felt good to be strolling along the sidewalk of the broad Unter den Linden boulevard. We were surprised and somewhat amused when we noticed that the limousine was following us at a slow pace, staying just a few meters behind us all the way to the Wintergarten.

Arriving at the theatre after a short walk, we could see our names prominently displayed on the marquée near the entrance, as well as photographs of us and other artists, under glass and placed along the walls next to the front entrance.

The theatre was enormous, and the stage was gigantic, much larger than any place Alma or I had ever performed. After our initial shock at the sheer proportions of the place, we were barely ready for a second shock: listening to our Spanish music being played not by a lone pianist or a small string orchestra, but by an orchestra comprising over forty musicians, many of them playing brass horns and trumpets. The subtle and delicate music of Albeniz and Granados was being blared now under the direction of the baton of a musical conductor who stood ramrod straight and had a demeanor more fitting to a Prussian general than a musician. It sounded more like a Wagnerian march than our accustomed Spanish melodies, but after three days of rehearsals and after getting used to the stage, we had to admit that our music sounded gloriously magnificent when played in this manner by such an impressive orchestra. Perhaps this was the main reason that the

Berlin press gave us such favorable reviews and perhaps the "Germanization" of our music accounted for much of our success during this time in Berlin. Newspapers published favorable reviews of the new Wintergarten revue, with special praise for "the outstanding performance of the Trio Arcaráz." Antonio was thrilled and was already talking about the great future he and I would have as a duo, perhaps one day even crossing the Atlantic and conquering the American audiences!

It was a nice dream, but the sad reality was that almost everyone in Europe now felt that war was inevitable. Our days were filled with fear and anxiety. These were the last few months of a precarious peace. The air was filled with tension and in our minds was the ever-present thought that war could break out at any moment and shatter all our dreams.

The man who ruled Germany at that time, their Führer, was a maniac, a dangerous individual who could no longer be trusted by any of the European powers. Through bluster and bluff, he had acquired territory without firing a single shot. More importantly, he had bought himself the time to finish re-arming Germany so that if war did come, it would come at a time of his choosing, when he was fully ready for it. Despite his reputation in the rest of Europe, in Germany he seemed to be worshipped everywhere and by everyone. His photograph was displayed prominently everywhere we visited. When his never-ending speeches were broadcast on the radio, all of Berlin seemed to come to a standstill so that the people could listen spellbound to his words for hours. Crowds would gather in the middle of the street, where tall towers with loudspeakers had been erected, to listen to and hang on to his every word. The voice that came through those loudspeakers sounded shrill and disagreeable in the extreme to me. In fact, I found his voice unpleasant to such a degree that I simply could not comprehend how that horrible sound of a human voice could mesmerize his listeners to the extent that it apparently did. To hear all that shouting, punctuated by the repeated "Sieg Heils" and "Heil Hitlers" of his multitude of worshippers was an annoying and frightening experience. I simply could not comprehend it. "What a bore this man Hitler is," I concluded. "He is an ugly man and most probably he is a mean person as well."

At my tender age – I was not quite eighteen years old at the time – I could not begin to perceive the depths of evil and depravity to which he and his followers would sink in the months and years to come.

After our nightly performance one evening, we were all called backstage by the theatre's "Herr Direktor." Alma and I, still in full costume and makeup, hurried to join Antonio and we sat down next to him. Already gathered there were the other performers: the outstanding gymnasts from Japan, the opera singers from the La Scala opera house in Milan, "Herr Gluck", the famous and beloved German clown, and the rest of the cast of the revue. Herr Direktor was visibly beside himself as he began to tell us what would be in store for us the following night. The theatre would be closed to the public, he went on to explain in his heavily accented French, and Hitler himself would be the guest of honor accompanied by his fellow high-ranking Nazis and the Diplomatic Corps, to commemorate and celebrate his birthday. Herr Direktor was clearly awed at the opportunity to entertain his beloved Fuhrer, whom he worshipped, and his entourage. As we returned to our dressing rooms, we noticed that the stagehands were already busy placing huge Nazi banners alongside the stage and red flags with the odious swastika were being raised all over the theatre.

When the special, and to me dreaded, night arrived, the sense of excitement at the Wintergarten was unbelievable. It was almost palpable. When I began to change into my costume, I could not hide my nervousness. We could hear the pounding of boot-wearing feet entering the theatre. When I snuck a peek at the Orchestra section, my blood ran cold and I felt the blood draining from my face. The sight in front of me sent shivers of fear through m spine. Throngs of men in uniforms were rapidly filling up the theatre. Khaki-colored uniforms were in the majority, but the front rows were filled by important and sinister looking men, straight-backed and cold-eyed in their black uniforms and polished black jackboots. Just the sight of these SS officers and the clearly high-ranking Gestapo officers seated among them was enough to almost paralyze me in terror.

Suddenly there arose a tremendous roar from the audience and the crowd that filled the vast room rose to their feet as if they were one person, their backs to the stage and their right arms outstretched in the Nazi salute, greeting their Fuhrer, who just at that moment was entering one of the boxes at Mezzanine level. Hitler stood there for a long time, acknowledging the greetings of his men. The scene is imprinted in my memory like a nightmare, the sight of all those fanatical human beings clamoring for their leader. What a strange and terror-inducing spectacle that was.

When we appeared on stage, we were received with wild applause. The audience enjoyed our show so much that they demanded encores and even after the second and final encore, the applause and the shouts of "bravo" continued. As the applause continued, I turned my glance for a moment to the box where the guest of honor was sitting. I stared at Hitler for a split second before averting my gaze. There he was, the most feared man in the world, applauding and obviously enjoying himself. The whole cast remained on stage while the German national anthem was played, "Deutschland Uber Alles." The cast enthusiastically returned the crowd's Nazi salutes at the conclusion of the anthem. All except for Antonio and me, which earned us a stiff reprimand from Herr Direktor afterward.

We had been told that absolutely no excuses would be accepted for not attending the reception that was taking place at the Chancellery after the show. We changed out of our performance costumes and into evening wear. Then the whole theatrical company from the Wintergarten gathered by the main door of the theatre and we were whisked away by cars. When we arrived at the Chancellery, a group of young soldiers ushered us inside and we entered a large room where a buffet table laden with food had been set up along a wall. For the first time, I noticed that in addition to all the scary looking men, mostly in uniform, there had been women in the audience as well and that they were all elegantly dressed, mingling easily with the crowd.

I had purchased an expensive evening gown for the occasion at a fashionable boutique on the Kurfürstendamm in the heart of Berlin's shopping district. I knew it was becoming on me by the enthusiastic comments from Antonio when he first saw me trying it on in front of a mirror. It was a simple white satin dress, very fitted to my body and with a low back. Alma, as always, looked stunning, tonight in her emerald green gown. Antonio, elegantly handsome in his dinner jacket, drew appreciative glances and comments from the ladies.

Someone had mentioned to me earlier that most of the German artists of the theatre and the screen would be present tonight. I was still somewhat discomfited by the presence of so many Nazi uniforms and I wasn't paying a great deal of attention to our theatre manager, the Herr Direktor, as he kept pointing out to me "the most powerful and mighty" among the guests, most of them people I had never heard of. Instead, I was preoccupied trying to catch a glimpse of Gustav Froelich, the German actor and director whom I had seen on the movie screen when I was a young girl in Madrid. I knew he was at this reception and I was excited at the opportunity to see a film idol of my childhood in the flesh. And finally, there I saw him, surrounded by a throng of women admirers. I was able to insert myself into the circle around him and introduce myself and tell him how much I admired his work. He bowed gracefully and kissed my hand and told me how much he had enjoyed my dance performance earlier that evening. So that evening was not a total loss for me after all!

The French ambassador to Berlin at that time was an old and dear friend of my father's. He and his wife were delighted at seeing me in Berlin and as an accomplished performer at that. He reminisced with me about the last time he had seen me, which had been in Madrid at my parents' house. I was wearing my school uniform then, with my hair still in braids. It was hard to believe that scarcely three years had gone by since then. He insisted that Antonio, Alma, and I attend a reception he was hosting for foreign dignitaries at the French embassy. Antonio and I accepted, but Alma excused herself, as she was at that time being courted and escorted all over Berlin by a dashing German diplomat with whom she was spending all of her spare time.

The evening of the French ambassador's reception, Antonio and I stepped out of the Hotel Adlon and began walking the short distance down Unter den Linden in the direction of the embassy, enjoying the cool evening breeze and the sight of the Berliners strolling happily among the sidewalk cafés. Once we arrived at the embassy, we became separated from each other. I had given up looking for him to rejoin him when I caught sight of him carrying on a lively conversation with a group of effeminate-looking young men. I left him to enjoy the company of his new friends and went to sit down on a sofa at the corner of the salon room. Before long, I found myself surrounded by a group of Italians. Luckily, I spoke a passable Italian and I was able to converse with them. Behind me, I heard the sound of a familiar voice, and as I turned around, I came face to face with Count Ciano.

I had not seen him since rebuffing his amorous advances in Venice less than two months earlier. He had an amused look of surprise on his face as he bent to kiss my hand. We chatted for a while and I was conscious that we were being watched by everyone present. Ciano seemed older than I remembered, an embittered expression seeming to cast a shadow over his face. I felt extremely uncomfortable in his presence. Too many things were happening in the political arena of the world now to ignore the reality that he too belonged to that group of individuals, contemptible at best, who apparently were determined to bring misery and total chaos to the world. The orchestra was playing in the adjacent room, but I turned down his invitation to dance and instead I excused myself and stood up to leave when I saw Antonio approaching with my coat under his arm.

That was the last time I saw Count Ciano. He would remain in power some years longer, but he was doomed and in the end his name would be added to the list of other names, the memory of those evil men of the twentieth century, their memories forever etched in infamy.

For the rest of her life, Isa would refer to that performance on Hitler's birthday as "looking out from the stage and seeing the gallery of Twentieth Century evil spread in front of me." She would shake visibly whenever she recounted the events of that evening and tried to describe what it felt like. I think it became even harder for her as the years passed and all the world came to learn what barbarities and atrocities those fanatics had in fact proved capable of committing. Those would have seemed inconceivable at the time, especially to an eighteen-year-old girl. In particular, she would refer to the memory of seeing the monstrously fat Goering, who as head of the Luftwaffe had coordinated the flyers of the Condor Legion who learned the business of terror bombing of civilians by bombing defenseless Spanish villages, and the twisted little monster Goebbels, whose propaganda had helped to fuel such hatred and vile actions. She could never speak of this without questioning how the "civilized world", the western democracies, had allowed this to happen and had not stopped Hitler when they could have.

Decades later, I visited Berlin myself several times and went on several long walks trying to recreate the paths my mother would have taken. I walked past the Adlon Hotel and the Brandenburg Gate and took long walks in the Tiergarten, that beautiful park in the center of Berlin that she had told me about. I got very excited to see that the Wintergarten Theatre still existed and wanted to go see a show in it to imagine what it must have been like when my mother performed there, but I lost interest when I found out that it was a new Wintergarten Theatre, in a completely new location. The most memorable sight I saw in Berlin was at Bebelplatz, a short walk down Unter den Linden from the Adlon Hotel. This was the site of the first official Nazi book burning, held in May 1933. I consider the memorial there one of the most touching memorials I have seen anywhere in the world, and I know that my mother would have been as touched by it as I always am when I visit it. One looks through a glass window and sees an empty library, with row upon row of empty bookshelves. Inscribed by the window is the quote from Heinrich Heine: "Das war ein Vorspiel nur, dort wo man Bücher verbrennt, verbrennt man am Ende auch Menschen." ("That was only a prelude. Where they burn books, in the end they will also burn people.")

Chapter 16

A Trip to Greece

Summer and Autumn 1939

The Danzig Crisis continued to escalate while Isa was in Berlin. Hitler continued his bellicose posturing and his demands, knowing that Poland would never agree to them. The German propaganda machine continued its constant denunciations of purported injustices being committed against the German population of Danzig. Meanwhile, Poland remained adamant in its refusal to accede to the German demands and moved to formalize and strengthen its defense guarantees from Britain and France. Europe seemed to be marching inexorably toward war. It now seemed only a question of when the war would begin, not if it would begin. Hitler continued to masterfully stall for time until the timing of war most suited him.

Europe remained on the verge of war throughout the summer of 1939. On August 23, the entire world was shocked to learn that the Soviet Union and Nazi Germany had signed a treaty, which became known by the names of their respective Foreign Ministers as the Molotov–Ribbentrop Pact. The formal name of this neutrality pact was the Treaty of Non-Aggression between Germany and the Union of Soviet Socialist Republics. This pact provided a written guarantee of peace by each country toward the other and an explicit agreement that neither country would in any way join an alliance with or provide aid to an enemy of the other.

In addition to the public declarations of non-aggression, the Molotov–Ribbentrop Pact contained secret protocols, or addenda, defining each other's sphere of influence in the region. In effect, this pact gave Hitler a free hand in Poland as far as the Soviet Union was concerned, with the secret proviso that Stalin was entitled to take a portion of eastern Poland as and when he wished. The immediate effect of this treaty was that Hitler could now invade Poland if he wished, without the fear of a two-front war.

"Miss Spain in Exile"

In response to the Molotov–Ribbentrop Pact, on August 25 Poland and Britain signed a mutual defense treaty formalizing Britain's obligation to come to war, if necessary, for Poland's defense. France had already promised in a treaty with Poland, signed in May, that if Germany were to attack Poland, France would in turn attack Germany within fifteen days of the German attack on Poland.

Poland deferred mobilizing its military until the last possible moment, in an attempt to prevent being blamed for the outbreak of hostilities. It would not have mattered. Although the Polish army was the fifth largest in Europe, including an army of a million men with almost 500 tanks, it was unprepared for modern warfare. It still included many horse-mounted cavalry units. The Polish army fought gallantly when the war inevitably came, but it never stood a chance against Hitler's Wehrmacht and the Luftwaffe.

On September 1, 1939, Hitler invaded Poland. World War Two had begun.

The reminder of our time in Berlin passed uneventfully. We still had a few more nights of performances at the Wintergarten, and when they were concluded, Alma and Antonio and I boarded the express train back to Paris. It was raining when we arrived at the French border. The soldiers and Gestapo entered our train and began going compartment to compartment to look at everyone's papers. Crossing the German border at the French frontier was as nerve-wracking as before, just because the soldiers and Gestapo staring at us and examining our papers looked so cold and ruthless.

They would approach each passenger and say "Ausweis, bitte!" ("ID card, please!") and though the tone of their voices was neutral, almost polite, their faces, especially their cold eyes, were so menacing that those words induced fear in anyone. Especially from the Gestapo, all of them in their uniform of long, black coat and fedora hat.

On the platform, there were soldiers in uniform standing guard to prevent anyone from sneaking off the train undetected. They had their dogs on leashes, German shepherds, but the dogs had been trained to snarl and look menacing and this added to the intimidating sensation that they wanted to create.

Our papers were in order and we were able to re-enter France with no problems. We were nervous enough this time that when our inspection was over and the soldiers and Gestapo raised their right hands in the Nazi salute and said "Heil Hitler" as they departed, we nodded and managed to mumble a "Heil Hitler" in return. The words stuck in my throat and I almost became sick to my stomach as I said them out loud. The officials left our compartment and the three of us sat back in our seats and sighed in relief.

Other than the attack of nerves, and the distraught feelings of utter helplessness that these men could induce – and that obviously was their intention – we were able to leave Germany and re-enter France with no problems.

The same could not be said for several unfortunate passengers, men, women, and children, who for whatever reason were not allowed to exit Germany. We watched from our compartment window as they were led off the train into the rain and then were herded into the small station under armed guard. These poor people looked terrified and I was horrified to think about what their fate might be. It brought back the awful memory of when we had crossed that same border just the previous year, with the forged dates on our papers, and what could have happened to us if we had been caught.

Years later, when we were living in California, our younger son wanted to have a dog, as his older sister and brother had had. For some reason, probably a television show or movie he had seen, he wanted a German shepherd. I took him to look at some at a kennel which specialized in raising and training German shepherds, and when I saw these dogs, I had the same reaction as when my son had come home wearing a long, black leather coat and it reminded me of the dreaded Gestapo. The sight of those dogs evoked a memory of those trained dogs in the hands of the Nazi soldiers and I was gripped by a visceral memory of terror that, try as I might, I could not control. In the end, we got him a Dalmatian puppy.

Curiously, probably because she had not traveled to Berlin with me and so did not share this memory, my sister Nuria did not share this fear of German shepherds. In fact, she raised several from puppies in her home in Mexico City in the years after the war and usually had at least one German shepherd, and sometimes several, sharing her home with her. She tended to name them after obscure Asturian poets, which was always a source of great amusement to the rest of us.

"Miss Spain in Exile"

We arrived back in Paris and Antonio and I immediately set to work developing and rehearsing our act as a duo. With Alma leaving, of course, we would no longer be the Trio Arcaráz. I enjoyed working with Antonio, who by now was treating me like the younger sister he had never had. We spent hours every day at the Studio Guelma trying out new ideas and rehearsing. He always listened to my opinion and began to give me a chance to contribute my ideas to our choreography.

Alma was leaving to return to Spain soon and I knew that our farewell was going to be a sad and painful one. We had become very close and after all the difficult times we had endured together, we had developed a love and mutual respect beyond the normal bond between cousins. It was an emotional experience for both of us to part company, after sharing so many happy moments, as well as some unhappy ones, during the years we had been living, traveling, and performing together.

We had been back from Berlin for less than a week, when the day came for Aunt Encarna, Alma, and Nanita to leave for Spain. Michel drove us all to the train station to see them off. We were all crying at the thought that we did not know when or even whether we would ever see each other again. Even little Moineau, usually so happy, seemed sad, as though he understood what this goodbye meant. As their train left the platform, we stood and waved goodbye until we could not see them any longer and Michel drove us all back to our apartment in the hotel on Rue Daru. The apartment now seemed too big for just the three of us and we knew it would be sad to stay there now without the company of the rest of our family. Mother and Nuria and I agreed that we would start looking for a new place to live the next day and Michel of course offered to help us.

The next morning was a beautiful spring day, as only Paris can have. The sky was a brilliant blue and the sun was shining and as I walked from the Metro to the Studio Guelma, I felt that this was going to be a special day. When I walked into the studio, Antonio immediately said, "Isa, I have great news! We are going to Greece and then to Egypt!"

"What? What are you talking about? Why are we going to Greece and Egypt? To dance?"

"Yes, of course to dance! What did you think, to join the circus?"

Antonio went on to explain that our agent had arranged for a tour

A Trip to Greece

of several months, first as the top-billed show in a nightclub and casino in Athens and then in clubs in Cairo and Alexandria. It was exciting news and I couldn't wait to go home later to tell Mother and Nuria. I just hoped we could all go together.

"My mother and Nuria can come, can't they?" I asked Antonio. "I don't want to be away from them for so long."

"Of course," he replied. "Why not?"

When I got home that afternoon, I excitedly told Mother and Nuria the news. They were delighted and we all agreed that we would go together. We would be leaving in just a few weeks, so now we didn't have to look for a new place to live after all. We could just stay in our hotel with the Russians until it was time to leave for Greece.

Antonio and I changed our stage name once more. From then on, we would be known as "Antonio y Isa" and as such we would debut our new two-person act on the trip that had been booked for us to perform in Greece and Egypt. We continued working on our act until we had agreed on the numbers that we would perform, with enough variety that we could change the show from time to time to avoid becoming stale.

Antonio knew Athens well, for he had visited it a couple of times in the past when he was a dancer with "Les Ballets de Monte Carlo". He kept describing to me how unbelievably beautiful Greece was but on one occasion he added, "But you know, Isa, the only thing I am afraid of is that one day you are going to fall in love with one of those handsome Greeks and I will lose you forever! How will I ever find another dancing partner as lovely as you?" We had no way of knowing this at the time, but before the year was over, Antonio's prophecy would be fulfilled.

Michel was heartbroken when he learned that we were going to be separated for over six months. We had remained fond of each other and had continued seeing each other often. Although he had never again mentioned the word "marriage", we were the best of friends and we continued to enjoy each other's company as much as ever. But lately, whenever we were together, our hearts would grow heavy with the thought that after I left Paris, we might not ever see each other again. Who could know what would happen in Europe and whether I would even be able to return to Paris?

One had only to go the movies and watch the newsreels of the week to be reminded how uncertain the situation in Europe was.

We would leave the theatre disturbed at the sight of Hitler's soldiers goose-stepping in unison in what seemed to be the endless military parades in German cities and towns. It was frightening to hear, inside the dimly lit movie hall, the noise of so many boots treading heavily on pavement as they marched through city streets. Austria and Czechoslovakia had already been occupied. Few people doubted that Poland would be next. One could feel the peace in Europe coming to an end.

Nuria had finished her school year at the Lycée with honors and, like me, she was excited at the idea of going to Greece. At the last minute, Antonio's mother, who also lived in Paris, in the room above her son's dance studio, had decided to come along also. She made arrangements to rent a villa on Glyfada Beach, a few kilometers south of Athens, where we could go to be together on the beach when our work schedule allowed. Our agent began making preparations for all of us to travel to Greece.

It would be the height of summer when we would arrive in Athens. I was looking forward to the chance to be near the sea, away from the heat and humidity of Paris that were becoming so oppressive. For me, it seemed like a vacation trip and I was delighted that my mother and sister Nuria were going to share the adventure with me.

When the evening of our departure arrived, Michel, always the gallant gentleman, drove us to the Gare de Lyon to catch the train for Marseille, where we would board our boat for Athens. He helped us to put our luggage into our compartment, then asked me to step out onto the platform with him so that we could say goodbye.

"I will see you when I come back to Paris, Michel. I promise," I said as I prepared to give him a last kiss goodbye.

"Conchita, ma chérie, I do not think you will be coming back to Paris. Not for a long time anyway. A war over Poland is unavoidable. Will it start this week or next month or in three months, who knows? But it will start. Then France will be at war with Germany, and who knows how long this will last.

Michel took my hands in his and looked intently into my eyes as he continued.

"Any day now, I will be mobilized again for the coming war and who knows where I will be sent?"

I knew in my heart that Michel was right in his prediction.

A Trip to Greece

"And anyway, my Conchita," he continued, "Any day now your father will send for you to join him in the New World and you will go there. Whatever happens, I will survive this madness and I will see you again. Someday, in someplace. Until then, do not forget your Michel."

With that, we said goodbye and kissed one last time. His letters to me became more and more infrequent and it was only later, after the war, that I learned he had in fact survived the conflagration of Europe when I ran into him by chance at a mutual friend's apartment in New York and learned that he had by then married the heiress to the Schrafft chocolate empire. Michel had never lost his talent for living a charmed life.

Our train left Paris and we arrived in Marseille in the early morning. It was a sunny day, with the bright sunlight reflecting off the too blue to be real waters of the Mediterranean. We spent the morning exploring Marseille, especially the bustling Canebière, the main street in the heart of Marseille's historic center, and had a lunch of delicious bouillabaisse, the hearty fish stew for which Marseille is rightly famous. From the edge of the port, we could see where the small liner, *The City of Cairo*, was anchored, scheduled to depart for Greece, with us on board, the next day. We found a small hotel and settled in for the afternoon. That evening, we went for another long walk along the Canebière, soaking in and enjoying the exotic atmosphere of Marseille. The next morning, we boarded *The City of Cairo* for our journey to Greece.

The City of Cairo was one of the many small liners, overgrown yachts really, that cruised the waters of the Mediterranean in those days, taking small groups of passengers from port to port in relative comfort. Our salary for our upcoming performances in Greece was such that we splurged and opted to travel first class on the voyage from Marseille to Athens. It was nice to set off on this adventure traveling in luxury! It was a delightful voyage. After departing Marseille, we made a short stop in Genoa. From there, we traveled south and after another short stop at a small port in Corsica, we sailed eastward through the Straits of Bonifacio. From the deck, we could see the beautiful islands of Corsica on our left and Sardinia on our right. The weather was beautiful and sunny and the sea incredibly calm for the entire time we were at sea. We were able to spend hours walking around the deck, enjoying the sights, or sitting in comfortable chairs on the deck, taking the sun and reading.

There were a few more short stops in ports along the way, and then one afternoon we arrived at Piraeus, Athens' port. The summer heat was almost unbearable, but the sight of the old, beautiful city of Athens, seen in the distance through a shimmering light that was almost diaphanous, was soul stirring. As we approached the city in our taxi, a glorious sunset bathed the Acropolis in fiery colors, the marble temple of the Parthenon atop the hill reflecting the lights of sunset and looking too beautiful to be real.

Antonio and I had been booked to dance at a nightclub in central Athens near Syntagma Square. It was a small and intimate club with a polite audience, and we enjoyed our performances there as the evening floorshow. We were scheduled to perform there five nights a week and our plan was to stay in a small hotel near the nightclub on days we were performing and escape to the house Antonio's mother had rented on the beach during our days off.

As Antonio had prophesied, or perhaps it was written in the stars, shortly after arriving in Athens I met the man, the "handsome Greek", who would steal me away. I met him on the third evening of dancing in Athens. I came out on stage and my gaze was immediately drawn to a handsome man, elegantly dressed in a white suit and sitting at a table just in front of the stage with two friends, equally elegant and well-dressed. He looked a bit like the French actor Charles Boyer, on whom I had had a bit of crush, and through my entire performance he kept his intense brown eyes focused on me. I was a bit disappointed when I returned to the stage after our short intermission that he was no longer at his table, and oddly relieved when only a minute or so into the second half of our act, he reappeared and sat back down. Almost without thinking about it, I caught his eye and smiled at him and when he smiled back, a strange feeling passed over me. I kept my eyes locked on his for the rest of my performance.

When I returned to my dressing room at the conclusion of my act, it was full of flowers, bouquets of red roses. At first, I thought, "Oh no! Not another repeat of the Count Ciano fiasco!" But attached to one of the bouquets of flowers was a note asking me if I would do Mr. Nicolopoulos the honor of joining him for lunch at the Hotel Grande Bretagne the next day, accompanied by a suitable chaperone of course. The next day, Mother accompanied me as my chaperone, and we went to lunch. The rest of the story was preordained.

A Trip to Greece

We began having lunch together almost every day and before long we were spending every spare minute that we had together. During my days off, he would come with us to the beach house that Antonio's mother had rented, or he would take all of us to Kifisia, the green suburb outside of Athens, to escape the city heat and breathe fresh air in Kifisia's famous park.

To my delight, he got along very well with Mother and with Nuria. He treated my mother with an elaborate old-world courtesy which she appreciated and thoroughly enjoyed, and he adopted Nuria as though she were a younger sister to take care of. He never really stopped treating Nuria this way, even years later when Nuria was a grown woman with children of her own.

This was George, the man whom I would fall deeply in love and later marry. He became my husband, the father of our three children, and above all, my companion and best friend for over thirty-five years. But my wedding day was still in the distant future, two years to be exact from that hot day in July when I first set foot on Greek soil and met my future husband. The wheels of fate turned, and we were swept in and caught by events we could not control. It would be in faraway Cuba where George and I, after leaving a war-torn Europe behind us in separate ways, would reunite and never leave each other again. Not until death.

George Nicolopoulos was indeed a remarkable man. He had been born in 1903 in a village on the Peloponnesus Peninsula of Greece, a village so small that it appeared on very few maps. Through sheer intelligence and force of will, he had made himself an educated gentleman. He came to America as a young man, learning English and completing high school in one year in San Francisco, then enrolled at Berkeley to study architecture. Unfortunately, this was in the late 1920's, when the United States was using a strict quota system to limit the number of immigrants from southern Europe, and he did not have the proper papers. During his second year at Berkeley, he was caught and deported back to Europe. Settling in Paris, he found a job as a bellman at a Paris hotel and resumed his studies, now at the Sorbonne. As it happened, one of the resident guests at the hotel at the time was the Greek writer Nikos Kazantzakis, who befriended George and used to feed him in exchange for his listening to drafts of Zorba as it was being written. He never forgot this kindness and he remained a loyal reader and admirer of Kazantzakis for the rest of his life.

When he returned to Greece, he made the first of the many fortunes that he would make and lose during his adventurous life. By the time I met him, he was a successful businessman, having acquired several concessions to represent Czechoslovakian businesses in the Balkans and in Egypt. That is what had caused him to be in Prague on the day of the infamous Munich Betrayal.

While I was in Athens, Hitler invaded Poland. Britain and France declared war on Germany and Hitler declared war on them in return. Mussolini's Italy remained neutral in the conflict between the Allies and Germany until June 1940, when he too declared war on France and Britain. The nightmare everyone had been fearing, and which in retrospect can be seen as having been inevitable, had arrived. The world war had begun.

Three months after the day of our arrival in Athens, George and I became engaged to be married. The hardest thing for me was to tell Antonio that I was quitting dancing and consequently that I would not continue with him on the next stop of our tour, scheduled to be Egypt. I had never seen Antonio cry before, and I was also moved to tears when we said our final farewells and he and his mother departed for Alexandria. He had become more than my dance partner and teacher. He really had become more like a brother to me. It was difficult to say goodbye to him. Like all the goodbyes during that terrible time, we said goodbye not knowing if we would ever see each other again or how we might fare in the chaos that our world was descending into.

Of course, the war soon affected Egypt. I received one letter from Antonio, from Cairo, telling me that he and his mother were doing well and that although he missed me, his act as a solo performer was going well and that he wished me all possible happiness in my life. I never heard from him again and I don't know what became of him and his mother or whether they survived the war.

Life in Greece for my mother, my sister, and me was becoming increasingly tenuous. The war was being fought not too far away and we awoke every morning with the fear that the Balkans, and Greece, would be the next victims on Hitler's agenda.

Mussolini by then had occupied Albania and there was little doubt in anyone's mind that Greece would be one of the next, if not the next, countries to be attacked by the Fascists.

George took charge of the situation and immediately we started following his advice to take the necessary steps to get out of Greece.

"You will go to America," he said in the deep and serious voice that he had. He spoke a beautiful and precise French, which he had learned as a student in Paris, and this was our usual language for communication, although he had a marvelous gift for languages and in a short time with me, his Spanish was already almost flawless. "You will go to America," he repeated, his eyes locked onto mine, "And I promise that I will meet you there one day soon. I promise." By then I knew what kind of a man he was and that if he said the words "I promise", then it would happen.

Just then, we finally heard from my father. He had settled into a stable new life in Havana, Cuba and was ready for us to come join him. We agreed that my mother, Nuria, and I would go to Cuba and wait for George there.

George and I were madly in love with each other and we were stricken with grief at the thought of having to separate. But I understood that he needed some time to put his affairs in order before leaving everything behind, including making sure his son from his first marriage was safe and taken care of or could come with his father to the new world if he so chose. George was eighteen years older than me and his son Leonidas, with whom I became very close, was almost exactly my age. He admitted somewhat embarrassedly to me years later that he had had a schoolboy crush on me when he was young, and I never told him that this was obvious to everyone around us. He was a lovely man who was a friend to me for the rest of his life and was a loving and attentive older brother to the children George and I would have later.

In the end, Leonidas decided to stay in Greece and during the Nazi occupation, he became a hero of the Greek resistance. He was captured by the Gestapo, who tortured him and sentenced him to death by starvation. He had the good fortune to be rescued by the British Army just in time. He eventually studied in England, at Cambridge University, and emigrated to Canada, becoming a professor at McGill University in Montreal. He never really recovered from what the Gestapo had done to him and he died a relatively young man.

One day, George told us that he had managed to get tickets for us on the ship *Nea Hellas*, which was sailing from Piraeus to New York in just two days. From there, we could make our way to Havana. Mother, Nuria, and I packed on our things and on the day of departure, George accompanied us to the ship and helped us

"Miss Spain in Exile"

load our luggage and stayed on board with us until the last possible moment.

It was a sunny, autumn day as we said our goodbyes. George kissed Mother and Nuria and said "Au revoir" to them. Then he took me in his arms and held me and said, "Take care of your mother and your sister and I will join you soon in Cuba."

Now, with the reality of our saying farewell to each other upon me, I could not bear the thought of saying goodbye.

"Please, George," I implored him, "Let me stay with you. We will leave together, with Leonidas if he decides to come with us."

With the tenderness and gentleness that he always showed toward me, George put his hands on my shoulders and stared into my eyes.

"Conchita, go to safety. I will follow you soon. I promise."

With that, he kissed me one last time and turned and walked away. I stood shaking and cried tearlessly as I watched him walk away. Mother and Nuria came to hold me and comfort me.

Once again, I heard the long and deep blast of the ship's horn announcing departure, just as I had heard it in Cherbourg saying goodbye to my father. And once again, I thought it was the saddest and most melancholy sound in the world. I followed George with my eyes as he made his way down to the pier below, where he stood, eyes locked onto mine, as our ship departed. I had to fight the urge that suddenly overtook me to leave the ship and run down to join him, but I resisted it and stood looking at him. He kept his eyes locked onto mine and I could see him mouthing the words "You will go to America and I promise that I will meet you there one day soon. I promise." I believed him.

We took several vacations to Greece together, as a family, when I was a little boy. When we were in Athens, we would go every afternoon to a popular café just behind the Grande Bretagne Hotel, Zonar's, for an afternoon snack. I especially loved their baklava, the Greek pastry made of layers of phyllo pastry soaked in honey and layered with chopped nuts. Zonar's would immerse their baklava in a tray with honey until it was totally saturated and when I was young, this was one of my favorite treats in the world. One time, when I was ten or eleven years old, Leonidas had come to see us in Athens and we invited him to come to Zonar's with us and he agreed, only to turn white and start shaking as we walked into the door together. Without saying a word, he turned and left, and we saw him walking down the sidewalk back toward the Grande Bretagne. I ran after him and asked him what was wrong. He could not speak to me; he could only stand there shaking.

I found out later that it was in Zonar's, while delivering a message for his Resistance unit, that the Gestapo had laid a trap and was waiting for him. As soon as he started to walk in with us, the memory assailed him, and he started reliving the terror of what they had done to him. Zonar's was never the same for me after that. Some years later, when I was visiting Leonidas in Montreal, he explained that episode to me. He told me that he thought enough years had gone by that he could walk into the café and enjoy it with us. But the memories were too strong.

I still travel to Athens fairly regularly. I can't stay in the Grande Bretagne without smiling at the thought of my father courting my mother over lunches there. Nor can I walk past Zonar's without shuddering at the thought of the Gestapo capturing my brother there.

CHAPTER 17

The New World

Autumn 1939

Within only two weeks of Hitler's army invading Poland, by September 15, Warsaw was encircled and under siege. The capital of Poland was being bombed mercilessly from the air by the Luftwaffe. On September 17, in keeping with the secret protocols of the Molotov–Ribbentrop Pact, Stalin's Red Army invaded Poland from the east. On September 28, after four weeks of relentless bombing had left much of the city as rubble, Warsaw surrendered. As my mother would emotionally recount later, when Radio Warsaw stopped broadcasting Chopin's Military Polonaise, *the world knew that Poland had fallen to the barbarians.*

By the end of September, with the fall of Warsaw, Poland had been occupied by the Nazis from the west and by the Soviets from the east. In the space of four weeks, Poland had simply ceased to exist as an independent country. The Nazis had developed a new method of warfare, which they called Blitzkrieg (literally, in German, "lightning war"), whereby combined air and ground attacks, including massive formations of tanks, quickly broke through, or went around, defensive fortifications to rapidly overwhelm their enemy. Having thoroughly rehearsed their Blitzkrieg tactics on the battlefields of Spain during the Spanish Civil War, the Nazis had been well prepared to brutally implement them on Poland.

Although a state of war now existed between France and Britain on the one side and Nazi Germany on the other, with Mussolini's Italy for the moment clearly allied with Germany, there was very little fighting going on at first. For eight months, Europe settled into that strange chapter of history known as the "Phony War" in Britain, the "Drôle de Guerre" in France, or the "Sitzkrieg" in Germany. During this period, there was only extremely limited military land

The New World

operations on the Western Front between France and Germany, with no major hostilities. The term "Phony War" was coined by journalists to describe this bizarre period, when after the Blitzkrieg attack on Poland and the rapid collapse of that country, seemingly nothing happened for the next several months. During the Phony War, there were several places along the Western Front where German and French / British troops were garrisoned within sight of each other but refrained from shooting at each other. Hitler took advantage of these eight months to finish rearming after the campaign in Poland, adding a million new soldiers, increasing his stockpile of ammunition, and tripling the number of tanks at the Wehrmacht's disposal. The strange pseudo-peace of the Phony War came to an end in May 1940 when German troops marched into Belgium, Luxembourg, and Holland, on their way to attacking France.

Despite the Phony War on land, at sea, the Battle of the Atlantic had begun. Many German warships were already at sea in the North Atlantic when war was declared. German submarines, the U-Boats as they were called, began attacking French and British shipping in the Atlantic immediately after war was declared. Although at that time, the German Naval Command had issued orders not to attack passenger liners, the first British ship to be sunk by the German Navy in World War Two was the passenger liner SS Athenia, sunk by the German submarine U-30 off the northwest coast of Ireland only hours after Britain had declared war on Germany. Among the 117 civilian passengers and crew killed as a result of the sinking of this ship were 28 citizens of the United States. The German high command feared that this might draw the United States into the war on the side of Britain and France and Germany denied any responsibility for the sinking of the SS Athenia until 1946.

It was into these dangerous waters of the North Atlantic that my mother sailed on the Nea Hellas with her mother and her younger sister.

The passenger list on board the *Nea Hellas* was composed of a number of nationalities. There were Jews from Eastern Europe on their way to Palestine, our first port of call. There were Arabs heading back to North Africa, our second port of call being Oran in Algeria. Finally, there were Greek-Americans returning to their adopted country and a diverse group of Europeans like us, trying to escape from the terrors of Europe to the haven of America.

During the bridge and other card games played in the salon every evening after dinner, Mother had become acquainted with an extremely elegant and polite gentleman who told us that he was a doctor from Vienna. He explained that he was traveling to America to stay with his dying mother in New York. He was a cultured and well-read man who spoke a beautiful and elegant French and we enjoyed our nightly conversations with him. Our surprise knew no boundaries when, on stopping at Gibraltar and being boarded by British authorities for a shipboard inspection, the gentleman was handcuffed and led off the ship by the police. One of the ship's officers told us that he was a Nazi spy and that the search party had been told he was on board the *Nea Hellas*.

Just before he was taken away, he somehow managed unobserved to slip an envelope into my mother's hand, saying that it contained a letter to his mother. "Please," he implored her, "Please, don't forget to mail this letter to her as soon as you reach New York." We looked at the envelope, and it appeared to contain just a normal letter and was addressed to a woman at a New York address. Mother agonized for days over what to do with the envelope and finally, just two days before arriving in New York, she took the envelope put of her handbag and without ever opening it to read the contents, she tore it into pieces and threw it into the ocean below. Later on, we read in the press that the man arrested in Gibraltar by the British was in fact a much sought after Nazi spy, as we had been told. I cannot help but wonder if that letter in fact did not contain information that would have been damaging to the Allies. Of course, I will never know.

It was beautiful autumn weather as we crossed the Atlantic and we had relatively calm seas for most of the voyage. But we could not relax and enjoy the sea voyage. We all felt too much apprehension about the possible dangers we faced crossing the North Atlantic during wartime. We had all heard about the sinking of a British passenger liner before we had departed, and we knew that the German and British navies were both active in the ocean that we were crossing. The arrest of Mother's bridge partner had reminded us that we were in the middle of a war. If there was one Nazi spy on board, who knew who else might be on board and what trouble could that cause for us if we were stopped by a German or British ship on our way to New York?

The sea voyage to aboard the *Nea Hellas* took a little longer to reach New York than had been anticipated. Twice as we crossed the North Atlantic, we were in fact ordered to stop by German submarines that were patrolling those waters. These were nerve-wracking experiences. Both times, we were boarded by submarine officers and crew who searched the ship to ensure it was not carrying military cargo of any sort and then interviewed the captain and officers of the *Nea Hellas* to be assured that this was in fact an innocent civilian passenger liner taking passengers to New York. Although we never had any direct contact with these German sailors – they never asked to see our papers or interviewed any of us passengers, seeming content to search our ship and interview its officers – in their own way, they were as menacing as the Gestapo and border guards that we had seen when exiting Germany. They were hard-faced and cold-eyed men and they gave the impression that their lives would have been easier if they could simply fire their torpedoes at us and sink us to the bottom of the sea instead of having to ask questions and then conclude that it was alright to allow us to continue on our journey. In spite of the luxurious amenities provided on board the *Nea Hellas*, we began to wonder if we would in fact make it safely to America.

Most of us had tears in our eyes when we arrived in New York and our ship made its way through New York Harbor. I shall never forget as long as I live the sight of that magnificent city and of the Statue of Liberty as we steamed past. That first impression of New York is forever engraved in my mind, the most fascinating view I had ever seen or would ever see. I was simply in awe at the sight and I was in utter disbelief that we had in fact arrived safely in the New World.

We remained in New York for almost a week. Father had made arrangements for us to travel to Cuba from New York and we barely had a chance to even begin exploring the city when it was time to board a train south to Miami. In Miami, we would catch a ship bound for Cuba, our new home. I vowed that I would come back to New York one day when I would be able to see it and enjoy it with George.

Father was waiting for us at the dock in Havana. I was overjoyed to see him again, but how strange it felt to see him in this unfamiliar environment. Father, who had always dressed so elegantly in Spain, and who managed to make even his Loyalist militia officer's uniform look like it had been expressly tailored for him, now went everywhere in loose fitting trousers, sandals, and a short-sleeved "guayabera" or Cuban shirt. He seemed enchanted by his new life in the tropics and it seemed to suit him. He looked happy and his usual smile had returned to his face, replacing the sad look of bitterness that the civil war had imposed on his features.

Mother had a little bit of trouble at first with the informality that characterized Cuban culture and society. Despite her somewhat leftist political orientation and being married to a staunch supporter of the Spanish Republic, Mother had never really lost her aristocratic bearing and she went through life expecting to be treated like the well-born and well-raised lady that she was.

Our second day in Havana, we all went to the drugstore together to buy some toothpaste and other supplies and Mother approached the pharmacist's counter to ask for some aspirin. Expecting the pharmacist to acknowledge her the way she would have been greeted in Spain, something along the lines of "Buenos dias, Señora, en que la puedo ayudár?" ("Good day, Madame, how may I help you?"), the smiling pharmacist instead asked her, in the lovely sing-song cadence of the Cubans, "Bueno, viejita, que quieres?" ("Okay, little old lady, what do you want?").

The poor man meant no harm, but Mother was not used to this level of informality and in a huff, she replied, "Para empezár, un poco de cortesía!" ("To start with, a little bit of courtesy!"). Having made clear her dissatisfaction with the way she was being treated, she spun on her heel and walked out of the pharmacy, leaving the confused pharmacist staring at her wondering what he had done wrong. Father and Nuria and I all burst into laughter. It was so nice for all of us to be together again!

Life on this sunny island promised to be pleasant enough. Father had found a small but comfortable apartment in Havana, not far from the beach, and there we all settled in, Nuria and I sharing a room as we had done throughout our childhood in Madrid. Every day, we walked along the Malecón, the beautiful esplanade along the harbor and the seawall. I became accustomed to and grew to love the warm and humid weather. I also came to love the happy Cuban people, with their loud music and their way of speaking Spanish that made almost any simple sentence sound like it was

The New World

song and who seemed to care more about music and singing and dancing than anything else in the world. After the years of building tragedy and sense of inevitable doom that had characterized Europe during the last few years, tropical and carefree Cuba was a welcome change!

The excitement of living in a new, safe place soon died down when Father lost his job suddenly and had to start looking for a new job. The next job he found would be as the news announcer for Radio Havana, the job he would keep for the remainder of our time in Cuba, but finding that job was weeks away and in the meantime, we were once again in the position of having to find a way to pay the rent and feed ourselves.

The immediate answer to the problem was for me to take up dancing again. My artistic career had come full circle. Here I was, wanting to or not, ready to go on stage once again. This time, I would not have anyone to help me. I would have to make it on my own. With quickly improvised costumes, strenuous rehearsals, and a lot of good luck, I did make it and the name Isa Reyes became well known, at least for a short time, not only in Cuba but even for a while in parts of the United States.

By pure luck, I happened to appear at the Hotel Nacional in Cuba asking for the chance to audition for their entertainment director the day after their long-standing floorshow performers had decided to quit and move on to more lucrative engagements in New York. The desperate man gave me an audition on the spot, and he liked my performance enough to hire me to appear as the evening floor show in the Hotel Nacional's dining and nightclub. Mother and Nuria helped me to improvise a costume and with two full days of rehearsing with the Hotel Nacional nightclub orchestra, we had put together an act of Spanish dances. It was a little rough at first, but after a week or so, we had smoothed the rough edges of the performance and my solo dance act had become quite popular.

My good luck continued. I had been performing at the Hotel Nacional for about six weeks when one evening, while doing my nightly performance, I was spotted by a theatrical agent who worked for MCA (Music Corporation of America). He was in Cuba on a vacation and was staying at the Hotel Nacional. He wasn't looking for a new act when he decided to spend an evening of his vacation with his wife at the hotel's nightclub and he loved my act. He looked me up after my performance and persuaded me to meet with him the next day to discuss a possible future with MCA. Within three days, I had signed a contract with MCA and told the Hotel Nacional that I would be departing after two more weeks of performances there. The entertainment director who had hired me was very understanding.

"Isa," he said to me, "I knew you would not be staying here forever. You have too much talent to stay forever at the Hotel Nacional. But at least you are giving more time to find your replacement than those ungrateful boors whom you replaced!"

"Yes," I replied, "But if it had not been for those ungrateful boors, I would not have had my opportunity here!"

"Ha, Isa, of course, you are correct! Come and I will get you a coffee."

We went to have our Cuban "cafecito" together, as we did after every meeting or discussion we had, the little cup of strong and heavily sugared coffee that the Cubans loved and seemed to drink dozens of each day.

My ensuing career under the contract with MCA was short but successful.

Soon, I found myself back in New York, with Mother and Nuria by my side. Father by then had been offered his job with Radio Havana and much as he wanted to come along on this trip, he had to stay behind in Cuba to start his new job.

I danced for two weeks at the Radio City music hall in Manhattan and appeared a few times at the then-glamorous Copacabana Nightclub. From New York, I went on tour and appeared to dance for several days each in Saint Louis and in Chicago and then finally in Saratoga Springs. It was an adventure to see these cities and it was exciting and fun to perform in front of the enthusiastic and polite American audiences.

Then came the big surprise and the unexpected highlight of this chapter of my life. One evening during a performance, a scout for MGM spotted me. He was trying to entice me to sign a five-year contract with MGM. It did not take long for me to be persuaded to sign with them, which I did with Mother's approval and Nuria's enthusiastic encouragement. Father expressed his enthusiasm by telegram from Havana. My dream of becoming a movie star, cut short in Paris some years earlier by an unexpected bout of the measles, had been revived, on a new continent and in the New World. MGM's stated intent makes me smile as I look back upon it

The New World

now. They said that they wanted to groom me to be the new star to appear in upcoming musical productions that were just then being planned. They said they would turn me into a cross between Carmen Miranda, Dolores del Rio, and a Latin version of Loretta Young. To my young self, it seemed an incredibly glamorous turn of events! I went back to Cuba to wait for them to send me the telegram telling me it was time to come to Hollywood, which they said would come within weeks. In the meantime, they would start arranging language lessons to improve my English, which they told me I could begin in Cuba.

But for the second time in my life, my chances to become a movie star were going to be cut short. This time it would not be because of a sudden onset of the measles, but because my true love had managed to escape Europe to join me. And this time, I would not regret the lost opportunity of perhaps becoming a star!

George had miraculously managed to escape Greece, through Albania, shortly after Mussolini's troops had invaded his country. Somehow, he had made it to New York. He had lost everything he had in Greece and he arrived in America with only $100 in his pocket. He spent $15 of this his first night in New York on a long-distance call to Havana to talk with me and let me know he was safe and had arrived in New York.

Despite only having the cash in his pocket, minus what it had cost him to call me, he knew he would be able to establish himself in the New World. George was a remarkably intelligent and ambitious man, with a will and sense of purpose that made him an unstoppable force when he decided he wanted to accomplish something. He spoke several languages fluently and soon found himself a job working for an American import-export firm with headquarters in New Orleans. Before long, he had saved enough money to come to Havana.

The happiest day of my life was when George and I were reunited. We could scarcely believe the day had come and that we could be together now, away from war-torn Europe. Now, the last thing I wanted to do was continue my dancing and acting career, with all the travel and time away from George that it would require. It was very difficult to break my contract with MCA, and even more so the contract with MGM, but with the help of a good lawyer and a little lie on my part, it was accomplished. We told the MCA and MGM moguls that I was secretly married and already pregnant and

"Miss Spain in Exile"

expecting a baby. In those more innocent days, that sort of behavior was absolutely taboo from an aspiring young star, and both companies finally released me from my obligations.

When he arrived in Cuba, George almost immediately became close friends with my father, who was only a few years older. They were close friends for the rest of my father's life. Realizing that Cuba would not offer a great future for them, every evening they would argue over their nightly game of chess about where we should all go next to build our family's future. My father wanted to go to Mexico, because the government in exile of the Spanish Republic was there and he wanted to try to resume his duties with the Diplomatic Corps of the Republic. George wanted to go to Brazil because he felt that a man like him could carve a fortune out of the Amazon. One night they decided that the time had come to make a decision and get on with things. They split a bottle of Scotch between them and then they flipped a coin. Mexico won. I sometimes have wondered what my life would have been like had the coin landed the other way and we had gone to Brazil instead of California.

George and I were married in Mexico City. Nuria met her husband, the surgeon Carlos Parés, there and they remained and raised their family in Mexico City. Carlos had also been a staunch Loyalist and had fled Spain after the Civil War. Following a harrowing period in one of the French internment camps in the Pyrenees, he had made it to Mexico City, where he established his surgical practice. Nuria kept her love of words and music her entire life and played the guitar until the arthritis in her hands forced her to stop. She published several books of poetry in Mexico and was well known in the literary and artistic milieu of Mexico City.

When the United States entered World War Two, George offered his services to the United States War Department and, among other things, built a plantation in the jungles of Campeche in the Yucatan Peninsula to grow castor beans in support of the American war effort. In those days, castor oil was important for use in aviation engines, and so was a strategic commodity for the war effort. As a result of this, and for helping to procure other important raw materials for the American war effort, he and I were invited to become citizens of the United States at the conclusion of the war. George was very proud of this, after having been unwelcome in the United States when he had come as a young man and was studying at

The New World

Berkeley. We moved to northern California, near San Francisco, where we raised our children, a daughter and two sons.

I have never regretted my decision to give up my artistic career. My life with George was never dull. He was an adventurous man, a bit of a gambler, and our life together was the happiest any woman could ever wish for. With him, I lived in the jungles of Campeche and the Yucatán, in the deserts of Arizona and Baja California, and in Mexico City early in our married life, before settling in California. George made and lost several fortunes during the course of his adventurous life. Our life was full, and we spent more than one summer, living as millionaires, in the playgrounds of the French Riviera, Spain, and the Greek islands.

Having lost our wealth to life's capricious turn of events, George and I moved to Maryland and took up residence in a suburb just outside of Washington, D.C. Our married daughter was living in Washington, our older son was living in Europe, and our younger son was attending university in Boston. But the sad reason behind this decision to move to the East Coast was that George was suffering from a fatal heart ailment and had only a few more years to live. He wanted me to be nearer our family when he would leave me for the last time.

I have had much and lost much in my life. Among the latter, the most traumatic and irreplaceable loss was the death of my husband in 1979.

Now, as I write these words in 1986, I still reside in Chevy Chase, Maryland. I work in the Sales Department and as a fashion adviser for one of the luxury boutiques on Washington, D.C.'s Wisconsin Avenue. Every July 17, I think about the start of the Spanish Civil War and how my young life was turned upside down by the events of that summer. Like that of countless other people, my life would have been entirely different if those events had not taken place. That summer day in July 1936 proved to be for me, not only a major turning point in my life, but the source of what my life became.

Epilogue

Isa lived for only a few more years after writing her memoirs. In 1988, she moved back to California to live with my brother George and his family. I also managed to come back to California in 1989 and my mother and I were able to spend well over a year together near the end of her life. I still treasure the memories of that time and I feel grateful that we were able to have it.

We took a lot of walks together during that year. We also cooked a lot of Spanish meals together and we watched a lot of old movies together. Our favorite movie was Casablanca, which we never tired of seeing. She would always burst into tears at the scene where the Nazis singing Der Wacht am Rhein are drowned out by the crowd of French, led by a Czechoslovakian, singing the Marseillaise. I would cry at that scene, too. I still do.

In 1989, she was diagnosed with ovarian cancer. Through sheer willpower, she beat it. Her oncologist referred to her as "The Unsinkable Conchita". Throughout the ordeals of the chemotherapy and other treatments, she never lost her sense of humor or her ability to make all of us laugh. Nor did she ever lose that iron streak of determination that, together with her sense of humor, had allowed her to survive so much in her life. Told that she should plan ahead and buy a wig because the chemotherapy would make her lose her hair, she announced that she had no intention of losing her beautiful hair. And despite the intense chemotherapy, she never did lose it.

If I had brought my guitar with me when I would go to visit her, she would still take out her castanets and click in accompaniment while I played. She could still switch effortlessly between the rhythm and the counter rhythm of the music. She loved it when I would play and sing the Loyalist songs from the Spanish Civil War for her, and when I would sing the songs of the Lincoln Battalion, she would still want to raise a glass of wine to those American volunteers. She continued to refer to them as "those brave

Epilogue

and idealistic young Americans, who came to Spain in her hour of need."

Then one day in 1991, she complained of stomach pains. We took her to the doctor and after a few days of tests, we learned the sad news that the cancer had returned. She now had an advanced stage of liver cancer. The doctors told us that an extremely aggressive and arduous regime of chemotherapy and radiation treatments might extend her life by a few months, but that her quality of life during those months would not be very nice. Really, they told us, it was too late to do very much for her.

She accepted the news when it was presented to her. It did not take her long to decide that she would decline any further treatment, telling us, "I miss your father. I want to go to be with him now."

We did what we could to make her comfortable and ease her last days, especially my brother George and his wife Jean, both of whom cared for her night and day. Toward the end, she was in a great deal of pain, but she never lost her ability to smile and she never stopped trying to make the rest of us laugh.

She spent the last few hours of her life in a semi-delirious state induced by the pain medications she had been given, half awake and half asleep. She murmured incoherently and barely audibly as waves of pain racked her body.

Then, slowly, a gentle peace settled upon her. Her body relaxed, her eyes opened, and her speech became steadier and clearer. She was having a waking dream, in which she thought she was back in Venice with my father. She had a broad smile on her face, her eyes appeared bright, and she looked like a young woman again.

In a clear and joyous voice, the voice of a young girl, she said in Spanish, "Oh George! Look how beautiful the Grand Canal looks today. I am so happy to be back here with you. Let's go to St. Mark's Square to have a coffee." Then her eyes closed, and she dozed off, still smiling.

Those were the last words she spoke.

Index

ABC (Madrid newspaper), 126, 127
Adrianus, 62, 68, 69–70
Alfonso XIII (King of Spain), 8, 40
Alma and Isa, 81, 82, 83, 85, 127–128, 168, 174, 188
Amsterdam, 111–112
Antonio y Isa, 203
appeasement, 6, 86, 109, 123, 148
Arcaráz, Antonio, 97, 140, 187–188, 190, 193, 202
Arpels, 126
Athens, 7, 147, 203–208, 210–211
Ávila, 1, 12–13, 23

Balcells Pinto, Ricardo, 3
  escape from Spain, 165–167
Balcells de los Reyes, Conchita, 1
Barcelona, 3, 9, 36, 37, 43–47, 50, 85, 92, 124, 153, 154, 166
Belmondo, Jean-Paul, 83
Berlin, 110–111, 149, 185, 187–189, 190–193, 195–202
Blum, Léon, 86
Bobino Theatre (Paris), 88
Boyer, Charles, 57
Brittany, 109, 113
Brussels, 111
Butcher of Asturias, 9

Canary Islands, 3, 10, 58
Cannes, 89, 94–96, 99
Cap d'Antibes, 96
Carretero, José María, 54
Cartier, 126
Casino de Paris, 88
castanets, 2, 3, 13, 49, 75, 77, 80–81, 84, 188, 222
Chamberlain, Neville, 123, 148–149, 151, 171, 172
Chautemps, Camille, 86

Chevalier, Maurice, 88
Churchill, Winston, 6, 33, 86
Ciano, Count Galeazzo, 180–184, 196–197, 206
Condor Legion, 33, 35, 59, 61, 197
Copacabana Nightclub (New York), 218
Copenhagen, 125, 142, 143–144, 148, 154
Czechoslovakia, 33, 108, 122, 123, 129, 141, 143, 148–153, 171, 172, 174, 181, 186, 204

Danzig, 146, 153, 185–186, 199
de los Reyes, 4
de los Reyes y Gonzalez Cardenas, Concepción, 3
de los Reyes y Gonzalez Cardenas, Teniente Coronel Alfonso, 40, 42
del Castillo, José, 8
de Waleffe, Maurice, 141–142, 145
Deauville, 157
Dinard, 157–159
Domergue, Jean Gabriel, 62, 69, 71–72, 142, 159
Duke and Duchess of Windsor, 82

El Baile de Luís Alonzo, 81, 84
Europejsky Hotel (Warsaw), 113
Exposition Internationale des Artes (Paris 1937), 61, 86

fascism, 6, 27, 74, 173–174
Fernandel, 57
Flamenco, 2, 13, 52, 74, 113, 155, 181
Franco, Francisco, 9, 13, 15–17, 21–24, 27, 33–35, 37, 48–49,

Index

54, 59, 75, 84, 86, 124, 126, 153–154, 164–165, 173–174, 176, 180, 182, 189–190

Gabin, Jean, 57
Gestapo, 49, 50, 59, 111, 119–120, 178, 191, 194, 200–201, 209, 211, 215
Girona, 3, 50, 166
Goebbels, Joseph, 197
Goering, Hermann, 33–35, 59, 178, 197
Grande Bretagne Hotel (Athens), 206, 210–211
Guelma Studio (Paris), 97, 140, 155, 187, 202
Guerlain, 126
Guernica, 59, 61
Guitry, Sacha, 56–58

The Hague, 161
Havana, 170–171, 209, 215–216, 218–219
Hermès, 126
Hitler, Adolph, 6, 9, 23–24, 27, 33–35, 59–60, 85–86, 108–110, 115, 118–119, 122–123, 129, 141, 148–151, 171–174, 177–179, 181, 185–186, 189, 191, 193–195, 197, 199–201, 204, 208, 212–213
Hitler's fiftieth birthday celebration, 189, 194–196
Hotel Nacional (Havana), 217–218

International Brigades, 23, 33, 48–50, 129, 153
  XII Brigade (Italians), 48
  XIII Brigade (Poles), 48
  XV Brigade (British and Americans), 23, 33, 48

Joinville Studios (Paris), 56

Kazantzakis, Nikos, 207
Koestler, Arthur, 33, 162

La Bagatelle Nightclub (Paris), 81–82, 87
Lanvin, 126

Le Boeuf Sur le Toit Nightclub (Paris), 82–83, 87, 98, 134, 154–155, 168
Le Monde (Paris newspaper), 124–127, 142
Les Perles de la Couronne, 56, 58
Le Vernet Internment Camp (Pyrenees), 162
Lido Nightclub (Paris), 88
Lincoln Battalion, 33, 47, 49, 153, 222
Los Cuatro Generales, 49
Los Cuatro Muleros, 49

Madrid, 1–5, 8–9, 11, 13, 15–16, 18, 24, 26–28, 31, 34–39, 42, 48–49, 51, 54, 83–84, 87, 99, 119, 123, 137, 154, 164–165, 167, 190, 196, 216
Malraux, Andre, 33
Masses, Federico Bertrán, 62–67, 69, 71
Maxim's Restaurant (Paris), 143
MCA (Music Corporation of America), 217–219
MGM (Metro-Goldwyn-Mayer), 218–219
militia, 27, 54, 84, 166, 216
Miss Europe, 125–128, 141–143, 145–147, 177
Miss Spain, 7, 124–128, 130, 141, 144–145
Monte Carlo, 87, 89, 92, 94, 96, 99
Montoya, Carlos, 5, 52
Morgan, Michelle, 57
Munich (Munich Betrayal), 33, 148–152, 171, 181, 186, 208
Mussolini, Benito, 6, 9, 23–24, 27, 35, 59, 85, 108, 130, 149–150, 172–174, 177–182, 184, 189, 208, 212, 219

National Theatre (Warsaw), 110–113, 115–116
Nea Hellas, 209, 213–215
Nicolopoulos, George, 206–207, 219–221
Normandy, 157, 162

Orwell, George, 24, 33

Index

Palm Beach Nightclub (Cannes), 89, 94–95, 97
Parés, Carlos, 162, 220
Parés, Nuria (née Nuria Balcells de los Reyes), 1, 4, 5, 11–14, 16, 18, 20, 24, 30–31, 35, 37–39, 41–42, 44–45, 51–52, 78–79, 87–89, 92–93, 96–98, 110–111, 113, 118–119, 124, 131, 134–135, 137, 139–140, 142–143, 154, 162, 165, 168, 175–176, 202–205, 207, 209, 210, 217–218, 220
Paris, 7, 36–37, 43, 46, 47, 50–52, 54–56, 61–64, 68–71, 76–77, 81–84, 86–89, 97–98, 110, 117–118, 124–127, 130–131, 133, 142, 148, 154–156, 161–162, 164–166, 168–169, 187, 190, 200, 202–205, 207, 209, 218
Paris-Soir (Paris newspaper), 126
Patou, Jean, 52–53, 126
Pedro Bernardo, 10, 12, 14, 15, 17, 19, 21, 23, 27, 59, 82, 169
Picasso, Pablo, 59, 61, 69

Queen Mary, 169

Radio City Theatre (New York), 218
Radio Havana, 171, 217
Raimu, 57
Reyes, Isa, 58, 82, 127–128, 140, 168, 174, 188, 217

Saint-Malo, 157, 161
Saint Tropez, 96
Sariñena, 33, 36, 37, 40, 41, 43–46
Schiaparelli, 126, 143
Sierra de Gredos, 1, 8, 26, 82
Sotelo, Calvo, 8
Spanish Foreign Legion, 22–23, 37, 40
Sporting Club (Monte Carlo), 89, 93, 94, 99
Stalin, Joseph, 23, 199, 212
Sudetenland, 122–123, 129, 148–150, 152, 171, 186

Trio Arcaráz, 140, 188, 190, 202
Trouville, 157

Valencia, 36, 38, 40, 54, 87, 124, 154, 156, 164–166
Van Clef, 126
Venice, 52, 130, 174–176, 178–179, 182, 184, 187, 189, 197, 223
Venice Casino, 174–175, 184

Warsaw, 110–111, 113–118, 120, 146–147, 181, 212
Wintergarten Theatre (Berlin), 187, 189, 192, 198

Zamora, José, 76

www.ingramcontent.com/pod-product-compliance
Lightning Source LLC
Chambersburg PA
CBHW052058300426
44117CB00013B/2194